Counselling Skills *for* Social Work

Lisa Miller

Counselling Skills *for* Social Work

SAGE Publications

London • Thousand Oaks • New Delhi

First Published 2006

 SAGE Publications Ltd
1 Oliver's Yard
55 City Road
London EC1Y 1SP

SAGE Publications Inc.
2455 Teller Road
Thousand Oaks, California 91320

SAGE Publications India Pvt Ltd
B-42, Panchsheel Enclave
Post Box 4109
New Delhi 110 017

British Library Cataloguing in Publication data

A catalogue record for this book is available
from the British Library

ISBN 1-4129-0714-4
ISBN 1-4129-0715-2 (pbk)

Library of Congress Control Number: 2005926722

Typeset by C&M Digitals (P) Ltd., Chennai, India
Printed on paper from sustainable resources
Printed and bound in Great Britain by TJ International Ltd, Padstow, Cornwall

Contents

Acknowledgements

Thank you to Caroline for all of your encouragement and support. I could not have done this without you.

Thanks also to Clare for all you have done to help with this book; to Marian, Gillian and Caroline E. for proof-reading and guidance; to East Ayrshire CAMHS for your humour along the way; to family and friends for believing in me; to Joy for giving me a place to start; and to Julie.

Preface

While working as a part-time lecturer with the University of Paisley and during my training in Systemic and Family Therapy with the Scottish Institute of Human Relations, I have developed an interest in exploring the complexities of communication within working relationships. As I have been exposed to different therapeutic approaches and experimented with them in social work practice, I have become increasingly enthusiastic about the need for a broader understanding of these models and techniques within our field. I have drawn upon case examples that have been significantly altered to protect confidentiality and have attempted to capture both the complexity and the simplicity of using the various approaches through these examples.

Through my current practice in Child and Adolescent Mental Health Services in East Ayrshire, I have found the inclusion of a broad range of techniques invaluable when matching the need of the individual or the family with an approach that would seem to be most helpful. While I do not advocate eclecticism to the point where the core of our practice would not have a knowledge-base at all, I have become a firm believer in practising social work as an art that evolves as we increase our understanding, experience and ability to work creatively. With this in mind, I am hopeful that other practitioners in the field of social work will be able to draw on some of the concepts within this book to develop their own art of communication.

During my own period of study towards qualification in social work at the University of Plymouth, I found that text books such as *Social Work Practice* (Coulshed, 1991), which offered practical steps to working with people, founded upon theory, enabled me to establish a foundation upon which I could build my practice. The structure of this book was influenced with this in mind, with the additional hope that readers would find enough detail to move beyond the basics of effective listening skills towards more specific techniques that can be used therapeutically with service users. Throughout this book, I am aware of writing from a white, female perspective.

Introduction

Social work practice relies on many aspects of knowledge and skill development. Service users sit at the centre of this practice in that their well-being and social functioning often relies on effective social work intervention. In the main, those people who use social work services are in vulnerable social positions for a variety of reasons. Social exclusion often limits proactive access to other non-social-work services that can prevent the escalation of problems. Financial limitations and factors relating to oppression invariably inhibit the ability of individuals and their families to resolve problems and find effective solutions more independently. In this context, this book aims to widen the scope of skills available to social work practitioners that are used therapeutically in other settings to communicate with people experiencing problems.

Using the following definition of social work (BASW, 2001), we can use counselling skills in our practice to communicate with people in the context of their environments and cultural contexts. 'The social work profession promotes social change, problem solving in human relationships and the empowerment and liberation of people to enhance well-being. Utilising theories of human behaviour and social systems, social work intervenes at the points where people interact with their environments. Principles of human rights and social justice are fundamental to social work.' Effective communication skills are thus essential if we wish to hear and be heard by those with whom we work. As communication is so often fraught with difficulties, having a broad range of skills and techniques to assist us with listening to people and helping them to experience change in their lives can be invaluable.

Social workers are required to engage with individuals, families and groups; form an assessment based on research and theoretical frameworks; and then intervene using a knowledge-base that draws upon communication skills (Compton & Galaway, 1999; Milner & O'Byrne, 2002a). The objective of practice is usually to enable change, from an undesirable emotional state, in behaviour, or from a position of social disempowerment that either impairs social development and participation or requires protection from some form of harm. The *process* of undertaking these tasks is the concern of this book by examining the utilisation of counselling skills in various forms.

Other texts examine listening skills in greater depth (Lishman, 1994; Seden, 2005). Listening skills form the foundation of practice and any use of counselling skills can only be made with this in mind. Lishman (1994) distinguishes between 'attending' and 'listening'. Attending to a service user involves punctuality, reliability and attentiveness to the conversation. Listening goes beyond hearing what a service user is saying. It involves the recognition of congruence and incongruence between verbal and non-verbal communication. While this is not fully explored in this book, the book is designed to build upon attending and listening skills to provide practitioners with a broader scope for communicating with people. With this in mind, readers would benefit from familiarisation with these skills before experimenting with the some of the more advanced skills contained within this book. It is hoped that this book, inclusive of many of the fundamental theories and approaches that have influenced social work practice over the years, will enhance engagement and forms of intervention by broadening the application of theory to social work practice.

Counselling and social work have long been connected. Counselling is defined by Feltham and Dryden (1993) as a 'principled relationship' in which practitioners draw upon a knowledge-base of psychological theories. As counselling is service-user-led and social work is governed by legislative and policy frameworks that often lead us to take a directive stance with service users, referring to 'counselling skills' in social work practice seems most fitting. The Barclay Report clarified the use of counselling skills in social work to be a means by which service users are assisted through the process of personal change or change of their environments. Counselling skills should also be used in social work practice to help people tolerate the emotional impact of their world (Barclay Committee, 1982). This also comes into conflict with some forms of 'therapy', in that emotional healing is not always possible without changes to an individual's environment. This is especially so in relation to abuse. This is discussed throughout this book, again reinforcing the use of 'skills' as the most relevant term to describe such 'therapeutic' activity within social work practice. Counselling and counselling skills are governed under the Ethical Framework of the British Association for Counselling and Psychotherapy (BACP).

Throughout this book, significant emphasis is given to the nature of the working relationship. The use of the self by practitioners within a working relationship is also a theme that is prevalent throughout the chapters. This concept is not new. Social work's foundations are based on the use of the self within a working relationship: 'casework' (Hollis, 1972). This book does not aim to move away from these time-established principles, while acknowledging that the socio-political context of social work has not been static (Brearley, 1995; Brown, 2002). Rather, the scope of the book is to incorporate traditional and post-modern therapeutic models into social work practice. This can enhance insight into the presentation of problems and widen the range of 'lenses' that we can use to understand communication (Hoffman, 1990). Due to the broad scope of the book, each chapter only offers a beginning to making sense of an approach and to applying it to practice. In all cases, further reading is recommended.

Organisation of the Book

The structure used throughout the book begins with an overview of the theory that underpins each approach. Each chapter then uses case examples, altered for anonymity, to illuminate the theory further, and applies the theory to a social work context. The skills required to incorporate elements of each approach into social work practice are defined to assist practitioners to experiment in practice. It is strongly advised that active reflection within supervision, either with peers or with line managers, be used to make sense of what went well and what did not when testing out these methods. Each chapter summarises with an outline of the key concepts discussed.

Chapter 1, on multicultural counselling skills, forms the foundation of this book. Developing awareness and sensitivity to cultural factors through increasing awareness of the cultural influences in our own history is the starting point, be that a position of privilege or disadvantage.

In **Chapter 2**, the generally well-known person-centred approach is offered. This chapter develops effective listening skills to include consideration of the personal qualities that are required of the practitioner for this approach to be utilised successfully.

Cognitive behavioural therapy and its contribution to therapeutic work are explored in **Chapter 3**. This model is significant in providing a framework for the way in which individuals develop core beliefs in early childhood that in later life set the course of interplay between thoughts, feelings, behaviours and physiological responses to stressors. Outlined are the skills required to use this model to make sense of anxiety problems and low mood that often stand in the way of change for service users.

Chapter 4 offers practitioners an insight into some of the psychoanalytic concepts that are often quoted in practice. This chapter also includes aspects of attachment theory that relate to the relational experience of working alliances. Fundamental is the principle of the temporary secure base offered in a therapeutic relationship and the skills that are required for practitioners to establish this with service users.

Narrative therapy is introduced in **Chapter 5**. This chapter presents techniques that help people to look beyond dominant stories of their lives, personal and political, and view the role of oppression in the composition of often unhelpfully rigid and problem-saturated stories.

Moving further away from the focus on problems and towards solutions, **Chapter 6** presents some of the principal concepts of solution-focused therapy. This chapter gives particular emphasis to techniques that can be included in conversations with service users when working towards change.

While the early chapters generally are directed towards working with individuals, **Chapter 7** overviews elements of family therapy and of families as systems.

Chapter 8 of this book explores using counselling skills to organise, facilitate and communicate within groups. As group work is often effective in assisting individuals towards change, this chapter draws on theories of change, theories relating to group processes and some of the skills that can enhance the functioning of groups.

The book concludes with a brief overview of the way in which theoretical models of counselling and therapy provide a basis from which we can expand the range of our skills when communicating with service users within working relationships. The **Conclusion** acknowledges the equal importance of values that underpin our practice. It also touches on the art and science of social work, arguing that we use both in practice.

I
Multicultural Framework for Using Counselling Skills in Social Work Practice

Key Concepts	Key Theorists and Practitioners
• Unequal Society as Context	• Hiro
• Ethical Dilemmas	• Dominelli
• Privilege and Disadvantage Positions	• Thompson
• Idiographic Framework for Practice	

Introduction

Britain, consisting of several countries, is by definition a multicultural society. In whichever region of our respective countries we live, a list could continue almost indefinitely when attempting to define cultural difference. It would include, but not be exclusively related to, differences in skin colour and facial features. This chapter aims to provoke thoughts about the multicultural aspects of society that are integral to our work, especially when communicating with others using counselling skills. By promoting the development of awareness of 'self' in working relationships, i.e. seeking to understand our own cultural history and position in society and how it impacts upon others, it is hoped that this can be achieved.

Emphasis is given to 'difference' and the resultant inequalities that exist in society. Race is given primary focus in relation to culture within the examples in this chapter but then broadened out to include other aspects that define life and experience. The purpose for this is that, regardless of skin colour, we all have a racial identity that has a history. It is an integral aspect of practice relevant to all practitioners, including those of us who are white.

Dominant groups within society have been defined by traditions of the superiority of some groups and the inferiority of others (Ahmed, 1986). These definitions continue today, despite ongoing political challenge from various sources to call for equity. Certain groups are without doubt more powerful than others. Those in a majority white position in society are more likely to be involved in defining policy than those in a minority black position, for example. There are 'close links between race and class' (Thompson, 2001). Gender inequalities are relevant to the positions of all males and females, with males generally being in a more powerful position than females (Thompson, 2001). To be a white female will be a different experience to being a black female, however, and to be in a position of higher socio-economic status will differentiate gender experience even further. That experience will differ again according to the country and region of the UK in which a person lives. This chapter does not intend to stereotype either the characteristics or experience of social groups of people, nor confine the discussion to race. However, it is impossible to make specific reference to inequality without identifying some core feature that links together those who experience oppression and those who do not.

As defined by Dalrymple and Burke (2003), the term 'black' is used 'in a political sense to reflect the struggles of non-white groups against the oppression they experience from white institutions ... we do not use the term "black" to deny difference and diversity'. However, this is not to limit the exploration of culture to skin colour, race and ethnicity. Rather, the intention is to highlight that cultural groups have different starting points in working relationships with practitioners as a result of assumptions made and the potential for prejudice and discrimination to disempower individuals. This can occur even with well-meaning intentions within practice. Notwithstanding, minority groups in a white majority society indeed experience disadvantage (Hiro, 1971; Dominelli, 1997). 'In counselling the culturally different client, the *practitioner* may unwittingly engage in cultural oppression, that is, the unconscious imposition of mainstream cultural values on to the client' (Alladin, 2002; my italics).

Social workers have been criticised by other professionals for being 'too politically correct', which devalues the efforts made to empower disadvantaged people towards a more equal participation in society. This chapter, in looking at the factors that lead to practices in which we can empower people in a multicultural context, does not aim to offer a surface presentation of the 'correct' language that will allow us to pay 'lip service' to matters relating to race and culture. Rather, an exploration of some of the theoretical components that can assist us to develop our counselling skills will be offered. This will be followed, as is the model in following chapters, with a case example and then summary of the skills that can assist us to integrate multicultural awareness and sensitivity into our practice. This chapter will emphasise the importance and difficulties of raising cultural awareness and cultural sensitivity. Specific reference is made to matters relating to ethnicity, gender, sexuality and social class. This is followed by a brief overview of an idiographic framework to using counselling skills in practice (Palmer, 2002).

The Complexity of Culture

Lago and Thompson (2003) emphasise the complex nature of the term and concept of culture. The historical roots of 'culture' are linked with the description of land, living environments and habitual practices in this respect. 'Culture' as a word is derived from various linguistic sources, each with their own inherent meaning. This chapter acknowledges the importance of recognising the complex nature of 'culture' in history as a forerunner to the meaning of the term in present-day society. Any definition offered here would only be a 'culturally programmed' view given by the author. Therefore, culture and its meaning can be both broad and narrow according to the context. For the purposes of this chapter, culture in relation to race and ethnicity, gender, sexuality, and social class and the interplay between these is the primary meaning given in this context (Atkinson & Hackett, 1995). References are occasionally made to regional cultural differences in respect of Scotland, Wales, England and Northern Ireland, to which unhelpful generalisations are often made by grouping the four countries under the one name, 'UK'.

Values

To place culture into a social work context, strong emphasis is made in training and continued development to values that underpin our practice. Fundamental as the bedrock of social work practice is the consideration of our personal values. Values held by an individual serve as the foundation for beliefs that translate into feelings and behaviour in different forms throughout our practice. Our feelings and behaviour about and towards people and their circumstances will dictate whether our practice counters prejudice and discrimination or whether we perpetrate oppression, either consciously or unconsciously.

Through becoming aware of the influences on our values as they shift over time, we can ensure that we do not inadvertently oppress service users through our language and behaviour. Equally, we can actively work to counter prejudice and stigmatisation in our working relationships with service users and with our colleagues and peers. While values held at a personal and societal level require open examination for effective social work practice, the connection between values and ethics also requires exploration.

To further consider the development of values in social work practice, we might make reference to radical Marxist practice, where 'divisions in society' result in an imbalance of power (Marx & Engels, 1965). Social divisions become structurally manifest in society through dominant belief systems being embraced by social policy and cultural norms. For example, western society is predominantly white, with a disproportionate number of white people, compared with people of other ethnic groups, in powerful positions making decisions about social policy. British colonialism is part of our recent past and many beliefs about superiority of one group over another still permeate our society.

As we develop our insight into the historical foundations of oppression, and develop our understanding of our own position in society – be that in a majority position or minority – we can then begin to explore the impact of our own culture and the assumptions we might make within a working relationship.

John had successfully finished his training as a qualified social worker shortly before this situation arose. His motivation for developing his career in the direction of a Youth Justice Service was a desire to assist young people through troubled times in their teenage years. He started his post with enthusiasm.

John had quietly struggled with the attention given to oppression and discrimination through his social work training course, believing that collaborative practice was 'good enough' to successfully engage with young people and their families. He believed that the course over-emphasised racial factors. John grew up in London, where he had been accustomed to multi-ethnic peers and associates. John had moved to rural Wales for his first qualified post, where the population was predominantly white. He had a white mother whose family had lived in London for many generations and a father of Nepalese origin. John had given little attention to the multicultural nature of his family history. He gave greater emphasis to his 'white English' family history, on account of his close relationship with his mother, and less emphasis to his 'Nepalese' family history, on account of his ambivalence towards his father and their distant relationship.

John met with service users after a two-week induction for his new post. On his first meeting with a young person, he had been shocked and disheartened to experience racial abuse from him. John had experienced racism on many occasions previously but not at his workplace. John had supervision with his team leader to explore his emotional reaction to this, where the team leader used counselling skills to enable John to express his feelings. John had been concerned that this experience could undermine this crucial foundation to his new career in social work and noticed that he had had an extreme emotional reaction to the situation.

John and his team leader started to explore the complexities of the experience in respect of the working relationship. The local authority had a 'no-tolerance' policy in respect of racism and John's team leader was supportive of this position. John was reluctant to disengage with the young person, a 12-year-old boy from a disadvantaged social background who had become involved with car theft with a group of older peers. John firmly believed that the young person required a service and that the young person was unlikely to have fully understood the impact of his choice of language. John took the position that he was more able to challenge racial stereotypes by working with the young person than he would be by disengaging with him.

During supervision, they also considered power issues. John was in a position of authority as a social worker with statutory duties. However, as a person with a Nepalese family history, with skin and facial features that expressed his ethnicity, he was also part of a minority group in a white majority society. John was troubled by the discussion as he had not fully explored the meaning for him of his own culture and family history before. He had previously avoided

(Continued)

(Continued)

thinking about 'minority' status and now was faced with acknowledging it with his supervisor who, because of his managerial position within the organisation, was in a more powerful position. The team leader was also white, putting him in a 'majority' social group. They discussed this factor also. This led to the outcome that acknowledging these directly relevant power issues allowed John and his team leader to communicate explicitly about the impact of racism.

Social Work Application

We often give thought to service users in powerless positions and consider the impact of disadvantage and oppression for them. However, oppression and its many forms, including prejudice and discrimination, is often evident in the workplace and can be experienced by staff as well as service users. Power issues are relevant in all forms of practice. They are complex and often no easy solutions can be sought. Hierarchical organisations bring with them managerial structures that distribute power and authority unequally. A practitioner might be powerful in one respect, i.e. with service users, especially when working with people according to statutory duties and powers, and in another situation might experience oppression and powerlessness, i.e. when working from a 'minority' position with a 'majority' client group. The same practitioner might also experience oppression in relation to more senior staff and possibly other agencies. Given power differentials in society between white and black people, males and females, able-bodied people and people with disabilities, heterosexual and homosexual people, for example, it is highly likely that those practitioners who are part of 'minority' groups, as well as service users, will experience some form of oppression.

When trying to make sense of the complexity of culture, we can therefore start with trying to understand our own social position. Are we from a privileged group of white, heterosexual males from families with high socio-economic status? If we are, then the starting point would be to examine the meaning of privilege.

Skills Component

- Accept that understanding cultural influences in communication is complex.
- Consider the meaning of our own social position as a starting point.
- Recognise that our own social position impacts on others, including peers, service users and supervisees.
- Power issues are central to thinking about the meaning of culture in working relationships.
- Incorporating cultural competence into the use of counselling skills requires a high level of personal awareness and reflexivity.

Cultural Awareness

As we develop our understanding of diversity within our society, we become cognitively or intellectually aware of the influence of culture. In order to build a contextual framework for multicultural counselling skills, the nature and history of British society requires acknowledgement. Ahmed (1986) outlines historical Britain's (especially English) belief of superiority over non-European and non-western cultures, played out through colonialism over the last hundred years and continuing to permeate 'the fabric of society'. 'Natural assumptions' of the superiority of British practices made at a 'subconscious level', such as regarding child rearing and life stage changes, are often made, instead of viewing 'different' non-abusive practices in equal terms, even by those of us aware of issues relating to racism and discrimination. This can inadvertently lead to 'pathologising' non-western parenting and relationship styles, instead of accepting them as 'different' from the white majority. Raising our awareness of the colonial roots of recent British history can assist us to make more conscious our assumptions about practices common to non-western originating cultures. Further, this 'pathologising' can extend to homosexual relationship styles, non-traditional families and imposing 'middle-class' values on those from different social groups.

Defining the nature of culture is complex in itself. While acknowledging race, we often confuse ethnicity and culture. Hardy and Lasloffy (1995) define culture as a 'broad multidimensional concept that includes but is not limited to ethnicity, gender, social class and so forth'. We could add religious beliefs, sexuality, regionality, migration patterns, skin colour and experience of oppression, among other factors. Hardy and Lasloffy define ethnicity as 'the group(s) from which an individual has descended and derives the essence of his/her sense of peoplehood'. Cultural identity, therefore, is the point where all of the dimensions of a person's life and history converge. This is as relevant for those with white 'British' histories as it is for those with different familial migratory patterns.

If we neglect exploration of our own histories, we deny ourselves the opportunity to make sense of our own beliefs that influence the assumptions we make about people and that can be prejudicial. Without developing awareness of our own cultural beliefs and assumptions, genuine acceptance of diversity becomes a stagnated process where at best we can only give surface attention to cultural matters.

Ahmed (1986) argues that we need to be cautious about over-reliance on cultural explanations for a person's circumstances and behaviour. This can lead to practice becoming culturally biased, i.e. overlooking other important factors that contribute to a problem by over-focusing on culture. This over-reliance can be a result of stereotyping groups of people and making assumptions about lifestyle and practices.

Viewing a person's culture as a dynamic part of identity, we can see problems in relation to other significant factors in a person's life. If culture is ever-changing, it is impossible to accurately stereotype people and groups by their common attributes and practices. With this in mind, this chapter does not advocate listing lifestyle practices ('first-order learning') for different cultural groups in order that they can be applied whenever we assume the situation dictates. Rather, this chapter argues that we develop a respectful curiosity about the beliefs and practices that are 'norms' within all service users' lives, regardless of skin colour or historical ethnicity.

During supervision, John began to raise his awareness of the meaning for him of his own cultural history. He had been able to identify that he had resisted discussions about race and oppression during his social work training as he found them uncomfortable and personally challenging. He acknowledged how these discussions had left him feeling guilty and ashamed of the racist assumptions that he had made about people from other cultures in the past. Difficult memories of racially abusive experiences were also triggered. As John developed his awareness of his own history and influences on his life through his family, he found himself more open to thinking about service users and the numerous cultural factors that also influence their lives. He started to make sense of what it meant to be perceived as not part of the white majority, despite having a white mother, white maternal grandparents and white aunts and uncles. He also started to think about what it meant to be male in a multicultural society. John's general understanding of societal inequality increased. He was able to relate this to many service users' experience of social exclusion and deprivation and therefore inequality through socio-economic status.

As John explored these factors through the supervision process, he found his focus for practice shifted from his thinking in terms of being an effective listener in working relationships to taking a more proactive stance when communicating with people. He began to incorporate thinking about cultural influences on behaviour and relationships with those with whom he worked. His style of questioning and reflecting back with service users became threaded with cultural curiosity. What did it mean to be a young person in rural Wales? What expectations were held regarding education, employment and relationships? Did the expectations differ between those of local communities and those of Education and Social Work Services? What did it mean to be black in the area that John was working? What was the migratory status of the young people with whom he was working? What did their families' migratory (or non-migratory) history bring to the young person's relationships? What did it mean to be looked after and accommodated by the local authority for young people? Did the family have religious beliefs that influenced behaviour and relationships?

As John developed his cultural awareness, he found that he would view individual behaviour in a less blaming way and was more open to perceiving problems in the context of societal, cultural and relationship factors.

Social Work Application

Cultural awareness begins with examining our own family history. History includes events, beliefs and traditions, passed down through generations through narratives, which influence current behaviour and relationships. For those who grow up away from their families of origin, the meaning of gaps

(Continued)

(Continued)

and lack of historical knowledge can be equally influential. By developing our awareness of how the roots of our own codes of conduct, our values and goals towards which we strive are bedded in our history, be it recent or not, we can be more appreciative of the influence of culture for service users.

Taking a humanitarian stance of individual uniqueness (Rogers, 1980), we can expect that all young people, adults and their families will have some differences, albeit some families will often share similar values and practices. With this in mind, we can avoid making assumptions about the meaning of behaviour and events for families according to the false stereotypical beliefs that are often held. The false stereotypes are usually generated from a white western view about people from 'minority' cultural groups. To avoid assumptions, we can respectfully enquire about cultural aspects to life with service users to assist us to make sense of beliefs and practices for the young person, adult or family in question.

Regardless of cultural diversity, social work practice is still inextricably linked to the legal system, and so diverse practices within different cultures cannot be overlooked where there is a breach of the law in whichever country within the British Isles we are practising.

Skills Component

- Develop awareness of our own cultural history by exploring the influence of generationally held beliefs and practices.
- Acknowledge the uniqueness of individuals and families.
- Avoid making assumptions about beliefs and practices based on stereotypes, often formed from a white western position.

Cultural Sensitivity

Cultural sensitivity moves a step on from cultural awareness by introducing an affective or emotional component. Hardy and Lasloffy (1995) distinguish cultural sensitivity from cultural awareness by introducing how affective responses can translate into action in a therapeutic setting by assisting us to attune to 'stimuli' with 'delicacy and respectfulness'.

We can draw upon our cultural awareness to increase our sensitivity in social work practice by developing 'cultural empathy'. Palmer (2002) identifies two dimensions to cultural empathy. The first, 'understanding', fits closely with the concept of cultural awareness; and the second, 'communication', concerns what we do with the understanding we have in various situations. We can use cultural sensitivity to ensure that our communication with service users from all cultural backgrounds meets the standards of 'delicacy and respectfulness' about cultural matters. Given that we also communicate with colleagues and people from other agencies, we can incorporate culturally sensitive styles of communicating as integral to our practice in all domains. This does not require us to avoid or ignore cultural factors to be respectful, but rather that we acknowledge the potential experience of difference within and outside of a working relationship with a service user in a respectful manner.

During his first year of qualified practice, John found that his growing awareness of cultural factors, especially in relation to his own life and experience, generated a greater emotional commitment to exploring experience with young people and to challenging oppression. This directly altered his practice of counselling skills. Prior to this work placement, John would be respectful to service users. He would take the time to listen, clarify and reframe aspects of discussion. He would be mindful of using a variety of open and closed questions and endeavoured to be reliable and offer positive regard. However, John had avoided questions relating to race and culture. This was not a deliberate position. Rather, he did not give cultural factors thought and so did not raise them with service users.

John's practice had evolved in that he was able to understand that people have different cultural experiences based on family background, ethnicity, religious or non-religious beliefs, ability, sexuality, gender and social status. As his understanding of difference grew, his understanding of shared experience of oppression in some respects also grew. John developed his repertoire of enquiring about cultural experience in respectful and non-critical language. He used a gentle tone of voice and sought permission to explore certain areas of a young person's life, to limit the potential intrusiveness of the subject matter.

John found that certain phrases assisted him to mention potentially difficult subjects in a non-intrusive way. He would often adapt, 'I have been thinking about what it must be like to … (be living in XY where lots of young people don't go to school); (live in a family who have moved to Wales from England); (be a young woman in a family of mostly males); (attend a school where most people are white)' … etc. He would then add, 'I wonder if it would be okay if we could talk about that?' John found that this form of questioning allowed him to bring often extremely emotive subjects into the discussion without imposing them on a service user. He adopted a position of 'not knowing' that allowed the young person to draw upon their own expertise and freed him from making assumptions about situations. John found that, on most occasions, the young people with whom he worked responded to this positively. When they did refuse permission to discuss a matter, the subject would often be raised by them at a later time. Using respectful cultural sensitivity freed John to explore the meaning of behaviours and relationships in a wider dimension than he had previously done.

Social Work Application

Social work practice, working with extremely vulnerable members of society, raises emotional or affective responses for practitioners daily. Often, organisational norms do not overtly offer caretaking of our affective responses to situations, although the use of the self in a working relationship is fundamental to social work practice. However, as our practice evolves, using our affective responses as indicators of how we are practising, and of how sensitive we are (or are not) to service users, can assist us in our progress. Cultural sensitivity requires us to be aware of our feelings and use them to make judgements in respect of the verbal and non-verbal communication that we use with service users. As we develop greater insight into our affective responses, we can develop a level of empathy that allows us to emotionally connect with service users. As always, becoming over-involved with service users is likely to be detrimental to the therapeutic relationship. Gaining insight into our own feelings can assist us to regulate our practice to enable an emotional connection to be made that is not too distant or too intrusive to undermine empathic communication.

Ideally, the supervision process will facilitate such discussions, and this can include formal and informal peer supervision. Sharing our feelings with service users is always fraught with potential difficulty. This is discussed more fully in Chapter 2.

Skills Component

- Practise recognising our own emotional responses to situations.
- Raise awareness of our own feelings in respect of culture.
- Use judgement to enable empathic communication to be at an appropriate level for service users.
- Be cautious about sharing feelings with service users – if in doubt, hold back.

Cultural Barriers to Communication

Lago and Thompson (2003) identify how misunderstandings can arise due to differing cultural norms in greeting and communicating with people, as well as assumptions made about culture that push people into stereotypical positions. The way in which assumptions are made and how they can hinder practice is highlighted above. However, thought needs to be given to the intricacies of communication that can create these barriers. This does not exclusively apply to assumptions about race.

Two people who are perceived to be culturally different, based on dress or accent of speech as some of many potential factors, can immediately be faced with difficulty when trying to interpret the meaning and intention of the other. We often take for granted the level at which we rely upon cultural conventions, both verbally and non-verbally, to create mutual understanding between two or more individuals. Perceptual assumptions are made at every level in society, most often between 'different' groupings of people where empathic understanding of the other is hindered by generalisations made. To broaden this, we can include assumptive beliefs formed about the capacities of those with disabilities by those with no similar impairment.

We are culturally programmed to make assumptions about appearance, behaviour, language and its meaning. Problems arise when someone from one cultural group tries to interpret the meaning of either verbal or non-verbal communication by someone from a different cultural group where the meaning of a statement or a form of behaviour is quite different. With this in mind, cultural sensitivity is at its most important. We need to be able to acknowledge and respect difference without drawing on assumptions derived from our own cultural perspective to attribute meaning that could easily be misguided. When differences in skin colour are introduced as part of this interaction, the level of assumption-making often increases.

Unhelpful assumptions can also arise from factors less tangible: individual systems of ethics and morals, perceptions about gender, status, religion and personal/institutional power, interpersonal projections, political differences, perceptions of the other based on personal history, and expectations of the other. While we might argue that unhelpful assumptions can be made between two individuals of similar cultural backgrounds, these assumptions are often magnified as cultural difference increases.

Thus to successfully diminish barriers to communication between members of different cultural groups, we need to increase our awareness of the potential areas in which assumptions are inadvertently made. As our awareness increases, we are more likely to develop cultural sensitivity as integral to our daily practice, instead of giving 'lip-service' to arguably the most fundamental principle underpinning social work practice.

Prior to discussing the impact of culture in shaping lives, through the supervision process, John had made many assumptions about the cultural practices of certain groups of people. He had drawn upon racist and homophobic stereotypes that were held among his own family and community of origin to make sense of the world. John became deeply troubled by this, as he had not realised that these stereotypes could have a negative impact for people. For some time, he struggled with the way in which he had perpetuated oppression through attributing stigma to certain groups. John spent significant periods of time reflecting upon this. He had been left with many unhelpful

(Continued)

(Continued)

emotional responses that for a while blocked his progress. Feelings of guilt and anger in relation to certain racist assumptions he had previously made initially had a detrimental impact on his confidence as a practitioner. Over time, John was able to reconcile his previous beliefs and actions as being symptomatic of the imperialistic views he had adopted in an attempt to 'assimilate' fully into white English culture. He had to forgive himself for this before he was able to rebuild his confidence in his practice. This painful transition allowed a metamorphic shift in the stance John would take when communicating with individuals that would not have occurred had he not developed his awareness of himself and of his own personal history and experience.

Social Work Application

Social work values require that we look beyond presentation and communication styles in order to empower people to increase control of their lives and work to reduce oppression. Being mindful of our own values and beliefs allows us to be more explicitly aware of the way in which we are likely to interpret the meaning of presentation and communication styles. Misinterpretation through assumption-making almost always leads to a block in communication. Raising our awareness of ourselves reduces the likelihood of stereotyping people according to their cultural attributes. Thus we are more able to work in a non-stigmatising manner with people.

When using counselling skills, the value base from which we build the foundations of working relationships is essential to ensure that our practice does not inadvertently oppress people. The 'fine' counselling skills, from numerous approaches discussed in later chapters, require this foundation before they can be effectively used in social work practice.

Skills Component

- Continue to raise awareness of our own values and beliefs to avoid inadvertently stereotyping people.
- Avoid assumptions about people's presentation and communication style, as they often lead to blocks in communication.
- Use awareness of self and of our values to build a foundation upon which to develop 'fine' counselling skills.

Culture and Ethnicity

Ethnicity is an important aspect of cultural identity. Whether we refer to ethnicity in relation to customs and practices common to a group of people or whether we broaden the term to refer to country of family origin is debatable, since there are often many regional differences in religion and customs even within one country. Scotland, for example, has many regions where levels of affluence differ, as do rural lifestyles as opposed to city living. Language spoken varies also between English and Celtic, with many regional variations in between. With this is mind, we need to question the use of ethnicity as a term to define skin colour and physical character-istics alone.

In social work practice, we have a responsibility to recognise and challenge inequity in society. Certainly prejudice and discrimination permeate the social, eco-nomic and educational structures of British society (Dominelli, 1997). Inequality in respect of race and skin colour continues to be a major social problem and requires specific recognition beyond 'lip-service' to 'politically correct' language. A starting point in using counselling skills in a multicultural society needs to be an acknowl-edgement of inequality and recognition that our position will automatically place us in either a powerful majority position or a less powerful minority position. Given the nature of a therapeutic relationship where there exists a power imbalance between worker and service user, we need to take account of the aspects of our own position in society that bring with them power or powerlessness. As we develop our under-standing of ourselves in this respect, we will be better prepared to develop sensitivity in relation to cultural difference.

Kingston had learning difficulties and attended a day centre where he would be encouraged to become involved in activities and became 'challenging'. Workers at the centre were increasingly frustrated at his 'behaviour' and he became the target for most of the discussions between the staff group. The manager of the centre overheard a conversation between two workers where racially derogatory language was used to describe him. The manager was appalled at the behaviour of the staff and speculated that Kingston was probably receiving a poor quality of service, based on the racist beliefs held about him by some of the staff and evident in the workers' use of language. The manager had not heard other 'non-compliant' white service users being referred to in the same way. As this problem was challenged and the staff group changed, Kingston was observed to be more settled at the centre and more willing to engage in activities. The manager surmised that Kingston's 'behaviour' had been largely the product of racism that he had been unable to disclose as he had been labelled a problem and his views were not heard. As the workers listened to Kingston, respected his ethnicity and tailored activities to suit his interests more, he gradually grew in confidence.

Culture and Gender

The interpretation of gender identity is an important aspect of communication. Awareness of the impact of our own gender on a working relationship with a service user is fundamental to drawing upon multicultural counselling skills. Social work literature abounds with references to feminist perspectives: see, for example, Parton and O'Byrne (2000) and Adams et al. (2002). This chapter does not intend to replicate critical analysis of the impact of gender in social work practice, although gender inequalities are fundamentally acknowledged. Attention is drawn, however, towards raising awareness and sensitivity to the importance of gender inequalities in society and in relationships that can marginalise women.

Expectations of roles according to gender can immediately impact upon the working relationship, as we and service users can make assumptions about each other in a working relationship. If left unchecked, these assumptions can lead us along paths of communication that can stereotype and therefore oppress. When we meet service users, our frame of reference for what we will enquire about, in what order, with how much emphasis and with whom, will be borne out of our cultural experience and our position within society. The author will see the world from a female perspective in western society where traditionally males have more powerful positions than females (Rowbotham, 1973; Weeks, 1986). To minimise discrimination or bias, we first need to explore our own position and experience in relation to gender.

Jenny had been a practice teacher for several years when she met Dave, a student social worker on his first placement. Initially Jenny found Dave polite and he seemed to be well organised for his placement. As they approached their first direct observation of his practice, Jenny noticed that their working relationship had become more strained. Jenny shared her feelings about this with Dave and suggested they attempt to explore what might be happening, before the observation took place. Dave said very little, although he did acknowledge the tension. Jenny introduced a discussion of power in the student/practice teacher relationship and highlighted that they could not ignore gender differences as part of this. Dave initially struggled with the discussion. However, he eventually identified that he had thought of himself as being sympathetic to feminist ideals but was alarmed that he had had intrusive thoughts regarding being assessed by a woman who was younger than him and had spent less time in the social work field, although Jenny had been qualified for some time. Jenny accepted Dave's struggles with this matter by spending some time with him exploring their source. Dave was able to recognise implicit and explicit ways in which women are marginalised in society and was able to put his intrusive thoughts in context. This non-judgemental discussion facilitated the working relationship to continue, allowing Dave to successfully progress through his placement.

Culture and Sexuality

Beliefs about sexuality are culturally held and, as with other factors of an individual's experience, left unexplored on the part of the practitioner can lead to either discrimination or bias. Satinover (2002) considers homosexuality from a political perspective in western society and identifies some of the sources of stigma and oppression that permeate today's 'British' culture. Field (1995) refers to inequalities between the more powerful heterosexual status in society and the less powerful homosexual status. While people who prefer homosexual intimate relationships are in the minority, sexuality as part of the human experience is relevant to all members of society: what it means to be heterosexual as opposed to homosexual, to be sexually active or celibate, to practise monogamy or not. Sexuality, therefore, is culturally defined and culturally governed.

Freedom to explore sexuality with individuals can also vary according to other social roles and the cultural norms that govern them. For example, in western culture, it might be acceptable to discuss the impact of sexual abuse on sexuality between two adult women as part of a therapeutic relationship but less acceptable between an adult male and female. Assumptions might be made about cultural boundaries that cannot be crossed for fear of perpetuating a form of intrusive abuse or for fear of sexual arousal in the other. Sexuality as part of social work practice is explored in depth in Brown (1998).

It is through the exploration of our own beliefs and values in respect of sexuality that we can raise our awareness of our behaviour and communication in practice. We can increase our confidence in understanding the impact of sexuality in a cultural context, and thus broaden our cultural competence in this respect.

Finton and his partner, Mario, were approached by social services after a neighbour anonymously alleged that Finton's seven-year-old son Toby was being routinely left alone in the house. Finton and Mario were angry at the intrusive response by social services, although reluctantly complied with an interview. Finton and Mario were able to demonstrate the childcare arrangements made for when they were both working and the social workers found no evidence that substantiated the allegations. Using sensitive and respectful language, the social workers responded to Finton's and Mario's belief about neighbourhood malice by enquiring whether their sexuality might be relevant. Mario disclosed that two households in the neighbourhood, known to be friendly to others, did not acknowledge them at all. This left the couple feeling vulnerable within the community and worried about the impact of discrimination on Toby. Although the family had been deeply upset by the malicious allegation, they were able to share their worries as a result of sensitive and well-timed questions regarding a central aspect of their personal lives.

Culture and Socio-economic Status

Parton and O'Byrne (2000) make reference to the history of social work practice in respect of social class. They describe social work since the late nineteenth century as occupying 'the space between the respectable and the dangerous classes, and between those with access to political and speaking rights and those who are excluded'. To effectively use counselling skills in social work practice we must first develop our understanding of the relatively powerless position of people from groups with lower socio-economic status and the privileged position of those in paid employment with higher degrees of social and economic power.

As we recognise the power imbalance between social groups in general, we can attune our communication skills towards not only effective listening, but effective listening to the content *and context* of a person's social position. In doing so, we are then better placed to actively empower a service user to access their rights, increase their socio-economic status or take a more active role in social functioning. As Thompson (2003) identifies, many assumptions can be made about a person based on socio-economically related matters, such as regional accent and education, which can mislead us into false beliefs regarding a person's capacity for understanding or their level of intelligence. Such false beliefs need exploring before we can fully embrace an empowering use of counselling skills.

Esther had six children under the age of 14. She lived in local authority rented accommodation and received state benefits. She had never worked and had a history of binge drinking. Her children had been accommodated previously and then rehabilitated back to her care after a degree of change had been achieved. Over several months, the children's school attendance began to decline and all of the children were presenting with emotional problems in different forms. After an incident of physical abuse towards one of the children, all six were accommodated on a voluntary basis. During completion of risk assessment, the social workers moved towards a position of seeking a legal order to prevent the children returning to their mother's care and to make plans for permanent alternative arrangements.

Throughout this assessment, the workers were acutely aware of the powerless position of the mother and the social barriers that stood in the way of change. The children had experienced emotional deprivation and abuse but this was compounded by social disadvantage. Using counselling skills alone would not have been enough to bring about change for this family. The lack of financial resources had compounded the stress experienced by Esther and had led to her 'giving up'. Empathic identification of this factor in discussions with her allowed the social worker to increase her understanding of the impact of deprivation but did not bring about enough change for the children to safely return home.

Social Work Application

Regardless of the social work setting, social workers are continuously faced with communicating with people from many various social and cultural groups.

(Continued)

(Continued)

As we move away from assumption-making and holding stereotypical views about people according to their culture, we are more likely to view their situations in a holistic way, considering the many factors that undermine social functioning.

As we develop our skills in recognising 'difference' and the powerless position to which being 'different' from the majority can lead people, we are more likely to be able to view people and their circumstances in context with society. The more we are able to recognise how oppression impacts on individuals as well as groups of people, the more able we will be to incorporate these matters into our conversations with service users and colleagues. This is not to advocate that we force people to discuss personal experience, nor that we impose our view of oppression on others. Either has the potential to be dangerous practice. Effective listening skills (see introduction) remain essential to hear and acknowledge people's own views. As experience is both an individual and a shared phenomenon, we need to respect the boundaries that people might set regarding how much they are willing to divulge about their individual cultural experience. However, being open to discussing oppression in its many forms can implicitly give permission for these matters to be discussed and can give a message that we are willing to hear.

Skills Component

- Acknowledge that many factors, including race and culture, can restrict social functioning.
- Recognise 'difference' and the link with less powerful social positions.
- Incorporate discussions of oppression in our conversations with people.
- Avoid imposing views on others.
- Draw on listening skills to hear the views of others regarding personal experience of oppression.

Idiographic Perspective

Palmer (2002) offers a multicultural framework for communicating with service users in a counselling or therapeutic setting. He terms this the 'Idiographic Perspective'. Ridley (1984, 1995) outlines a 'multi-modal' approach to counselling and therapeutic intervention that fits with the values and ethic of social work practice. Palmer draws upon Ridley's work to advocate exploring the concept of an individual's culture and ethnicity within the context of roles and status relating to other factors: 'the idiographic approach supports the concept of differential but non-discriminatory' practice (Palmer, 2002). This method allows us to acknowledge the possibility of several sources of oppression without the risk of stereotyping an individual.

Each individual will have several roles that sit alongside culture, ethnicity and socio-economic status to form a whole identity. These will include whether an individual is a parent, a son or daughter, the birth order if one of a group of siblings (i.e. eldest, youngest, middle), whether they are employed or not and, if so, the nature of the employment, their social class (of family of origin and currently), their region of residence, their gender and ethnicity. Palmer argues that it is the point where these 'overlapping identities' converge that should be the focus for using counselling skills from an idiographic perspective. Although Palmer does not weight these 'overlapping identities', we might assume that for each individual the level of influence or perceived influence of each factor could be different.

Ridley (1995) cites 12 points that can assist us to integrate idiographic counselling skills into practice (my italics):

1. Develop cultural awareness
2. Avoid value imposition
3. Accept *our* naivety as multicultural *practitioners*
4. Show cultural empathy
5. Incorporate cultural considerations into *practice*
6. Do not stereotype
7. Weigh and determine the relative importance of the client's primary cultural roles
8. Do not blame the *service user*
9. Remain flexible in *our* selection of interventions
10. Examine *our* counselling theories for *cultural* bias
11. Build on the *service user's* strengths
12. Do not protect *service users* from emotional pain

Paro, a 13-year-old young woman with parents who had migrated to the west of Scotland from southern Pakistan before she and her two siblings were born, came into conflict with her parents over peer relationships. She was a popular young woman with her peers and for some time had wanted to join them at a local youth disco. Her parents objected, believing that any form of dancing was degrading and an act of 'enticement'. Paro became increasingly resentful towards her parents and started to truant from school in an act of defiance. Her declining attendance and visible low mood following an overdose of tablets led to Paro being referred to social work services. The presenting problem perceived by the social worker was that Paro was struggling with the competing demands of two cultures – that of her parents and that of her peers within the local community.

However, as the social worker met with Paro and her parents, other factors became apparent. Paro's father had had a stroke approximately a year before and although he was left with some right-sided paralysis, this was not open for discussion within the family. He had lost his employment and the family were

(Continued)

(Continued)

still trying to adjust to a lower socio-economic status. Paro's mother was an anxious woman who worried every time Paro was away from home. Paro was aware of this and felt constrained by her mother's anxieties. Her parents valued their independence and were uncomfortable with asking services for help. Paro also resented her two older brothers, both over 16, whom she perceived as having more freedom than she to go out with their peers. Paro attributed this to her gender and to the over-protectiveness of her parents. While the social worker had been aware of the cultural factors relating to Paro and her life, she had also given time and consideration to other important aspects of Paro's identity as a daughter, a popular schoolgirl, a talented academic, a sister and youngest child and a carer for her father. She acknowledged that she did not understand what family life for them must be like and used her 'not knowing' position to draw upon the family's expertise to explain cultural and familial beliefs and practices. Rather than narrow her focus on cultural aspects alone, however, an idiographic approach allowed her to communicate with the family regarding a broad range of social and relationship factors.

Social Work Application

This model provides a useful framework in which counselling skills can be used to acknowledge cultural influences in individuals' experiences without dismissing other important factors. Using this framework alongside models of assessment, important cultural and relational factors can be included in data collection and analysis. In addition, drawing upon this model when communicating with service users, pointers as to what to be curious about in our conversations with people are thus provided. While ever we avoid making stereotypical assumptions and focus on cultural factors above all else, we are able to integrate this framework into and alongside other models, including assessment and counselling approaches. Using a framework does facilitate focus and although eclectic practice certainly has value in that it allows flexibility, the focus of a framework prevents practice becoming too broad and diffuse.

Skills Component

- Draw on features of this framework to include consideration of cultural matters alongside other factors.
- Use this framework in conjunction with other models of assessment and alongside techniques gained from models of counselling.
- Use a framework flexibly to maintain focus in practice without becoming too diffuse.

Summary of Key Concepts in Multicultural Counselling

- Understanding **Cultural Experience** is **Complex**
- Social work **Ethics and Values** require that there is a balance between individual need and accountability to society as a whole
- The foundation for using counselling skills in a multicultural context is the acceptance that **Society is Unequal**
- Understanding that 'minority' groups are in less powerful positions within society than 'majority' groups assists us to develop **Cultural Awareness**
- Accepting that people and their beliefs and practices have **Differences and Similarities** assists us to further develop **Cultural Awareness**
- Insight into our own **Cultural History** is essential to developing **Cultural Sensitivity**
- Recognising the impact of **Cultural Difference** for individuals and families allows us to further develop **Cultural Sensitivity**
- **Cultural Sensitivity** facilitates us to communicate with people with respect and delicacy regarding cultural matters
- **Assumptions** made about presentation and communication styles can block effective communication
- An **Idiographic Framework** integrated into practice allows us to view culture within the context of many aspects of people's lives
- We can become **Authentic Chameleons** as we selectively use counselling and other theoretical models fitting best with service users' needs for assessment and intervention

---

Conclusion

All areas of Britain are multicultural in nature. This includes, but is not exclusive to, skin colour. Wherever we practise social work, we will find that people have similarities and differences in their cultural histories, in their values, in their beliefs about themselves and the world, and in the way in which the rituals of life are practised. The concepts presented in this chapter are fundamental as a basis upon which a broad range of 'finer' counselling skills can be built. As we take time to reflect upon our values in respect of culture, we can become more 'tuned in' to recognising the impact of cultural difference in a white, heterosexual 'majority' society that holds social progression, economic status and individual achievement in high esteem. As we 'tune in' to difference we start to understand oppression, and as we understand oppression we can develop our affective responses to be sensitive to the service users with whom we work. As cultural matters can so often become either an afterthought or caught up in relentless 'political correctness' that can be seen to devalue this important aspect of life, this chapter aims to promote multicultural counselling approaches as the absolute foundation to social work practice.

Further Reading

- **Palmer (2002)** provides a series of papers that explore a broad range of issues when using counselling skills multiculturally. Inclusive is his own chapter outlining the idiographic framework to practice. While social work practice is not the focus of the text, it is helpful in increasing understanding of the complexity of cultural factors in therapeutic relationships.

- **Lago and Thompson (2003)** focus heavily on race in respect of culture. The chapter on 'Cultural barriers to communication' and the chapter discussing 'Non-western approaches to helping' are especially useful for social work practitioners to draw on to improve counselling skills in this respect.

- **Speed and Burck (1995)** offer a selection of chapters with a range of perspectives on gender and power relationships. While it is an older text and not specifically designed for social work practice, the book is very useful for considering gender, power and culture in working relationships.

- **Thompson (2003)** draws upon culture to explore communication and language in written and verbal forms. This book provides an in-depth analysis of the style of communication cross-culturally and the meaning of different styles of communication in various contexts.

- **Brown (1998)** considers sexuality in a social work context in significant depth, including an exploration of factors relating to inequality and prejudice. This book is of fundamental importance in general social work literature.

2
Person-centred Approach to Using Counselling Skills in Social Work Practice

Key Concepts	Key Theorists and Practitioners
• Self-actualisation • Self-concept and Self-structure • Unconditional Positive Regard • Working Alliance • Congruence • Empathy	• Maslow • Rogers

Introduction

The person-centred approach is an influential model that strongly informs our use of counselling skills. This chapter aims to achieve two objectives. Firstly, it will provide a brief overview of the person-centred approach, which will be outlined and applied to social work practice. As with other chapters, this is not all-inclusive and further reading is strongly recommended. Secondly, some of the skills associated with this approach will be examined in detail within a social work context. Contained within this is an exploration of the three fundamental therapeutic attributes for effective communication with vulnerable people in need, building on listening skills: congruence, empathy and unconditional positive regard (Rogers, 1957).

The Humanistic School

The Humanistic School (Nelson-Jones, 2000) is named as a result of its value base, advocating that human beings have individual potential that needs to be achieved in order to experience satisfaction with life. This is referred to as actualisation (Rogers, 1977). It is reached by 'experiencing ... feelings' in order to bring a form of 'harmony' between thoughts, actions and underlying tendencies, and then to generate autonomous thoughts and actions. The Humanistic School firmly believes that all of us have tendencies that are unique and all of us have a capacity for understanding the self. Thinking and acting that is out of harmony with these tendencies results in distress, dissatisfaction and a lack of fulfilment in life. Self-reflection aided by therapeutic support helps to bring our lives back into harmony with these tendencies (Rogers, 1977).

Carl Rogers (1942, 1980) is the dominant theorist in this perspective. A historical account of his life as such is given by Nelson-Jones (2000), who provides the context in which his ideas evolved. Rogers seems to have acknowledged areas of disharmony in his own life and appears to have been striving to fulfil self-actualisation and to find more internal–external harmony. As social workers we are interested in political influences and we need to view Rogers' beliefs about human potential in a political context if we are to objectively evaluate the usefulness of this approach. His commitment to the emancipation of people from the dominant voice of society and from their parents sets a foundation for the notion of individual potential and for the challenging of authority in various forms (Rogers, 1980).

As with other approaches that follow in subsequent chapters, a person-centred approach has theoretical underpinnings that are based on beliefs that have been tested in practice over time. Critical social work practice requires that we keep a firm hold on the origin of theoretical concepts and do not fall into fixed, repetitive practice, where we accept theoretical models on face value as 'absolute truth'. There are, however, benefits to including elements of this model into social work practice.

Theoretical Underpinnings of the Approach

Rogers (1961) was wholly concerned with people's internal processes that lead to environmental stimuli being experienced by them as a unique and entirely subjective form of reality. Individual emotional and behavioural reactions to experience and the unique meaning of those reactions cannot therefore be globally categorised or predicted, even in the context of culture. Tolan (2003) includes scope for the influence of culture in the development of personality within this approach but the meaning given to experience remains an individual phenomenon. In this respect, labelling emotional and behavioural problems as disorders that lead to broadly defined and prescribed 'treatments', pharmacological or psychological, would not easily fit with this approach.

Self-actualisation

Rogers' most significant and distinguishing theoretical concept is that of actualisation (1977). Drawn from other theorists of his time, including Maslow (1962, 1970), Rogers identifies that human motivation functions to assist us to reach our individual potential. In so doing, we strive to achieve internal harmony between what we feel and what we experience. By a process of internally evaluating experience we individually evolve by change and adaptation through the means of self-regulation. This includes congruent awareness and expression of feelings evoked by experience: we recognise, then express, what we feel about an experience. Self-regulation allows choosing satisfying experiences over dissatisfying ones. The actualisation process is thus a motivational system from which our individual evolution and development occurs. Competing against this, however, is the conscious self (Rogers, 1959; Maslow, 1962), where blockages to the actualising process occur.

The actualisation process in Humanistic theory applies over the life span. The self-actualisation drive is not a static concept but one that is continually in progress through the triad of experiencing, perceiving feelings linked to experience, and expressing or acting upon feelings in congruence with the experience. Reaching human potential does not have a ceiling of age and is unique to each individual. The actualisation process becomes blocked and internal disharmony results when incongruence between feelings and experience, expression or action occurs. In such a situation, inner conflict is generated and emotional and behavioural problems can develop.

Immediately, the potentially conflicting elements – individual tendencies and social structures – become apparent. For example, it is a legal requirement for children and young people to participate in education. The educational structure that exists in our society inevitably results in some young people's tendencies, i.e. their talents, strengths, activities through which they can thrive, do not easily fit with the system. Therefore, disharmony for such young people becomes evident through their behaviour and emotionality. Quiet withdrawal and acceptance, possible low mood or 'acting out' through challenging behaviour can all occur.

The education system is one example of how young people are required to fit with a system that does not meet the needs of all of the children and young people in society. This obviously highlights a conflict for social work. We are required to work within socio-political and legal boundaries. Awareness of the lack of fit between some individuals' needs and the social structure does at least give social workers the opportunity for insight into difficulties that are not intrinsic to the person. This offers us an alternative perspective to one suggesting a person is either mentally ill or has a disorder that leads to 'dysfunction' within a specific environment. Raising awareness can also lead to creative exploration of solutions within those social structures, even if it does not result in changing the structures themselves.

Gregor presented as extremely quiet when meeting individually with Ajay, his social worker. He was known within his peer group, however, as a bold and charismatic leader who would often be the instigator of offending behaviours, especially car offences. Gregor was a 16-year-old young man, the middle child from a family of three brothers and a single mother, who was an exhausted woman who had been asking for help with Gregor for several years. Gregor had a long history of truanting from school, this having been a pattern of behaviour since primary school. He had gradually become involved in car theft and was recognised among his peers for his deftness and his daring for fast

(Continued)

(Continued)

driving. He had long been involved with the Children's Hearing system in Scotland and was subject to a Supervision Requirement under Section 70 of the Children (Scotland) Act 1995. Gregor's offending behaviour had peaked and declined over the years, mostly in response to threats from Children's Panel members that if his behaviour continued he would be accommodated by the Local Authority due to moral danger and being beyond parental control. Gregor was frightened by the thought of being accommodated and these threats regulated the extent of his offending behaviour periodically. This was enough to legally maintain him at home but did not assist in any way to understand the reasons for his behaviour, nor alter the course his life was taking. Gregor had had difficulties maintaining his focus on academic work when at school, especially with subjects that required reading, which he found challenging. He had greater interest in technical studies but as these classes were limited, his interest was not enough to encourage him to remain in school, and, when he did, he became angry and very aggressive, as he did at other times.

In several ways, Gregor had not been reaching his 'organismic' potential, either in the past or presently. His talents in technical subjects had little opportunity for substantial development, as this was only a small part of the school curriculum. He had acknowledged his feelings about his difficulties with the more literary subjects at school but avoiding these through truanting led to the Children's Hearing system becoming involved and exacerbated the fraught relationship between him and his mother. He often expressed boredom the community in which they lived. Gregor did experience internal conflict, which was evident through his aggressive behaviour. The self-actualising drive was being inhibited by a combination of lack of opportunity for skill development attuned to his needs, and lack of social opportunities due to living in a deprived area of a small, rural town. Inner conflict between lack of opportunities for development alongside social disapproval of offending behaviours that did provide him with both status, a form of social development and gratification, created emotional disharmony that was expressed through aggression.

Gregor's self-actualising drive was in action in that he continued behaviours that matched his needs through self-regulation. However, inner conflict was also being experienced. His mother, his social worker and the legal system were attempting to limit his offending behaviours in conjunction with a lack of alternative opportunities for Gregor to seek the same level of gratification and skill development in socially acceptable activities.

Social Work Application

Gregor had become known to social work services initially through poor school attendance and later through offending behaviour. Although other approaches

(Continued)

(Continued)

can be helpful to work with these types of problems such as cognitive behavioural therapy and family therapy, as social workers we can try to make sense of what can motivate different behaviours through the theoretical components of a person-centred model. We can accept that social structures often do not fit with individuals' needs and we can therefore avoid pathologising responses such as aggression or avoidance of difficult settings as a problem entirely located within the individual. Although this approach is primarily about an individual and whether internal conflict exists, we must hold to the notion that internal conflict is usually a result of an individual adapting to an environment that does not fully meet their needs. The drive to reach our potential is strong and, as with Gregor, the motivation to meet unmet needs may eventually become apparent though the drive for self-actualisation. We can seek to recognise where self-actualisation might be motivating an individual into activities that are not socially acceptable in the same way as we can learn to recognise when this drive is being blocked.

As a fundamental principle of communicating with others, we must first learn to accept the individual nature of human development and be willing to notice that people have needs that do not always fit with social structures. While some general rules might apply to social development, such as all children requiring certainty and predictability coupled with opportunities for exploration of the world, we cannot actively accept and listen to another person's position if we do not accept the value of individual uniqueness. This is intrinsic to social work practice.

Gail was a young woman who had struggled with feelings of hopelessness and general low mood for many years. She was a bright, intelligent young woman who had been finding it hard to make progress in her chosen career and to have her voice heard. Her participation in social activities had gradually declined, where she used to keep herself fit by regular gym attendance and had been very involved socially with other young people. She no longer pursued intimate relationships, denying her need for this. Her determination to be successful in life led her to dismiss feelings of sadness and loss since she had had 'the accident' several years previously. She believed such feelings to be 'weak' and 'unproductive'. Gail used a wheelchair since she had damaged her spine in adolescence.

Gail was not congruently connecting her experiences with her feelings. Feelings of anger, frustration and sadness were pushed aside and she refused to accept these as relevant. She was not reaching her 'organismic' potential socially, intellectually or sexually and, as a result, the drive for self-actualisation left her with feelings of inner conflict and distress that she found hard to name.

Again, as with Gregor, Gail was not reaching her potential and this led to disharmony in her life. The social work task in applying the theoretical concepts of the person-centred approach would be to accept firstly that in

(Continued)

(Continued)

some way her potential was not being met. Her feelings had not been congruently linked with her experiences. For communication to be effective, as social workers we can recognise incongruence in the way in which people speak and act. Before moving on to use this approach in a therapeutic way, we need to develop and improve our observational skills in this respect. Thompson (2003) offers a clear outline of how we can do this in his chapters on verbal and non-verbal communication.

Skills Component

- Understand the actualisation process and the need for congruence between feelings and experience to create internal harmony.
- Recognise and hold to the value that individuals are unique and have unique needs.
- Become aware that social structures do not always meet the needs of every individual.
- Accept that the lack of fit between social structures and individuals does not translate healthy emotional responses into pathology.
- Improve skills in verbal and non-verbal communication to tune into observing incongruent responses indicating the source of distress.

Self-concept and Self-structure

An important element within the theoretical framework of a person-centred approach is the development of self-concept as distinct from the self: the self, or 'true' self, is where underlying tendencies are generated as part of being a living organism that has experiences over time.

Self-concept begins during infancy as we begin to have experiences that are given meaning – whether we are fed and comforted, for example. We could compare this with attachment theory (see Chapter 4). We take experiences, attribute meaning to them through our feelings and use this as feedback to form a picture of how we see ourselves and the value that we have to others (Rogers, 1951). Tolan (2003) broadens this, using the term 'self-structure' as a wider framework for the development of beliefs and values that an individual will hold of him- or herself, of individual experiences and of the world in general. This links to some extent with George Kelly's (1955) 'personal constructs' that formed the basis of what became schema in cognitive behavioural therapy (see Chapter 3). The self-structure develops over time and is separate from actual experience, or receiving information about the world through the five senses; experience in itself and without the application of meaning, is thus neutral. Tolan refers to the self-structure as a 'framework of familiarity', which helps us make sense of our lives. Implicit is the self-concept as part of the self-structure. She focuses on experience and the development of the self-structure rather than innate tendencies, in her interpretation of the approach. However, implicit in the self-structure is the idea that tendencies develop as part of the organisation of the self-structure through a life-long evolutionary process. The self-structure is thus an individually unique organisation that allows the self to function and perceive the world.

Sometimes awareness of the impact of experience is not directly available to us if we have had to adapt it to survive or function adequately in a difficult environment. This could range from subtly difficult, i.e. a child experiences a parent offering a secure home environment but dismisses the validity of their feelings, to obviously traumatic, i.e. in the domain of abuse. Tolan (2003) suggests that experience is 'symbolised' in awareness. Levels of awareness can improve gradually as we re-experience events through discussion and recall, i.e. as part of a therapeutic relationship. She describes this as 'loosening' the self-structure to accommodate denied or distorted feelings linked to previous experience by reflection. As situations, and thus repeated experience, change over time, the need for denial or distortion of feelings related to experience often becomes less, which then space for this 'loosening' to occur.

For example, feelings of fear generated by repeated physical abuse from a parent could lead a child to be extremely anxious and unable to tolerate the presence of that parent if their feelings were being actively acknowledged at the time. Most often a child is aware of his or her dependency on the parent to provide basic care needs so this fear would be counter-productive. Functional to day-to-day living is either denial or distortion of feelings of fear, where the child could make sense of the experience through self-blame, freeing the parent to continue to offer some form of care. The child then re-attributes blame to themselves. The child's self-concept starts to incorporate negative beliefs about self-worth, which would likely result in the child becoming either withdrawn, acting out or displaying other emotional problems.

The self-structure, which includes the child's beliefs about the world, could come to include a general distrust of adults. At the time of the abusive experiences, this creates a wariness of other adults that serves to protect that child from further harm. This part of the self-structure is functional to the child's survival in his or her home environment and is therefore rigidly held. However, once the child grows and leaves the household, and providing he or she then lives in a safe situation, denial or distortion of that fear is no longer a necessary function of day-to-day living. Therefore, where rigidity in the self-structure in childhood, for functional reasons, was useful, it can hinder emotional growth and development in later life. Therapeutic work, however, can lead to the opportunity for a loosening of that structure. It can thus provide a window for denied feelings to be reconnected with previous experience and so loosen the level of emotional rigidity.

The fundamental difference here is that the person's environment has changed. Implicit is that a child with a functional, rigidly held self-structure will not be able to loosen their self-structure in a therapeutic setting if the experiences and the environment in which difficult experiences occurred have not changed. This would apply similarly to an adult in an environment that generates negative feelings, such as domestic violence. Unless that person is actively seeking change and help and is therefore already experiencing a loosening of their self-structure, the imposition of therapeutic intervention will not necessarily facilitate a change in thinking or beliefs.

Hence we should not be overly hasty in encouraging or coercing individuals into therapeutic work.

Seeking objective truth that is separate from meaning ascribed to experience by individuals is not the concern of the person-centred approach (Rogers, 1980). Again obvious limitations are striking for social workers, such as our commitment to counter racism and other forms of oppression. These are recognised in the social work field as structural problems that have an impact on every individual. Reducing structural racism and other forms of oppression to an individual experience denies wider societal beliefs of superiority for those in privileged positions, including white, able-bodied, heterosexual people and people in economically secure positions. While we might accept that each individual will have a unique experience of prejudice and discrimination, we cannot deny that more universal experiences of oppression do not exist.

Gregor's view of the world was that of adults, most significantly in authority positions, being only motivated to criticise him and keep him in line. He believed that the Children's Hearing system was punitive and that his behaviour, although highly gratifying to him, should not be the concern of others who were only intrusive in order to be controlling of him. He could see no clear opportunities that he desired for either self-development within his local community or for achieving the levels of status and excitement he found when involved in car theft. Car theft did seem repetitive at times and his need for developing more skills on a broader level was stagnating. He was aware of the danger to himself and others and fully aware of the illegal nature of his activities. As he continued to be involved in offending behaviour he developed a self-concept of 'badness' as a 'criminal', with little regard for others and therefore 'very selfish', despite being very protective of his peers. He believed only those like him would respect him and the influence of his peer group remained very strong. He saw the world as a hostile and unforgiving place where each person must fight for his or her own survival by aggressive means. Gregor had little awareness of any of his talents or positive attributes other than through car theft. Both his self-concept and his self-structure (being inclusive of this and of the world in general) were shaped around these strong beliefs. Ajay, his social worker, had recognised the incongruence between Gregor's feelings and experiences and had started to actively listen to him during their meetings in a non-directive way, since many other directive approaches had had little impact on his behaviour.

Social Work Application

From a person-centred position, a social worker would be seeking to assist Gregor to connect his feelings with his experiences in a non-directive way. This does pose problems in that the legal system, such as the requirements of the

(Continued)

(Continued)

Children's Hearing system to keep both Gregor and the public safe, might be frustrated with a less directive approach. However, this aside, the essence of Gregor's difficulties in achieving change was the lack of gratification in other areas of his life that was not linked to crime. He had not received an education that offered him hope of a future where he could channel his skills and improve them. He felt marginalised from society due to his social status, living in a deprived area with few amenities outside of education. His mother was in receipt of benefits and did not have the available resources to allow Gregor to travel to become involved in activities. His environment had not offered Gregor opportunities for gratification through skill development, which had become a need and a tendency as part of his self-structure. As Gregor's feelings were not symbolised in awareness, the actualising drive was only partly in progress as he was seeking gratification through offending, albeit that this was limiting for him, but he was unable to self-regulate his behaviour to direct his energies into other channels where a greater level of gratification could occur.

There are times in social work practice when a less directive stance through an approach such as this is more helpful. Gregor would have the opportunity to make sense of his frustrations by reflecting back on missed education and the feelings that had generated for him. Being 16 and no longer required to attend school, he had a changed environment which could allow a loosening of his self-structure enough to reconnect feelings and experiences. Adult education, which tends to be broader in vocational terms, was more of an option and so the limited opportunities of childhood could change in adulthood. Most importantly, though, Gregor was starting to feel limited by the constant repetition of scenarios through car theft and was therefore experiencing a greater degree of inner conflict. Through a non-directive person-centred approach, Gregor could re-evaluate elements of his self-concept and self-structure that were both negative and limiting his personal progress. The communication skills required for effective non-directive listening are outlined below in the section on application of the person-centred approach. However, key skills exist at this stage for recognition of where inner conflict might exist and where timing as to when to use this approach is crucial.

Gail had always been a determined individual whose self-structure included a self-deterministic view of the world. She would focus her time and attention to achieve whatever she set her mind to. She had not encountered social barriers to achievement and success until the accident occurred. She saw herself as a strong independent individual who had no need to rely on anyone. Following the spinal injury, she continued to view herself in the same way to the point that she refused any practical help and developed coping skills through the use of her arms to manage day-to-day life. She also refused to acknowledge the accident had an emotional impact. Only as time passed and

(Continued)

(Continued)

she encountered social barriers relating to physical disabilities did feelings of inner conflict emerge. Her self-structure of beliefs that she could achieve anything she set her mind to had been seriously challenged. Most of all, she noticed that often people would ignore her in the wheelchair and speak about her to a companion standing next to her. Rather than accept feelings of anger that were evoked, she denied them. Eventually her mood became so low that she left her job, started to neglect her personal care and was referred by the family general practitioner (GP) for help. A social worker taking a non-directive approach to listening provided her with the opportunity to reconnect her denied feelings with her experiences. This had become possible as she had a changed social environment and the denial was no longer functional to her needing to tolerate working.

Skills Component

- Recognise that the self-concept and self-structure shape the way in which experiences are given meaning to individuals.
- Heighten awareness of negative self-concepts and possible areas of incongruence suggesting denied or distorted feelings.
- If the timing for a non-directive approach does not fit with the circumstances of a referral, selective use of the principles within the approach might be more appropriate to incorporate within a different model, i.e. crisis intervention.
- Judging whether the timing best suits the situation involves consideration of whether the environment leading to experience has changed sufficiently for an individual to reflect upon this, 'loosening' the self-structure.
- Balance the demands of the legal system with the needs of the individual to judge whether this is the most helpful approach.

Positive Regard from Others

Self-concept is influenced by our sense of worth, learned and developed from feedback from others over time (Rogers, 1959). Elements of this fit closely with cognitive behavioural theory as outlined in Chapter 3. Positive regard from others is an important concept that can motivate action. For example, a young person might receive recognition by peers and adults for sporting skills and this positive regard will become an integral need for feelings of self-worth as part of an individual's self-concept. McMillan (2004) draws on Rogers' (1959) description of a 'regard matrix' that develops as we filter these experiences. Experiencing positive regard from others is necessary to feel 'good enough' among others. It thus intertwines with self-concept to influence behaviour.

Many vulnerable people who become known to social work services have either experienced little positive regard from others or received conditional positive regard based upon some form of attribute or behaviour. Rogers (1959) suggests that we are motivated by the need for positive regard. Feelings can easily be denied or distorted as we attempt to meet this need, leading to behaviours to continue that do not necessarily fit with the experience of the true self. This might include being very quiet when angry for fear of being rejected, or distorting feelings of anger after being highly criticised into inadequacy and self-blame.

When we repeat behaviours for acceptance from others to continue feelings of worth, we can find ourselves acting incongruently with our tendencies intrinsic to our true selves. Self-actualisation becomes blocked if we continue to recreate conditions that result in specific forms of positive regard from others. For example, compliant behaviour in school could be motivated by fear of recriminations if a teacher became angry. Further, spontaneity and creativity could become blocked and development might be hindered. Likewise, a young person repeatedly involved in offending behaviour could be strongly influenced and motivated by the need for peer acceptance, following negative or conditional regard from family. The positive regard from the peer group has the more powerful voice to the individual and positive regard from them is sought after more than that of the family.

Denial or distorted beliefs about strengths or positive attributes in other areas of that young person's life that might be neglected, would limit individual growth. Continuation of this form of offending behaviour, even when the peer group has changed, fits with denial of other positive aspects of the self. This denial minimises any conflict between perception and experience, i.e. problems fitting in with majority society, public disapproval. Denial also allows previous patterns of need-fulfilment to continue.

Receiving positive regard from others, be it real or perceived, is the central motivating factor for behaviour that is linked to the self-concept (McMillan, 2004). Further, the level of congruence between feelings attached to behaviour and self-regulatory reflection and action, will determine the level of individual harmony and satisfaction in life.

When repeatedly behaving in ways that are not motivated by the need to generate positive regard from others, we are acting upon tendencies from the 'true' self, from which satisfaction is derived. For example, a young person who chooses to join a specific club, e.g. hockey, rather than run with the local 'gang' in his or her local community, might be acting in congruence with his or her individual tendencies: in this case to develop sporting skills. He or she might experience a level of social isolation within their own community but this does not motivate behaviour that would generate positive regard from the local group. We could refer to attachment theory here (see Chapter 4), which would suggest, in humanistic terms, that the young person receives adequate positive regard, or a secure enough base, from his or her social experience to resist the need to seek it in other areas of life.

In most instances, acting in harmony with our tendencies is viewed as positive, i.e. that young person might avoid becoming embroiled in offending behaviour, which is common within that particular 'gang'. There are some types of behaviour, however, that can harm others and are both socially and legally unacceptable, even when it could be argued that an individual is following his or her organismic tendencies. An example might be the sexual abuse of a child, that is, a behaviour that is unilaterally harmful to another and thus cannot be condoned in any circumstance, even if an individual's tendencies lead him or her towards such behaviours. Self-actualising therefore requires limits based on restricting that which might harm others. As social workers working within a legal and social policy framework, we cannot view the drive towards self-actualising without boundaries and cannot work to facilitate the congruence of one person's tendencies with their actions when it would be harmful to another.

Gregor received status and admiration from his peer group for his daring feats and for his charismatic leadership. This positive regard was completely conditional, however, upon certain forms of behaviour, and thus his continued involvement in car crime maintained his position and leadership within the group. Gregor received little positive regard at home. He was seen as an 'embarrassing disappointment' to his mother, who believed he had 'something wrong with him', which led him into the behavioural patterns that had become so entrenched. Gregor's mother was highly critical and negative of him to the point where she struggled to recognise any positive attributes at all. His older brother was mainly dismissive of him and his younger brother, the only one without any history of behavioural problems, feared him. Gregor valued the acceptance and admiration of his peers above all others and denied any need to be accepted within his family. Thus his motivation to continue with offending remained high. His mother's view of any future acceptance of him by her was dependent on his behaviour changing. This was too high a goal for Gregor to achieve at that point to attain her approval of him as a worthwhile individual. He stopped trying.

Ajay recognised that Gregor had not received any form of acceptance as a person in his own right, regardless of the behaviours he presented. Ajay, through drawing on a person-centred approach, demonstrated that he accepted Gregor as an individual and that his behaviours did not lead to him to be either critical or rejecting of him.

Social Work Application

In social work, our interest in positive unconditional regard is twofold: we can model this form of acceptance in the work we do within the remit of communication skills; and we can recognise where those with whom we work have received positive regard where it has only been conditional.

(Continued)

(Continued)

During Gail's early years and through her adolescence, she had received praise and recognition from her family and from teachers for her academic and sporting abilities. She was what would typically be known as a 'high achiever'. Her parents had high expectations of her – she would go to university, have a successful career, achieve financial independence. The times when Gail was struggling with her focus and had wanted to receive comfort and nurturing were met with dismissal of her feelings. Gail shaped her self-structure around this feedback and found herself shaping her behaviour around ways in which she would receive positive regard. This was functional until she lost the use of her legs.

Her experiences of using a wheelchair and of people's reactions to her no longer provided her with positive regard through her achievements and abilities. Some of the barriers that she faced included people using patronising language and tone when speaking to her; and ignoring her and treating her as if she could no longer think in the same ways as she did previously (her job being one that involved a lot of thinking). One of the greatest impacts of her disability was the loss of positive regard that had motivated her for so long.

Both Gregor and Gail had one experience in common. They had both experienced *conditional* positive regard from parents and peers. Understanding the theoretical component to this is an element of the person-centred approach that is most useful, even when the approach is not being incorporated into practice in full. How to use language and feedback to place ourselves in an unconditionally accepting position is offered below. However, if we can find ourselves integrating this principle into our thinking with people, then immediately we can free up an avenue of acceptance that might allow people to share with us their own thoughts, feelings and opinions.

Skills Component

- Recognise where service users seem to have received conditional positive regard and how this can motivate behaviour.
- Project a **genuine** message that we accept the service user as a worthwhile human being regardless of behaviour (see exceptions later in this chapter).
- Be consistently accepting of the service user through reliable availability, time-keeping and using meetings to keep our focus on listening to him or her.
- Accept the service user's **motivations** for behaviour as needed and functional to them at the time the behaviour patterns developed (e.g. car theft).
- Do not challenge these motivations as being flawed or wrong. This only gives the message of rejection. This is different from stating the legal position or the stance in which our role places us, which might not be condoning of the behaviour.

The Person-centred Approach in Action

To apply the above concepts into practice requires firstly an understanding of the theoretical elements to the approach and secondly a level of awareness of the impact of our own experiences. To help service users resolve inner conflict by congruently matching feelings with experience, we need a level of congruence of our own. Practice becomes dangerous and potentially harmful to vulnerable people when we loosely apply concepts to situations without an understanding of their meaning and of our impact on the process as individual practitioners.

As engagement with service users (Compton & Galaway, 1999) is a core and arguably a social worker's most important task, the person-centred approach's emphasis on this is offered as the starting point to using this model in practice.

The Working Alliance

In practice, the person-centred approach relies on a working alliance between service user and worker (Rogers, 1962). This is largely the crux of the approach in practice. The medium for facilitating change is engagement with people; this is also crucial in a person-centred approach, and is termed the working alliance. This is not a passive stance taken by practitioners, but a highly active one that requires ongoing thought and attention to our own position, emotional reactions and behaviour. Too often we are caught up in the belief that engagement is an area that requires brief attention at the beginning of contact with someone, and then, once formed, it remains sufficient for some form of intervention to occur. Thinking of the engagement process in terms of forming a working alliance allows us to think beyond our first contact and embark on a process of constantly reviewing our own position within the working relationship.

First Steps to Engagement

Tolan (2003) suggests that all relationships have a set of rules that govern how relationships progress. The working relationship is no different: it has a power imbalance, the social worker having a knowledge base upon which problems are understood and intervention often, although not always, being of a statutory nature. With this in mind, a service user is reliant on the worker to set boundaries around what is and is not acceptable behaviour within the working relationship, such as how much a worker discloses about him- or herself, the context in which the worker and service user plan to meet, i.e. how often and where. Other rules which need to be thought about prior to meeting with an individual are frequency of contact, worker capacity to be available and reliable, and the purpose of contact.

All too often someone experiencing a problem is allocated to us and we make contact, without giving prior thought to these matters. We find ourselves in a turbulent ocean of problems, desperately trying to find direction. This is neither time-efficient, confidence-inspiring nor helpful to a vulnerable person in distress. The primary concern before meeting an individual or a family is then to be extremely clear about our role and our capacity for meeting with that person, and whether the frequency is sustainable, given other demands.

A contract between service user and worker provides a foundation for agreement from which both parties can make explicit such matters as boundaries to the relationship, and practical arrangements such as frequency of contact, how to manage cancellations and the opportunities and limitations of the service. This is requisite, using a person-centred approach, during the initial meeting but does not need to be within the first few minutes. Judgement is required in timing to allow a service user to feel at ease as much as possible and to be acknowledged as an important person in the process. Thus beginnings are not purely about meeting people and gathering information. They have an essential role in building elements of safety and some certainty about what will happen and why for service users.

Ajay was introduced to Gregor after his previous worker had left. A variety of approaches had been tried previously to achieve change in the direction Gregor's offending was taking, but success had been limited in the long term. Ajay decided to use a person-centred approach in communicating with him and spent several individual sessions trying to form the basis of a working alliance that was borne out of clear boundaries, listening intently to what Gregor did and did not say, being clear with him around the social work role and legal framework, and exploring of the limits of confidentiality.

Social Work Application

The focus of the first sessions with Gregor was to form a working relationship with him. As many attempts to bring about changes in his behaviour had failed over the years, Ajay did find himself under pressure from his department and from the legal system to bring about change quickly. However, he decided to use the first few meetings to focus solely on developing the relationship, which would serve as a foundation for facilitating future sessions that could explore Gregor's previous experiences, his feelings attributed to them and resultant behaviours that continue to concern the legal system.

We might question how we know whether we have formed an adequate engagement with a service user. As individuals are unique, there are no uniform responses that allow this judgement to be made. However, spending time with service users to explore their understanding of our involvement with them, their feelings about it and what motivates them to meet with us is a starting point. This does not mean we fire off these questions, make a note of the responses and move on to the 'real work'. Exploring these matters might take several meetings. Taking time here is effective as it begins to build elements of trust and of mutual understanding that can make the difference between effective and non-effective intervention.

> **Skills Component**
>
> - Prioritise engaging with service users by spending time developing a working alliance.
> - Use the first few sessions to ensure a service user is clear about our role and where boundaries lie, including confidentiality.
> - Resist pressure to rush the engagement process to the detriment of the working alliance and therefore of the success of any intervention.

Congruent Practice

If one of the aims of using a person-centred approach is to help people to reduce inner conflict that causes emotional problems affecting behaviour, then congruent practice is a means to assist people to this end (Rogers, 1962). Essential in this process is enabling people to sift through the imposition of others' ideas and opinions of them and of the world until they are able to find their own 'true' reality through matching their experiences with their feelings. If a person has spent many years believing in a distorted self-concept of their strengths and abilities, to begin to match feelings and experience involves learning a new skill. This is modelled by the practitioner by offering congruent feedback within discussions regarding the practitioner's own experience and feelings relating to the discussion or event occurring at the time. A person can learn to recognise their own feelings linked to both past experiences and present experiences as they are felt in the present. This skill is termed 'reflexivity' (Schön, 1991).

Caution is required here for congruent practice to be both timely and useful for a vulnerable person. Indiscriminately offering our own feelings could easily be perceived by a vulnerable person as judgemental, patronising or rejecting. To model linking feelings to experiences requires a high level of skill and practice and an equally high level of self-awareness of what we are feeling, to what it appears to be linked and the possible impact of sharing our feelings with a service user. Reflexivity in action requires all of these elements to be processed by us as practitioners *while discussion takes place* so that a *measured* response can be given. We need to be continually monitoring our own responses to events that occur within the service user–worker relationship and then use our judgement to assist us to know when sharing our own thoughts and feelings would be helpful to a service user and when it would not.

It is always possible that we might catch ourselves having thoughts or feelings that are not based on values that are in keeping with social work. Any such judgemental or prejudicial feelings should not be denied or distorted by us, leading to incongruence in our own feelings and experience. We need to accept their occurrence and challenge the basis of our prejudice during our own time for reflection. Supervision should be a forum in which these matters can be freely discussed and resolved. During the conversation and as these responses occur, these need to privately become symbolised in our awareness, acknowledged by us and then filtered through our own internal monitoring to ensure that they do not inadvertently impact negatively upon the service user. We can then choose not to share any judgemental responses that are likely to be unhelpful. As a general rule, if we are not sure whether to share our feelings, then to err on the side of caution is likely to be least detrimental.

Self-awareness is the first and foremost step to the way in which the person-centred approach uses the self as practitioner. In an emotionally accepting environment, we help service users 'loosen' their self-structure enough through reflective, congruent feedback to re-evaluate their own experiences. It therefore follows that as social workers we need to have a highly developed level of self-awareness to help us to use elements of this model successfully and become congruent practitioners. It might be that many of us require an opportunity to reflect upon our own life experiences in a therapeutic environment before we are ready for this.

After several meetings with her social worker, Gail started to describe her low mood and the impact this had on her motivation to find another job and to socialise. She explained in detail how people had started to treat her differently after the accident and how she no longer saw herself as an important person. During the meeting, her social worker, Barbara, found herself feeling angry that an intelligent woman such as Gail should find herself so marginalised. Barbara reasoned that Gail possibly could be angry, contributing to her low mood, but was denying that feeling and blaming herself as inadequate instead. In an attempt to assist Gail to connect her experiences with her own feelings, Barbara decided to share her feelings of anger with Gail about this social injustice.

Barbara was making a statement from her own frame of reference with a view to assisting Gail to 'loosen' her self-structure enough to accommodate her feelings. This was not a spontaneous statement, but one that was reasoned through Barbara's perception of Gail's self-structure and self-concept. Barbara's feelings of anger were genuine and so were congruent with her statement, made in a calm and matter-of-fact manner.

Had she shown high affect, either by raising her voice or using hand gestures to express her feelings, this could have been interpreted by Gail as either aggressive or as imposing her views. Making reasoned and well-timed statements in this way simply models to others that feelings can be connected with feelings and then verbalised.

Social Work Application

There are many situations that as social workers we find ourselves in, evoking emotional reactions within us. Often we are meeting the most vulnerable

(Continued)

(Continued)

people within society and their experiences can touch us, often very deeply. Emotional reactions to difficult events are not wrong. We too are human organisms, and hearing about trauma and where people have been abused and excluded from mainstream society is extremely emotive. Our awareness of our feelings is fundamental to our work, whether using this model or others outlined in later chapters. Time spent in supervision or with trusted peers to share our emotional responses to the encounters we face can allow our experience of social work practice to be symbolised into awareness. Taking time to do this goes some way to prepare us for working with service users and to guard against untimely and reactive emotional responses that are more about our own needs than those of service users. In busy environments, time for reflective supervision is an oft-neglected task. However, to use a person-centred approach effectively, it is arguably the most important element of the work, without which we are likely to revert to the demands of our own actualisation drive for precedence.

Skills Component

- Recognise our own emotional responses to situations with service users.
- Take time to share these responses with peers and supervisors.
- Cautiously share our feelings from time to time with service users regarding specific matters, only after reasoning whether this is likely to be in their interests.
- Do this in a gentle manner without high affect.

Empathy

To be an empathic practitioner we must learn to see the world as another person sees it. This does not mean we can ever fully feel another's feelings or wholly experience an event or situation that another person has experienced. Rather, it is a means of communication where we attempt to perceive the world from another person's frame of reference and communicate to that person what we have perceived (Rogers, 1957). A person's frame of reference includes their experience, values, feelings and perception. It is more than the spoken word, but that which is communicated along-side non-verbal communication such as body language, tone of voice, facial expression and overall demeanour. Our attempts to see the world from another's frame of reference is not with a view to analysing or interpreting experiences but to enable someone to experience being as fully heard as possible. Non-verbal communication skills are explored in greater depth in Thompson (2003).

There are several important stages to becoming an empathic practitioner (Tolan, 2003). We need to learn to be able to summarise statements made to us and reflect them back in our own words. Added to this is the skill of listening for feelings, which are rarely explicitly given. This does call for a degree of interpretation of what we see and hear of another's communication to us. Effectively it is a hybrid between an informed guess and a question that is then communicated back to the service user. We need to resist giving in to any desire to interrupt by giving advice or offering a solution. Doing so takes us back to our own frame of reference and not that of the service user.

As we learn to stay with a service user's frame of reference, we can develop the capacity not just to hear single statements made but to capture the essence of what is being communicated in total. This includes thoughts, feelings or beliefs that have not been voiced. We can then offer what we *think* we have heard but has not been voiced, such as, 'you sound as though you feel totally helpless', in a way that is both uncertain and open for confirmation or clarification from the service user. The service user takes the lead in the direction of the conversation. We, as social workers, try to stay with the conversation and, at the same time, gain an understanding of the service user's world at that moment in time. We must be open to the service user correcting our reflections of that which has been perceived. For example, in response to the above statement, the service user might reply, 'No, not totally hopeless but just not sure where to turn next.' There is no requirement for the practitioner to always 'get it right' when offering reflective statements but perceived feelings that are not expressed by the service user would continue to be vocalised by the practitioner, such as, 'You seem very frustrated by that'. If the service user refutes these feelings: 'No! Getting frustrated wouldn't change anything so there is no point', the practitioner might question whether experiencing such a feeling is difficult for the service user. For example, 'So it is hard to accept your feelings of frustration?'

There are many occasions where a social worker's role and task necessitates a more directive stance. We might have our own objectives for a meeting with a service user, which are dictated by either statutory concerns or policy objectives. An example might be a social worker meeting with a service user to undertake a specific type of assessment, such as in respect of child protection or at the request of a Court or Children's Hearing. In such a situation, our role requires that we use some structure to discussions in order to meet our statutory objectives. However, we can incorporate empathic listening into a non-directive part of a discussion. This can assist a service user to feel heard in what is often an extremely powerless position for them.

Skill development in being empathic is a slow process that requires reflection on practice over time (Schön, 1991). We do not become empathic practitioners by reading about a concept and testing it only. It is a highly developed skill that becomes fine-tuned as we use it and then evaluate our progress through honest critique. We require also a willingness to examine the quality of our feedback as a valuable source of learning.

Gregor and Ajay were meeting on a regular basis. Gregor had made a level of engagement with Ajay, in that he continued to attend sessions, although he would share very little. Ajay had been tempted to revert to using a different approach from

(Continued)

(Continued)

the person-centred model but resisted, knowing that Gregor had completed all the worksheets he knew about, which were filed in Gregor's case notes. Ajay was reticent to try approaches that had already had limited success.

Ajay attempted to use the sessions instead to try to stay with Gregor's frame of reference and together gain some insight into Gregor's motivation for offending. Gregor had clearly expressed he did not want a career within the adult criminal justice system but could not explain why he carried on with car theft. Gregor stated that he had hated school and that he was bored in the evenings where, in his local community, there was 'nothing to do'. Ajay listened intently, tuning in to two major indicators of where Gregor had not been meeting his potential. He explored with Gregor what it was about school that he hated, using open questions, pausing to allow him to reflect and tolerating what often felt to Ajay long and painful silences. Over the weeks, Gregor started to connect his long-standing anger and frustration with school. He had denied these feelings, believing instead that he had no talents and that his intelligence was very low in learning. The only exception was with his peers when stealing cars. Gradually, Gregor began to remember times when he did do something well, small incidents that dated back to primary school. During these conversations, Gregor was starting to 'loosen' his self-structure enough to include these experiences as part of his view of himself. As he recognised that he had other strengths, he started to show some interest in developing himself in ways other than offending behaviour.

Ajay could have imposed his own views on where he thought Gregor's strengths were. Other workers had often been very positive and given him lots of praise. However, this had not been incorporated into Gregor's self-structure as it had not been from his own frame of reference. Ajay's ability to resist doing this and to stay within Gregor's frame of reference allowed Gregor to alter his own self-concept to a more balanced one that included his positive attributes.

Social Work Application

We are often charged with the task of offering a timely service and of bringing about change quickly. If these expectations are not explicitly given by our agencies, then caseload matters often lead us to impose this upon ourselves. We can miss a vital opportunity that using this approach offers if we rush in to a situation and impose our own timescales and our own agenda for change. Often we do have a specific role and task to undertake but this need not result in our moving completely away from another's frame of reference. In all circumstances we are meeting with people who have feelings and vulnerabilities. For social workers, the art of the profession is being able to hold on to this notion, while making clear our remit and reason for involvement.

(Continued)

(Continued)

It is often a fine balance that rarely can be slotted into one form of 'counselling'. However, we could argue that attempting empathic listening is possible within any social work situation.

Skills Component

- Draw on listening skills, including attentive listening, tolerating silences, staying with the conversation and being aware of verbal and non-verbal communication.
- Stay with the service user's frame of reference by checking out what they seem to be thinking or feeling about a matter.
- Reflect back what might be the meaning of seemingly denied or distorted feelings that do not seem to fit with a person's overall presentation.
- Resist offering praise that is sourced from our own frame of reference.

Unconditional Positive Regard

Learning to have unconditional positive regard for the people with whom we work is also a skill that we need to consistently develop (Rogers, 1961, 1986). This necessary condition in a person-centred approach requires that practitioners accept a person and their feelings in the present without conditions imposed. Implicit is that we need to accept that people have their own reasons for their behaviour, albeit not always consciously known.

We have learned by looking at congruent practice that as practitioners we must not deny our feelings or distort them as they occur through the worker–service user relationship. We need to be able to catch ourselves having thoughts and feelings that are generated through therapeutic conversations and moderate whether we share them or not. When thoughts and/or feelings fall into a category of being judgemental, without awareness on our part, this can inadvertently translate into our behaviour through reactions and responses and we can lose the capacity for unconditional positive regard. Any judgemental thoughts, which are born out of prejudiced opinions held within our own self-structure, need to be noticed as they occur. They can then be metaphorically put aside so that they do not directly impact upon feelings of acceptance for the service user in the therapeutic encounter. Other forms of judgemental responses can include attributing individuals with labels that seem to fit behaviour patterns, such as 'defensive', 'hostile' or 'manipulative'. This use of labels, globally ascribed, blocks us from being able to hear and acknowledge the minutiae of communication as it occurs in conversations, and from staying with the service user's frame of reference.

To clarify a commonly held myth, unconditional positive regard does not mean we should be seeking opportunities to offer praise to a service user. From a person-centred perspective, this moves us into responding from our own frame of reference rather than from that of the service user. If we are seeking to assist the service user to connect with his or her feelings regarding experience we need to be cautious not to impose our own. This way a service user can move away from feelings and opinions relating to experience which belong to other people and have become part of that person's self-structure. The self-structure can then loosen enough to allow their own feelings regarding an experience to move into symbolic awareness – not ours. In time a person can develop confidence in their own feelings and perceptions of experience. Such an individual will no longer need to deny or distort their feelings to fit with others, or accept another person's interpretation of an event as being more meaningful than their own.

If we can consistently use moderated, congruent practice alongside empathy we are taking steps towards accepting a person with unconditional positive regard. We learn to resist making statements from our own frame of reference: for example, stating 'your hair looks lovely' when a person complains it has been cut too short, or 'you handled that really well' when a person is angry that the outcome of a complaint was not what they had hoped for. Instead we can create an environment in which a person can become more aware of their own thoughts, and in which a practitioner will accept them with these thoughts unconditionally. Rather than try to console the person with some form of praise, which inadvertently undermines the person-centred therapeutic process, we refrain and listen to the whole context of what is being communicated. For the person dissatisfied with a hair-cut, we accept their dissatisfaction and communicate to them that we acknowledge it, saying, for example, 'Your image is very important to you?' and 'You seem disappointed and frustrated with the outcome of your complaint?' Using this response, we accept the person regardless of their feelings and acknowledge their feelings as being important. This validates them as worthwhile individuals in the process.

We must offer a consistent emotional environment of **genuine** warmth and acceptance for our acceptance to be congruent. In busy work environments we often thrust ourselves into meeting people with little if any preparation, either on a practical level or an emotional one. Without some form of mental and emotional preparation, we are more likely to make reactive responses rather than moderated ones through a reflexive process. Reactive responses can often be prejudiced or judgemental, as they arrive directly from our own self-structure. We therefore need to allow time for preparation if we are going to make full use of this approach. We need to be mentally and emotionally prepared for the therapeutic encounter.

Boundaries to unconditional positive regard exist, for example where a service user is physically or verbally aggressive to a practitioner. We have a responsibility to keep ourselves safe. With statutory responsibilities, we can expand this boundary to include forms of behaviours that are harmful to others and which the legal system defines as prohibited in our society: for example, child abuse and other offending behaviours.

Ajay did not approve of Gregor's lifestyle. He believed that his highly dangerous behaviour put both himself and members of his community at risk. However, Ajay recognised that Gregor's motivation for these behaviours was not out of malice or 'badness' but was a way of seeking approval from his peers. Ajay recognised Gregor's positive attributes, although he resisted verbalising them to him so as not to impose his own frame of reference onto Gregor. By recognising these attributes, Ajay was able to offer Gregor genuine warmth and friendliness, rather than cold criticism and rejection that could have been a feature of his communication if he focused only upon Gregor's activities. While Ajay did not condone Gregor's offending behaviour, he did not reject him because of it either. He found a way to give unconditional positive regard that was sustainable throughout their contact.

Social Work Application

Engagement with service users requires us to show some level of positive regard, otherwise a working relationship could not be formed. There are very clear restrictions for social workers being able to offer unconditional positive regard when directed at accepting behaviours. In a social work context, to usefully incorporate a person-centred approach into our practice, either as a form of communication with service users or as a mode of intervention, we need to be absolutely clear about the nature of our role and task. If we have a clear mental framework of what we can accept in a non-judgemental manner and what we cannot, through therapeutic discussions, we are more likely to achieve a workable balance between congruence, empathy, unconditional positive regard and directive engagement.

We can accept the person unconditionally, however, if we are unable to accept the behaviours of a person. This would mean separating out behaviour from the core self, accepting that the motivations people have for their behaviour are, in this model, born out of the self-concept and the self-structure. We can accept that as a human being in his or her own right, a service user will have feelings linked to experience that impact on the day-to-day functioning of life. For example, we might cut short a session where a service user becomes verbally abusive to us, but allow them the dignity of choosing not to behave in such a manner before we do. A statement such as 'You are clearly very angry with what I have just said. It is okay for you to be angry but it is not okay for you to swear at me. We can carry on if you choose to stop swearing at me or we can finish now and meet again at our regular time next week. Which would you like to do?' We accept the person and the feelings but not the behaviour. Within the boundaries set as above, we can continue to show unconditional positive regard only if we genuinely feel it. If we do not, then our verbal and non-verbal responses will be perceived by the service user as insincere and engagement will be sabotaged. In this respect, if we as

(Continued)

(Continued)

individuals hold prejudice towards others, such as racist feelings, homophobia or ageist beliefs, then our non-verbal reactions will plainly indicate that we are not sincere in our acceptance of another person regarding race, sexuality or age, among other matters.

Skills Component

- Be extremely clear in our own thinking about which behaviours preclude unconditional positive regard being shown.
- Explore our own feelings of prejudice, as part of our self-structure, that could interfere with unconditional positive regard for others.
- Accept a service user's thoughts and feelings even if we do not agree with them to enable them to develop congruence with their own feelings and experiences.
- Accepting feelings and then exploring them from the service user's frame of reference can move us between unconditional positive regard and empathic listening.

Endings

The person-centred approach requires that ending involvement is given significant emphasis if the work undertaken is to be consolidated (Tolan, 2003). Abrupt endings, in which the service user has no part in decision-making, leave room for the event to be interpreted as a rejection or abandonment. Continuing to offer unconditional positive regard requires involving the service user in a process of working towards an ending in a planned, staged manner.

As Gregor moved away from offending behaviour and out of the legal system, Ajay recognised that Gregor's progress indicated that an ending would need to be negotiated. He had mentioned to Gregor at their first meeting that their contact would be time-limited, and revisited this from time to time. He and Gregor negotiated when to start reducing the frequency of sessions until the final meeting. Gregor attended all but the last session, which Ajay surmised was Gregor's way of retaining some element of control and limiting the experience of sadness at saying goodbye.

Social Work Application

We do not always have the luxury of ending in a staged way. Often service users disengage from services, workers move on to other posts and workloads can often result in harsh decisions regarding who can receive a service. However, as far as is possible, endings should be planned and allow service users to retain some degree of control. This is not to advocate that endings should be postponed to avoid the often painful emotions felt during goodbyes. This only dilutes the focus of the work and increases the risk of service user dependency on the service. Trevithick (2000) discusses this further in a social work context.

Skills Component

- Think about endings with service users during each stage of the work, including at the beginning.
- Help the service user to recognise from the beginning that involvement is not without ending, although how and when might not be clear at this stage.
- Include the service user in decision-making as far as possible regarding endings.

Limitations of the Person-centred Approach

As outlined above, the person-centred approach does have limitations for social workers. Our role is often with a clear agenda, such as with child protection matters or problems relating to criminal justice, where the impact of one person's behaviour could be harmful to another. If we are clear about our role and remit, it is possible to include elements of this approach within our work. However, we need to be assured that if we are embarking on using a person-centred approach as a form of intervention, then our role and responsibilities do not interfere with the non-directive flow of the work. As with other models for using counselling skills later in this book, we need to be selective about what we do and how we do it.

Oppression and the forms it might take are only implicitly threaded through this approach. To take a feminist stance in the work that we do requires a more directive approach than the person-centred model would advocate. We would be challenging gender oppression and raising awareness as an integral part of our practice. This does not easily fit with this approach, which suggests that people need to come to their own conclusions about the meaning of their own individual experiences. To take an anti-racist stance as part of this approach poses similar difficulties. As there are exceptions to what we would accept unconditionally, described above as violence and abuse, it could be that we can take the same stand on racism, gender oppression and other forms of discrimination. This highlights the need for us to be very clear about the stance we take at the beginning of any meeting with a service user.

Summary of Key Person-centred Concepts

- The **Humanistic School** provides the value-base for this approach, in that humans are unique and need to meet individual potential for satisfaction with life to occur
- Moving towards self-satisfaction is driven by **Self-actualisation**
- An individual's view of the world and of the self is contained within the **Self-structure** and **Self-concept** and can be distorted by the lack of **Unconditional Positive Regard** during early development
- In practice, the **Working Alliance** is central to the change process
- **Congruence** is required to allow genuine engagement within the working relationship
- The practitioner shows **Empathy** towards a service user, which allows the **Self-concept and Self-structure** to be challenged
- **Endings** and their management are fundamental to this approach

---

Conclusion

There are many core principles in this approach that are valuable to social workers for communicating with others. An overview of some of the most relevant aspects is included within this chapter. A clear theoretical understanding coupled with clear reasoning for using some or all of the concepts within a person-centred approach can allow effective incorporation of the model into our use of counselling skills in social work practice, if at times in a selective manner. However, the directive stance often required for social work practitioners can conflict with a person-centred counselling model. At its best, we can incorporate key elements of this model to engage with individuals, families and groups to assist them through change.

Further Reading

- **Tolan (2003)** offers a detailed exploration of the skills upon which this chapter is based. In addition, Tolan's book examines the nature of psychological contact with people.

- **Seden (2005)** uses a process model to consider the stages of social work practice from engagement to intervention with counselling skills in mind.

- **Palmer and McMahon (1997)** give a social context to counselling in various settings, although do not directly include social work. However, later chapters draw upon the person-centred approach as a useful model for themes of problems, including race, bereavement, abuse, disability and health-related problems.

- **McMillan (2004)** provides a theoretical exploration of the principles of person-centred counselling.

3
Drawing on Cognitive Behavioural Therapy in Social Work Practice

Key Concepts	Key Theorists and Practitioners
• Cognitive Schema	• Kelly
• Automatic Thoughts	• Beck
• Connection between Assumptions, Thoughts, Feelings and Behaviour	• Ellis

Introduction

Cognitive behavioural models of therapeutic intervention have a well-established place in practice for those working with vulnerable people. For this reason, the approach has been included as integral to this book. However, the model can only be successfully incorporated into practice with an understanding of the theoretical underpinnings to the approach. This chapter has a weightier emphasis on the theoretical components of the approach compared with most other models incorporated in this book. There is as much of an emphasis on tracking and understanding service user thought processes and how they lead to certain behavioural responses as there is to using techniques to change them. This focus on 'understanding' thoughts and feelings is reflected in the content of this chapter.

This chapter aims to provide those in social work practice with a broad understanding of the principal components that contribute to cognitive behavioural therapies, and develop these aspects to show how social workers can use these skills in practice to facilitate change. As the emphasis of this approach is on individual functioning rather than on social factors that can directly contribute to emotional and behavioural problems, as social workers we need to be equally mindful of environmental influences to problems, such as poverty and oppression.

Within this chapter are several diagrammatic models to highlight the circular link between how we think and how we behave. The theoretical aspects to the approach, as in other chapters, are linked to case studies and to some of the skills that we can develop to use this approach in a social work application.

Theoretical Underpinnings of Cognitive Behavioural Therapy

Cognitive behavioural therapy derives from an integration of two therapies, cognitive therapy and behavioural therapy, the amalgamation of which started in the mid-1970s. Behaviourism refers to the ways in which behavioural outcomes can be manipulated to either increase or decrease as a result of the consequences that occur. Cognitive theories are concerned with thought processes that impact on individual functioning, leading to undesirable changes in mood and emotion.

Behavioural therapies were the first to develop, beginning with Adler and Watson in the early 1900s, followed by Skinner in the mid-1940s. These therapies moved away from the dominance of psychoanalysis to develop learning theories, and became almost revolutionary in the therapeutic field. Behaviourism in its infancy included classical conditioning, the learning theory that behaviour is conditioned by repeated exposure to stimuli of the same nature. Behaviour becomes conditioned to react to the expectation of an event, when corresponding stimuli are experienced. These events include the well-documented experiments by Pavlov (Hawton et al., 1995) who conditioned a dog to respond to a bell by salivating. The bell was paired with food at first and then rung without food. The food led to the dog salivating as an unconditional response, linked to hearing the bell. As the bell was repeated with no association with food, the learned behaviour became extinguished.

Operant conditioning (Skinner) developed from this starting point. Hawton and colleagues (1995) define this as '... the "Law of Effect" ... behaviour that is followed by satisfying consequences will tend to be repeated and behaviour that is followed by unpleasant consequences will occur less frequently'. Behaviour followed by satisfying consequences, and thus increased, is termed 'positively reinforced'. Reinforcement and thus an increase in a form of behaviour can also result from an unpleasant but expected consequence not occurring. This is termed negative reinforcement.

In working directly with people, behaviourism became a forerunner of work with problems such as anxiety and low mood and later with more severe mental health problems, including psychosis, although the results of research into what reinforced changes, and how, appears to have been hotly debated.

Cognitive therapies became integrated into behaviourist therapeutic techniques as the limitations of a purely behavioural approach became apparent. Behavioural therapies did not address the thought processes linked to emotional influences on behaviour. Concepts such as motivation and general mood, whether optimistic or pessimistic regarding the future, could not be directly explained by behavioural theories. Rational emotive therapy (Ellis, 1962, 1999) developed alongside cognitive therapy

(Beck, 1970) to offer theoretical ideas that allowed an individual's thought processes and the behavioural and emotional consequences that followed to be more easily understood.

Blackburn and Davidson (1995) outline the way in which an individual will interpret an event through a filter of '*a priori* structures of knowledge'. That is, interpretations of events are filtered through past experience, socio-cultural history and the prevailing mood of an individual at any given time. Cognitive theories recognise the influence of early experiences that shape individual belief systems that in turn shape thinking. However, contrary to the focus of psychoanalytic psychotherapy, cognitive therapy is concerned with thought processes that occur in the present, and thus the therapies tend to be structured and time-limited in their nature.

As the two therapies integrated, there became a greater recognition that thought processes strongly influence behaviour, either in motivating an individual toward a course of action or leading to behaviour that results in avoidance of certain situations or experiences. The two therapies have not become one. However, cognitive therapies often work alongside behavioural techniques to focus on changing both thought processes and behavioural outcomes where either or both cause some form of distress for an individual.

This integrated approach does not discount the systemic nature of problems, such as environmental influences that continue to reinforce thinking and behaviour. Rather, environmental experiences are viewed as causal factors for problems in conjunction with interpersonal relationships and individual traits. A combination of these factors, in various degrees, can lead to one individual experiencing emotional and behavioural problems where another might not. Resilience to problems in individuals is not discussed here, but equally can give insight into the differing extent to which people experience emotional problems as a result of their experience.

Central Concepts

Cognitive Schemata

Beck's 'schemata' or 'schema' (Beck & Emery, 1985) are defined by Blackburn and Davidson (1995) as 'stable knowledge structures which represent all of an individual's knowledge about himself [*sic*] and his world'. Knowledge structures consist of an individual's beliefs about people and the theories we hold about the actions people might take in given circumstances. They also consist of theories about the world around us and about ourselves, including our self-image and our sense of worth. Beck's theory about schemata was influenced by Kelly's (1955) 'personal constructs'.

The development of cognitive schemata begins in early infancy with experiences that are given core, or established, meaning over time (Beck & Emery, 1985). That is, as experiences build on one another, a set of beliefs and theories begins to develop for each individual that acts as a type of lens through which people, relationships and the world in general are perceived. Experience becomes subjective rather than objective.

It is viewed through structurally developing filters that allow interpretation of events and assumptions about the meaning of each experience that occurs.

As infants grow older, these experiences continue to build and shape the way in which the core structures are formed. In childhood and early adolescence, these structures or schemata remain pliable enough to be changed and shaped in accordance with different experiences that challenge core meaning structures already formed. However, these core structures become consolidated during adolescence and more fixed in early adulthood (Friedberg & McClure, 2002). Consequently, working with individuals to change problematic core beliefs is progressively more difficult as a child matures, often requiring direct therapeutic intervention by adulthood when significant emotional problems arise. Conversely, changing environmental experiences for younger children has a greater probability of altering the knowledge structures that shape the interpretation of experience.

Using this theory to map likelihood of generating changes in children's core knowledge structures that shape emotional health through the filtering of experience could be seen on a continuum. The younger the child, the more likely that changing environmental and interpersonal experiences will positively impact on the development of that child's core cognitive schemata. The older the child, or the more severe the nature of the early adverse experience, the less effective changing the environment alone would be likely to be in creating more positive core beliefs about the world and the self.

The nature of schematic material contained within these core structures is believed to consist of early-experience non-verbal images alongside verbal material that combines over time to develop an 'attributional style'. This attributional style relates to an individual's tendency to view the world and/or the self either positively or negatively. While this style is formed in childhood, it might not be until adulthood that the effects of the attributional style emerge through mood, thought patterns and behaviour. In general, schemata lie dormant until a situation perceived as a stressor triggers automatic thoughts that are based on schematic interpretation of the meaning of that situation. These automatic thoughts that arise are skewed by negative assumptions about the situation, as opposed to more positive assumptions, deriving from the core beliefs in someone struggling with emotional problems.

Aaron is a white man in his early forties with a female partner and a family of four children; he is the birth father of two, but the eldest two, living in the household, have a different paternity. Aaron has been unemployed for nine years, although he is trained as an electrician. Aaron met a social worker, Gillian, when his youngest child, aged eight, disclosed in school that Aaron had hit him with a shoe, leaving bruising. During and following the completion of child protection procedures, Gillian became aware of the persistent low mood experienced by Aaron and its impact upon his and his family's life. She observed that he viewed life extremely negatively, with a sense of hopelessness about the future. He believed that it was 'his fate' to 'end up in

(Continued)

(Continued)

jail' for 'just trying to manage the kids'. He presented as though his life was completely out of his control and as though he had to endure difficulties with resigned passivity. From time to time, life events would build to become overwhelming and he would become extremely angry to the point of rage. It was during one of these rages that Aaron had hit his son. Gillian observed that Aaron appeared to have a negative attributional style.

Social Work Application

When we meet with vulnerable people who often have had adverse experiences and difficult personal relationships, it is probable that many of these people will have cognitive schemas that leave them feeling anxious and/or hopeless about the future. Developing our knowledge of this theoretical concept can allow us to make sense of how a set of core beliefs and theories about themselves and their world might have formed. Often we can be perplexed about behaviours displayed by people, especially if on the surface these behaviours do not appear to fit with the social context in which they live. We can often find ourselves explaining away certain behaviours when we link them to poverty, deprivation and oppression. However, these experiences might not be visible nor found in the present. It is our responsibility as social workers to think about the environmental context in which someone exists and work to empower an individual to improve it wherever possible. However, when historical experience is influencing and impairing life experience in the present for service users, thinking about cognitive schemata can be a useful starting point for change.

Skills Component

- Develop an understanding of the formation of core knowledge structures that consolidate through adolescence to become an attributional style.
- Use listening skills in communication with individuals to track themes of negativity, hopelessness or fear in conversation.
- Assist individuals to share their views of life and life experience relating to past, present and future.

Automatic Thoughts

Automatic thoughts are the thoughts based on assumptions that immediately occur, like a habitual reflex action, following a stressor that is perceived and interpreted as either negative or as a threat (Beck, 1976). Ellis (1999) refers to these as 'self-statements'. Automatic thoughts occur in every individual and are based upon our individual cognitive schemata. Each of us, therefore, has 'cognitive vulnerabilities'. Whether automatic thoughts regarding events develop into severe emotional problems is not a matter of health versus pathology. Rather, whether automatic thoughts are problematic depends on a subjective measure regarding the frequency of these thoughts and level of intrusion on day-to-day functionality. The more unhelpful assumptions that occur as automatic thoughts, the more vulnerable a person is likely to be to experiencing emotional and behavioural problems. Also, the more likely it is that a wider range of stressors will trigger these unhelpful automatic thoughts.

For example, a woman who believes that traffic lights do not adequately control traffic flow, and whose core beliefs include a view of the world in general, and traffic specifically, as unsafe and unpredictable, finds that every time she is a passenger in a car and goes through traffic lights, she starts to have panicky feelings. Tracing her automatic thoughts at this time reveals assumptions that traffic chaos prevails at junctions, which generates her fear that she is going to die in a car accident when going through a set of traffic lights. The worst possible outcome is thus anticipated, referred to as catastrophising. This leads her to avoid forms of transport, which restricts her lifestyle to some extent. Other than a fear of roads, this woman might not have significant problems in day-to-day living, although her core beliefs about the unsafe nature of the world would probably become activated in stressful situations.

The degree of intrusiveness of unhelpful assumptions and automatic thoughts will vary from person to person. In social work practice we acknowledge that individuals with more severe emotional problems are not 'pathologically' different from those of us without, but that some of us are more cognitively vulnerable than others.

As Gillian and Aaron spent 'therapeutic' time together following the registration of the children on the Child Protection Register, Gillian recognised that Aaron seemed to be preoccupied with the future being bleak for him and his family as a consequence of Social Services involvement. He interpreted the registration of the children as the 'step before they are taken away'. While Gillian used listening skills to hear and acknowledge Aaron's view, she hypothesised that this was not enough to facilitate change for this family. Working with Aaron to track some of his automatic thoughts revealed that when the children, especially the youngest, became argumentative, he felt powerless to manage the situation. He would shout and try to reason with them but it made no impact on their behaviour. He believed this was an indication of his failure and inadequacy as a person and would give up trying. The automatic thoughts that surfaced as a result of these beliefs included 'I am a useless father'; 'I am a useless husband'; 'there is no point trying'; 'I don't know what to do'; 'nothing will ever change'.

Social Work Application

The nature of social work requires us to have conversations with service users and use communication skills as the central tool in bringing about change.

(Continued)

(Continued)

Through our conversations with people, we can become attuned to listening for themes as to how beliefs about the self and the world can translate into specific assumptions that influence feelings and behaviour. As with schemata, knowledge of the theory relating to the formation and impact of automatic thoughts can give us direction to help a person to make changes in their lives. We might find ourselves working to create opportunities for different experiences to the ones service users have day-to-day, such as empowering a socially isolated woman to attend a group of other women in similar circumstances. We might then become frustrated that the woman does not attend, even though she seemed willing at the time of discussion about it.

While individual choice needs to be respected, it could be that negative automatic thoughts about how she would perform in a group, whether the group would accept her and whether it would help could all limit the extent different opportunities could be utilised. Making sense of automatic thoughts in this respect could more helpfully inform our thinking about the woman not taking up services than perhaps believing she is resistant to change. Using this concept could also empower us to adapt our practice and care plans that we formulate to better suit the needs of individuals.

Skills Component

- Develop an understanding of how automatic thoughts are generated and the impact they can have on choices and behaviour.
- View resistance to intervention as indicative of an individual's automatic thoughts about the nature of the work.
- Recognise where automatic thoughts are having a negative impact on a service user's life by enquiring about what stands in the way of change, i.e. fear that 'everyone will laugh at me', 'there is no point'.
- Incorporate conversations regarding these thoughts and their impact into communication and intervention (see below).

Cognitive Distortion

As above, we can understand from cognitive behavioural theories that stressful situations trigger assumptions and then automatic thoughts that occur like reflexes to provide us with a filtered interpretation of an event. All events that we experience are not objective, free from interpretation. Rather, they are individually subjective, made sense of through this filter of previous experience and interpretation. Automatic thoughts become unhelpful when they distort an experience to fit with the core belief system, the cognitive schemata.

For example, a child who has been removed from their family of origin due to neglect and placed with foster carers might receive a higher level of care and nurturing from the carers. However, initially when moving to the new family, the child will be viewing the care received through the filter of their core beliefs, albeit that these core beliefs are not yet consolidated. If the new experiences of nurturing do not fit with the child's beliefs and assumptions about how adults behave, it is likely that nurturing experiences will be rejected and given less weight than more neglectful experiences. Thus the cognitions or thought processes become distorted.

As the cognitive schemata are not consolidated in children, it is likely that different experiences alone would change some of the core beliefs of a child about adult behaviour. However, in adults, these beliefs being more fixed often require some form of direct intervention to enable changes to occur. Thus an adult who is consistently critical of services might be filtering these experiences through their core beliefs to negate or distort more positive experience. However, using a post-modern perspective to critique this model, we might remind ourselves of the difficulties in defining 'reality', and so what is 'real' to one person will be very different from what is 'real' to another. We might also question the definition of 'distortion'. On this basis, only when thinking patterns negatively impact on a person's life to the point where it is either harmful to themselves or to others, where the person is requesting help, can we justifiably intervene to try to change unhelpful assumptions about life.

With Aaron, his thoughts and perceptions of his family had led him to a violent act that required statutory intervention. He had filtered his experience of family life to become wholly negative; a view that was not shared by other members of his family.

Aaron's youngest child had been mostly well behaved at home, according to Jan, his partner. Jan noticed that her relationship with Aaron was often very warm although Aaron would withdraw 'into himself' and would be difficult to talk to for days at a time. However, Aaron could not recognise any times when he was relating well to his children or his partner. He would filter out these experiences as 'meaningless'. He discounted these experiences, which left his core beliefs and theories about himself and the world intact.

Social Work Application

As we continue to communicate with service users about their lives and their behaviours, we can become aware of when some life experiences are given recognition and when some are dismissed. Other chapters give consideration to how we construct reality and how dominant social discourses filter experience to exclude opinions and beliefs of minority groups. This is not to dismiss the fundamental social work principle that experience is highly subjective and that we cannot impose our view of truth and reality on another person. Aaron has a right to his view of 'reality', although by filtering out more

(Continued)

(Continued)

positive interactions with his family that are experienced by others, he maintains his belief about his worthless status within the family. This belief had been a contributing factor to a serious incident that left a child injured. For practice to be ethical, Aaron would need to give consent to a social worker exploring with him unhelpful assumptions about life that do not seem to fit with the specific environment in which he lives.

There needs to be caution exercised here when contemplating whether a person's experience is 'distorted'. We could be dismissing experience of abuse in various forms if we interpret a person's negative statements about life as evidence of cognitive distortion. In social work practice, we are constantly thinking about risk and risk management. To effectively use this concept, we need to view statements made in the light of other information before making an informed judgement as to whether a cognitive behavioural approach would be in the best interests of a service user. If a person is experiencing a form of abuse, then viewing assumptions as distortions would undermine a person's view of reality and their confidence in their own perceptions. It could also give a message that the abuse is acceptable behaviour and that we are colluding with the perpetrator by ignoring it.

Skills Component

- Listen to unhelpful assumptions made consistently by individuals to track whether they appear to be dismissive of more positive feedback from others or of their successes.
- Be mindful of theoretical models that introduce the individual and social construct of reality.
- Exercise caution in viewing all negative statements about others or the self as 'distortions'.

Cognitive Behavioural Model

This model demonstrates the way in which thoughts are generated, then established, leading to emotional, behavioural and physiological reactions. The cognitive behavioural model of emotional and behavioural problems helps explain the development of problems over time and how these problems might impact upon several significant areas of a person's life.

Content-specificity Hypothesis

Content-specificity hypothesis is a term for a framework for recognising automatic thoughts that maintain and perpetuate schemata or core beliefs and theories. Cognitive

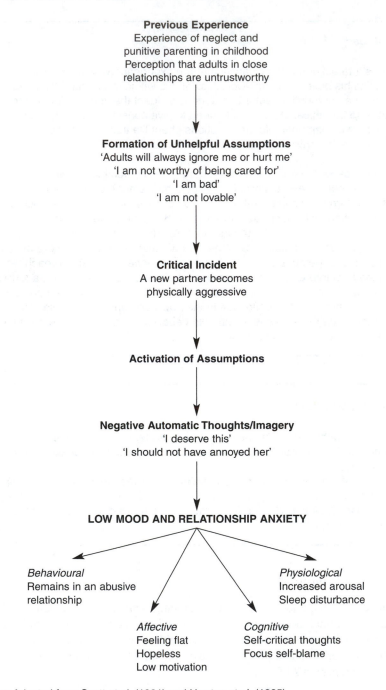

Previous Experience
Experience of neglect and
punitive parenting in childhood
Perception that adults in close
relationships are untrustworthy

Formation of Unhelpful Assumptions
'Adults will always ignore me or hurt me'
'I am not worthy of being cared for'
'I am bad'
'I am not lovable'

Critical Incident
A new partner becomes
physically aggressive

Activation of Assumptions

Negative Automatic Thoughts/Imagery
'I deserve this'
'I should not have annoyed her'

LOW MOOD AND RELATIONSHIP ANXIETY

Behavioural
Remains in an abusive
relationship

Physiological
Increased arousal
Sleep disturbance

Affective
Feeling flat
Hopeless
Low motivation

Cognitive
Self-critical thoughts
Focus self-blame

Source: Adapted from Scott et al. (1991) and Hawton et al. (1995).

theory is based upon the premise that different emotional states result from specific organisations of cognitions that are unique to each state. Thus characteristics in thought and in beliefs are grouped into several distinct groups, such as depressive or anxiety states. As social work practitioners, we are not concerned with the grouping of individuals with a view to labelling them or 'medicalising' their presentation. However, awareness of the theory of how certain thought processes are linked through research to certain states of mood and resultant behaviour can help us to choose the most effective form of communication to assist individuals with working towards change.

Several hypotheses are useful for social workers. The 'negative cognitive triad' (Beck, 1976) links people with chronic low mood experiencing unsatisfactory events by criticising and blaming the self, even when external factors were outside of that individual's control. Thus a 'self-critical' view of problems, and preoccupation with past (unfavourable) events, lead a person towards a generally pessimistic view of the future.

In contrast, problems with anxiety have a different hypothesis in cognitive therapy. The core structures of cognitions or thoughts are developed to be more future-orientated in people with anxiety problems. The content-specific hypothesis for anxiety is that people will be preoccupied with potential dangers that the future could bring, but which have not as yet occurred. Catastrophising about the worst likely future outcome of a given situation, regardless of other information that might suggest the worst outcome is unlikely, is also a key feature of this hypothesis.

Without falling into the diagnostic/symptomatic arena, knowledge of content-specificity hypotheses for emotional problems that are often part of a complex picture of vulnerable individuals or families within social work practice can enhance our practice threefold. Firstly, we can hone our use of counselling skills for communicating about emotional problems. Secondly, we can expand our understanding of the development of emotional problems over time to make sense of the evolution of low mood and anxiety. Thirdly, we can be more selective about the techniques we require to draw on to bring about change with people.

Aaron had, over many years, probably originating in his early experiences, developed core beliefs that, through his thoughts, culminated in his negative view of himself, of others and of his future. Gillian was able to recognise the pattern of these negative thoughts, which offered her a focus for choosing certain therapeutic skills over others to facilitate change. Aaron was clear about his remorse for assaulting his youngest child and was able to take responsibility for his actions. He also demonstrated commitment to the children in that he did not want to lose contact with them. While he did not ask for therapeutic intervention for his low mood, Aaron's motivation for working

(Continued)

(Continued)

therapeutically with Gillian was to maintain contact with his children. Gillian used her knowledge of cognitive behavioural approaches to assist her to communicate effectively about the problems and to use this communication to bring about change. Aaron gave consent to be engaged in ongoing work and so progress began. As Gillian helped Aaron to identify some of the triggers that maintained his low mood, including his perception of events, his feeling of powerlessness reduced alongside the extent of his rage.

Social Work Application

As previously stated, the social work role does not take us into the domain of categorising problems into groups that some other disciplines might label as illness or disorder. The content-specificity hypothesis could be used by some disciplines as a diagnostic tool. However, for social workers we can use the concept of common themes with thought patterns to assist us with targeting communication and intervention at a level that best suits the problem. We do not need to be caught up in the stigmatising implications of labelling problems to do this. We can selectively use language that is inclusive and empowering rather than categorising individuals as having an intrinsic problem. We can refer to an individual having problems with low mood or worrying, and work with people to limit the impact these problems have on social functioning through considered therapeutic intervention. It does not require a label for this type of work to be valid.

Skills Component

- Become familiar with the general patterns of thought development that influence perceptions of the past, present and future.
- Work with people to explore these patterns through the therapeutic relationship.
- Use language that defines the nature of the problem rather than labelling an individual in general and stigmatising terms.

Techniques used in Cognitive Behavioural Approaches

The Therapeutic Relationship

In social work practice, we are first and foremost interested in engaging with service users in a working relationship. In many forms of counselling and therapy, including cognitive behavioural approaches, this process is described as the therapeutic relationship. Wills and Sanders (2002) indicate that the emphasis on the therapeutic relationship has not always historically been a core component of this approach, the technical aspects being favoured. Wills and Sanders, among other theorists and practitioners, have recognised this lack and emphasise the importance of the engagement process, more fitting with a social work model.

As many people with chronic and entrenched problems are likely to have interpersonal difficulties, the need for nurturing of the therapeutic relationship cannot be understated. Thus some of the features of Rogers' work (1951, 1959, 1986) (see Chapter 2), including warmth, genuineness and unconditional positive regard, have been incorporated into cognitive behavioural approaches. The requirement for transparency, i.e. avoiding hidden agendas, is important for a trusting relationship to be formed. Social workers in various fields often have grave concerns regarding an individual or a family's situation, and being open and transparent about serious concerns is often a challenge. However, to be genuine in our interactions with a person, we need to develop our ability to assertively state our position regarding concerns in order that we can be transparent in our working relationship.

Collaboration is an aspect of the working relationship that requires all of the above features but acknowledges the reciprocal nature of the therapeutic alliance. Often in social work practice we demonstrate enthusiasm with regard to developing a positive working relationship, especially in statutory work where service users have a legal obligation to work with us. Collaboration, however, involves a step-by-step building of a relationship, involving feedback and reflection, as well as a sense of both parties working towards a common goal. This approach removes the emphasis on the service user alone being expected to make changes that can be perceived to be dictated by another, i.e. the legal system, child protection procedures. Rather, the collaboration between the worker and the service user generates the changes, without reducing the responsibility for individual behaviour being removed from the service user.

When Gillian first met with Aaron and his family, her social work role, in this instance regarding child protection concerns, required that she engaged with the family and was explicit about her involvement. This initially evoked an angry response from Aaron and his partner and so Gillian and her colleague used communication skills to remain calm and non-threatening while retaining an assertive stance regarding the social work role. As the crisis was addressed, Gillian's transparency regarding her agenda and her continuing reliability, consistency and respect for the parents through the investigative process had begun to establish a level of trust and collaboration. Gillian was fully aware of the need for collaborative understanding to be established before she could work with the parents to bring about change.

Social Work Application

The therapeutic or working relationship is fundamental to the nature of social work practice. As social work practice has evolved in the twentieth and now twenty-first centuries, the core element to practice remains this relationship. As we meet with individuals, we emphasise the importance of this relationship through the engagement process. Engagement means more than a service user being available for visits or meetings. It is based upon a transparency of role and purpose for involvement, respect through reliability and consistency and developing a level of mutual trust. A truly collaborative working relationship maintains clear boundaries to behaviour, including the level at which a practitioner will disclose elements about the self. As these boundaries become clear and accepted, the relationship can provide a secure enough temporary base within which difficult experiences and feelings can be explored. This is covered in greater depth in Chapter 4.

Skills Component

- Prioritise the importance of forming a working relationship at the beginning of any work.
- Maintain engagement through continuing attention to the therapeutic relationship as intervention progresses.
- Be clear about the role and purpose of intervention before meeting with a service user, to facilitate transparency.
- Give attention to the foundations to engagement, including time keeping, reliability and consistency of approach.
- Enable the service user to have an active role in the working relationship by drawing on listening skills.

Problem Identification and Social Work Assessment

As social workers, we are concerned with the assessment process to make sense of what factors might be contributing to an individual's difficulties. A broader social work assessment framework (Parker & Bradley, 2003) requires us to take account of social, economic, political and relationship factors as well as individual patterns of thinking and behaviour. The cognitive behavioural model allows us to focus in on thoughts and behaviour *after* considering the contributing environmental factors such as the impact of poverty and deprivation, significant life events and history. Thus, identifying problems for social work practitioners using this model would most likely be useful as part of a more general assessment.

For adults, it might be easier for them to identify problems related to low mood or anxiety. For children and young people, this is more complex. Often it is not children themselves who request services or who are developmentally able to hypothesise about the impact of their problems on their own lives or on others. Using this model, problem identification is related to tracking where and when unhelpful emotional and behavioural responses to situations in life impair functioning as social and emotional beings. The model requires an approach that targets specific behavioural and emotional responses using a framework of techniques to bring about change in a time-limited period. Most adults are able to identify these problematic areas. However, with children and young people, a greater emphasis is required on the engagement process and on a more practical approach to identify feelings and worries, such as using simple worksheets, pictures and toys to allow children to communicate their feelings and worries in a non-directive manner (Geldard & Geldard, 2002).

An assumption is made, as with any other therapeutic model, that the practitioner will offer a warm and uncritical, responsive working relationship to generate trust and open participation in discussion regarding the nature of problems. This closely fits with the requirement for social workers to develop working relationships with people as part of the engagement process.

Problem identification in this instance was threefold. For Gillian, a social worker using child protection policies and the legal system as a framework, the problem was the contributing factors that led to a child being assaulted. The problem for Aaron was that he believed the world was against him and that he was powerless to make any changes, other than when he became angry, and people, including his children, listened to him through fear. From a cognitive behavioural perspective, the problem was related to Aaron's negative attributional style, based on his core beliefs about the world. Gillian was able to hold the three angles to problem identification enough to satisfy the legal and local policy requirements to protect children from further harm – this being her first priority. She was also able to hold Aaron's view of the problem in mind, him being the perpetrator of the physical abuse, and the focus of change if he was to remain in contact with his children. She did this by listening to his views and accepting them, although they could not override child protection requirements. Following the initial crisis, Gillian used cognitive behavioural theories to work with Aaron regarding the core beliefs that governed his interpretation of experience, with a view to facilitating change for him and for his family.

Social Work Application

As part of the assessment process, problem identification is a fundamental part. We need to give consideration to what is a problem for whom. Often

(Continued)

(Continued)

those who refer vulnerable people for social work services have concerns about the behaviour or social functioning of an individual. They will have identified a problem which they hope social work practitioners will be able to resolve. This does not always fit with an individual's view of a problem, however. Before problem identification can be undertaken from a cognitive behavioural perspective, thought needs to be given to who believes what is a problem, and whether there are any requirements of the legal system that would influence how much choice an individual has and what are the consequences if the problem is not addressed.

Skills Component

- Identify who is most concerned about the service user and who is most motivated for problems to be resolved.
- Consider the demands of the legal system in problem identification.
- Seek permission from the service user to explore problems relating to feelings and behaviour using this approach.
- Explore the consequences that denial of permission for intervention might have, i.e. in relation to the legal system or child protection systems.
- Accept that cognitive behavioural approaches can be viewed as intrusive to some people who are not ready or willing to examine the contributory factors to their mood or behaviour.

Using the Cognitive Behavioural Model in Practice

Outlined above is the cognitive behavioural model. Incorporating the model into practice requires a timely coordination of intervention in social work practice, especially when statutory matters require primary consideration.

Following matters relating to child protection being undertaken, Gillian embarked upon a programme of work with Aaron to identify some of the thought processes and behavioural consequences that led to the assault of his child. Using the cognitive behavioural model, she found that working collaboratively with him to make sense of events unveiled the contributing factors.

Aaron had had on the surface an unproblematic childhood. However, when he gave more thought to his experience, he recognised that, in his busy family of four children in which he was the quieter third child, he often found that he

(Continued)

(Continued)

did not have a voice that was heard. He found that he would withdraw rather than try to let his family know his thoughts about matters. This would lead to feelings of anger and resentment regarding his family. He began to believe that his opinion was not important and that he was worthless as an individual.

This led to several unhelpful assumptions developing that he would make about himself, other people and about the world in general. He assumed that his opinion about 'things' was less worthwhile than those of other people. He assumed that people in general would not listen to him unless he became really angry. He assumed that the world was a busy, fast place that did not allow a space for his opinions to exist. He assumed that he had no skills to change this and that he was completely powerless for life to be experienced differently.

A critical incident had occurred. Aaron's partner had been promoted in her place of employment at the same time that his youngest son had been especially challenging around times to go to bed. This 'critical incident' on the surface might not appear to be out of the ordinary but for Aaron, who was not working and having his authority as a parent challenged by his son, became critical enough to activate his assumptions about life. Negative assumptions including 'I am worthless', 'no one listens to me' and 'everyone else has their say heard' generated several cognitive, behavioural and physiological responses.

Aaron's cognitive response was increasing thoughts of his own worthlessness and of others' disregard for him; his physiological response was an increase in arousal – raised heart rate and 'fire' in his muscles; his affective response was feelings of overwhelming anger leading to rage; and behaviourally this manifested in the assault on his son.

Gillian effectively used the model to enable Aaron to make sense of his actions and create some specific areas whereby changes could be made.

Social Work Application

Once a service user has given permission to explore the various factors that generate unhelpful thoughts and feelings, this model can be used to make sense of how early experience can link with core beliefs, and thus assumptions, that directly impact on present perceptions of events and their outcomes. We might debate how useful actually seeing the model might be for service users, or whether the practitioner should use it as a therapeutic map from which to ask questions and make sense of reactions to experience. Since the emphasis of

(Continued)

(Continued)

cognitive behavioural approaches is on awareness raising and teaching of how beliefs shape feelings and behaviour, some service users will respond well to a visual aid. Others might find the theoretical model threatening and difficult to understand and so judgement is required in this respect. Sharing the model could be perceived as being transparent about the theories we use, or it could be perceived as hierarchical and disempowering in the same manner that using jargonised language can set practitioners apart from service users.

Skills Component

- Use judicious caution as to whether to use this model explicitly with people or as a therapeutic map.
- Seek the service user's opinion on whether seeing a model and learning more about it would be helpful to them.
- Draw on the model to make links between historical experience, development of beliefs and assumptions and how events are perceived and reacted to by service users.

Cognitive Behavioural Assessment

The focus of this chapter, or indeed this book, is to provide practitioners in social work with a range of counselling skills drawn from several therapeutic models. Models for assessment in social work can be found in other literature (Milner & O'Byrne, 2002a); however, the emphasis on tracking the details of emotional and behavioural problems within this model requires some attention being given to cognitive behavioural assessment.

The first concern with a cognitive behavioural assessment is to track the onset of the problem: for example, when did the first experience of anxiety emerge? The problem could either have had a gradual onset from which the problem worsened, or it could have developed suddenly, usually following a traumatic experience. We would be interested in whether the problem has persisted steadily or had a more fluctuating course. While a time-line for the problem is important, it is the way in which it impacts on present-day functioning that is most relevant for a cognitive behavioural interview.

To elicit the information required to connect the problem with an individual's core beliefs and assumptions, the focus of the discussion would be on the fine detail of how and when the problem occurs and what impact it has on a service user. Self-monitoring is an integral aspect of cognitive behavioural assessments, using charts such as an A-B-C chart – Antecedents, Behaviours and Beliefs, and Consequences (O'Leary & Wilson, 1975). These are useful in mapping what preceded a stressful event and what was the outcome. This has been developed to include the cognitive aspects of a situation (Hawton et al., 1995). The example below shows how a chart can be used to map mood, precipitating behaviour and behavioural outcomes.

Date	Mood and how strong 0–100%	Activity/ thoughts before event	Urge to harm self before cutting 0–100%	Cutting occurred	Relief from cutting 0–100%
2 Feb.	Angry 80%	Arguing with partner	40%	Yes	20%
8 Feb.	Worried 60%	Daughter late home	60%	Yes	35%
12 Feb.	Angry 45%	Arguing with son	20%	No	–
14 Feb.	Upset 70%	Partner forgot Valentine	30%	Yes	5%

Greater detail of the problem, i.e. self-harming through cutting in this instance, was achieved through charting the events and outcomes. This does rely, however, on service users engaging with the model and being able to read, write and use numerical skills. It can equally be used to map the occurrence of other mood and behavioural problems, including offending behaviours, unhelpful parenting strategies and behavioural outcomes of low mood.

Defining the details of what triggers and maintains unhelpful behaviours or mood states is undertaken in a cognitive behavioural assessment by six areas of exploration:

1. Situational – what environmental factors were present
2. Behavioural – what did the person do
3. Cognitive – what thoughts were present at the time
4. Affective – what emotional reaction occurred, i.e. overall mood
5. Interpersonal – who else was present
6. Physiological – what bodily reaction resulted

Other significant factors can be gaining insight into a person's beliefs about a problem as well as taking into account psychosocial factors that would be part of a broader social work assessment.

Using cognitive behavioural assessment, Gillian extended her understanding of the incident when Aaron physically injured his son. This provided her with a greater insight into the risk factors that would indicate whether it was likely to occur again and also gave Aaron insight into contributing factors in order that he could make changes.

Gillian asked Aaron to track his thoughts, feelings and behaviour over a week-long period.

(Continued)

Date	Mood and how strong 0–100%	Activity/ thoughts before event	Urge to lose temper 0–100%	Temper lost	Relief from losing temper 0–100%
18 May	Angry 80%	Partner started new job	60%	Yes	20%
19 May	Angry 30%	Went to Jobcentre	10%	No	–
21 May	Angry 70%	Children noisy	70%	Yes	10%
24 May	Rage 90%	Partner late home	80%	Yes	10%

(Continued)

From this Gillian and Aaron ascertained that Aaron could control his anger, as was evident from his feelings leading to a different behavioural outcome in the Jobcentre. The influence of a different situation, i.e. with other non-family members around, changed the automatic thoughts that Aaron had when feelings of anger arose. This awareness allowed him to recognise his ability for self-control and for exploring his core beliefs that led to the shift in automatic thoughts. Aaron also gained insight into the general level of dissatisfaction that losing his temper gave him. Losing his temper meant that in general he would raise his voice and at times he would break household items. He was surprised to find that, after losing his temper, he would feel an exaggerated sense of worthlessness that exacerbated his problems. This feeling was absent when he returned from the Jobcentre.

Aaron also realised that the people in his life that he valued the most, i.e. his family, were the ones with whom he would lose his temper. Non-family members appeared to have a modulating effect on his mood and behaviour. When exploring this further, Aaron realised that his core beliefs led him to expect his family to remain with him unconditionally out of duty, where he had a greater fear of rejection and reprisals from others. Only when Aaron had had to leave the family home during the child protection investigation had he realised that his relationships with his family were not as certain as he had once thought.

Social Work Application

A cognitive behavioural assessment considers only the factors present when an individual has an unhelpful emotional or behavioural outcome to an event on a basis regular enough to be impairing social functioning. What this assessment lacks from a social work perspective is a broader exploration of the social and relationship factors that could also be maintaining an emotional or behavioural response. The assumption with this model is that some form of

(Continued)

(Continued)

cognitive distortion exists, as outlined above. However, we need to be mindful that experiences of poverty, oppression in various forms and social and emotional deprivation can also generate problems with anxiety and low mood. Unresolved traumatic experiences can create anxiety problems that do not always fit with a person's current circumstances and could be overlooked if this approach is adhered to without some degree of openness to other influencing factors.

This form of assessment would mostly best fit with social work practice after wider social factors have been given attention. Trying to resolve problems through therapeutic intervention when environmental triggers remain for an individual might only deny experience rather than resolve its impact. This assessment appears to be most useful in social work practice as part of an assessment and intervention process that has identified a service user having unhelpful thought patterns that impairs their social functioning, alongside an assessment of contributing social factors.

Skills Component

- Firstly, use problem identification as part of a broader social work assessment to highlight problems of mood or behaviour.
- Draw upon a cognitive behavioural assessment to give greater depth to the manner in which unhelpful thoughts and behaviours interfere with social functioning and relationships.
- Explore the six key areas of an event to give a level of depth as to triggers, thoughts, feelings and impact on self (service user) and others.

Socratic Dialogue

Therapeutic conversations from a cognitive perspective are based upon the Socratic method. This method has three fundamental features: systematic questioning, inductive reasoning and constructing universal definitions. Systematic questioning requires the practitioner to be curious about several key features of the problem and be open as to what the answers to these questions might be.

Rutter and Friedberg (1999) outline a five-part process in developing a Socratic dialogue:

1. Elicit and identify the automatic thought
2. Tie the automatic thought to the feeling and the behaviour
3. Link the thought–feeling–behaviour sequence together with an emphatic response

4. Obtain collaboration on steps 1–3 and agreement to go forward
5. Socratically test the belief

This form of dialogue to be undertaken with a service user takes the theoretical concepts above and brings them into direct practice. The problem-identification step needs to be undertaken before attempts are made to link a person's core assumptions with their thoughts, feelings and behaviour. Without engaging the service user in this form of intervention prior to this stage, successful collaboration with service users is unlikely.

To elicit and identify automatic thoughts, direct questioning, such as 'what went through your mind then?' can be useful if timed with a service user's description of a problematic event. The service user then has the opportunity to track and share automatic thoughts that occurred alongside an unhelpful emotional or behavioural reaction.

Guided questions to broaden the service user's description of a situation where the problem occurred can also assist in this process. For example, when discussing extreme anxiety at traffic lights with the woman referred to above (whose fears are triggered by her interpretation of the chaotic and dangerous nature of these junctions and the belief that she as passenger and the driver will die if they go through them), we might ask certain guided questions to test the evidence for these core assumptions. We could enquire whether there were other road users at the lights, whether the other drivers were adhering to road safety laws, whether her companion adhered to the road traffic laws at the lights, etc. Thus automatic thoughts can begin to be challenged by evidence recognised by the service user that her automatic thoughts are based on distorted cognitions, not on what was evident in the situation. Alternative explanations, i.e. regarding the level of safety for car passengers at traffic lights, can be sought in the light of the new evidence. Automatic thoughts can thus be challenged in a non-critical and collaborative manner. Examining and evaluating the evidence to support or challenge automatic thoughts is called distancing from the problem and adopting a more realistic position.

The final component of the Socratic dialogue is to construct universal definitions. Often people with emotional and behavioural problems define themselves and their world in narrow terms based upon negative and unhelpful beliefs and assumptions. These narrow definitions restrict a person's ability to view their more positive attributes and those aspects of the world around them that could give them joy and pleasure. Using this technique we can help a service user to broaden their definition of themselves and their world, through challenging cognitions and using activity schedules to alter behaviour.

During their work together, Gillian used Socratic dialogue to track some of Aaron's automatic thoughts. This allowed Aaron to extend his awareness of his thoughts, feelings and behaviour and gave him a greater sense of self-control. She did this by carefully listening to how Aaron described himself and his world, noticing themes that indicated general negative assumptions that did not always seem to fit with those of others around him, including his family.

(Continued)

(Continued)

Asking Aaron what went though his mind at trigger points to certain events made his automatic thoughts more explicit. She then considered with Aaron some of the assumptions he had made explicit about his world and his relationships to explore with him whether the evidence that feedback from others gave really did fit with his assumptions. Using distancing, Aaron and Gillian were gradually able to formulate a broader definition of who he was and what his world was like. This created therapeutic space for more positive attributes to be included alongside the negative ones.

As Aaron began to recognise more of his strengths, he became more assertively able to share his thoughts and opinions. This in turn left him feeling more in control of his life, and his feelings of anger lessened.

Social Work Application

The Socratic dialogue offers us, as social work practitioners, a framework for forming the content and sequence of questions that can be used to illuminate a service user's unhelpful automatic thoughts. The dialogue in itself is not enough for skilled communication. We still need to give emphasis to the ongoing maintenance of the therapeutic relationship by being consistent, respectful and reliable. We need to draw upon listening skills to ensure that we are attentive to the service user and the service user's feelings. As mentioned previously, without consent to question people about their automatic thoughts and the core beliefs upon which these are based, this technique could be viewed as threatening and intrusive. If a service user perceives our intervention in this way – unless this is stipulated by statutory requirements – he or she is likely to withdraw engagement with us or with the work, either overtly by avoiding meeting with us or more subtly through an emotional withdrawal.

Skills Component

- Become familiar with the Socratic dialogue as a framework for forming questions.
- Use it in conjunction with skills to promote a working relationship, i.e. respect, reliability and consistency.
- Incorporate the dialogue into other forms of communication to retain focus on engagement, i.e. listening skills and attentiveness.
- Re-visit the service user's consent to the work to avoid withdrawal from perceived over-intrusiveness.

Other Cognitive Behavioural Techniques

Reattribution

Reattribution concerns assisting service users to reattribute negative outcomes of events or experience away from perceived internal and self-critical causation to external influence. Reattribution is not intended to move people to avoid taking responsibility for their lives and their actions. Rather, it works to facilitate an individual to move away from unhelpful negative emotions that debilitate self-control and self-action when faced with unsatisfactory outcomes.

Aaron had become self-blaming for many of the negative experiences he had had, including being out of work for many years. He viewed his long period of unemployment as a reflection of his lack of skill, and his unattractiveness to potential employers as somehow unworthy of finding a job. He had internalised the problems which in consequence led him to view his future prospects as extremely bleak.

Gillian assisted Aaron to consider the local employment situation and to make sense of the lack of industry in his area that led to a decline in the opportunities for someone with his trade. They also explored with employment agencies the kind of attributes and experience that were sought to secure alternative employment. Aaron realised that he had some of those attributes and took steps to re-train in a different skill. As he began to reattribute some of the barriers to finding work to societal factors, he felt more optimistic about the future and was empowered to take active steps towards changing his future.

Social Work Application

Our social work values require that we assist people wherever possible to take more control of their lives. In doing this, we are thinking about matters relating to various forms of oppression, deprivation and social exclusion that prevent people fully participating as members of their local communities. Furthermore, we assist people to take responsibility for their actions and to consider alternative paths that are either less harmful to others or have less impact on the safety and well-being of the local community. When this includes offending behaviour or forms of abuse, reattribution techniques would not be helpful.

However, as we can see with the work undertaken by Aaron and Gillian, some of the unhelpful beliefs about the world and of the opinions of others that contributed to Aaron physically assaulting his child were reattributed to socio-economic factors, but not his responsibility for the assault itself.

(Continued)

(Continued)

This allowed Aaron to have a broader view of his own positive attributes that he had previously ignored or filtered out of his perception.

While reattribution techniques do not always fit with social work practice, especially when a service user is struggling to accept responsibility for behaviours that have been harmful to others, it does offer the distinction between responsibility and blame. Aaron needed to accept responsibility for the assault and the consequences that followed but was not wholly to blame for the social circumstances of his early history and his present situation. Using this technique does allow the distinction to be made between responsibility for individual behaviour and blame for socio-economic circumstances that can be restrictive and oppressive.

Skills Component

- Distinguish between behaviours for which the law requires that an individual takes responsibility and societal factors for which an individual does not accept personal blame.
- Assist service users to take responsibility for their own thoughts, feelings and behaviours.
- Assist service users to reattribute blame for the generation and shaping of beliefs and assumptions over time as a result of situational factors, i.e. societal, economic, political, religious and from early negative experiences of relationships.
- Use the reattribution process to free individuals to change their core beliefs and assumptions that can result in different automatic thoughts, feelings and behaviours.

Challenging General Rules

General rules are the beliefs and theories that emerge from the cognitive schemata in raw or abstract form, that then influence the perception of experience or likely future experience. These general rules are the basic blueprint for how we experience and anticipate life: for example, 'people are untrustworthy'; 'life lets you down'; 'things are too good to last'. With vulnerable people whose life experience has been difficult or traumatic, we often find that this blueprint, or the general rules applied to life as a whole, is largely negative. As these general rules continue to be applied to life, exceptions that challenge them can be missed. The times when a friend remains loyal and trustworthy, or when a good experience has not 'gone wrong' are not acknowledged and so the general rules remain unchallenged.

Cognitive behavioural models can assist us to challenge negative 'general rules' through distancing from a problem enough to consider evidence that either supports or negates basic beliefs, using the Socratic technique, detailed above, to weigh up advantages and disadvantages for maintaining the belief.

Blackburn and Davidson (1995) outline some techniques for 'extracting' or making sense of 'general rules', that are useful for social work practice. These include using specific examples given by the service user and tracking 'common themes'. Rules that are then applied by service users for their personal lives can be traced by the times statements are made about what they 'should' be doing. The worker and the service user can explore the implications of these rules and how they have developed to form automatic thoughts, by applying the technique detailed in the example below.

The aim of these techniques is not to create a crisis for an individual, whereby all sense of understanding of the world is challenged. Instead, the primary objective is to *gently* assist individuals to make their own gradual shifts in their belief system and thus their automatic thoughts, to incorporate more flexibility in their perception of events.

In discussing family relationships, Aaron had described how 'everyone' in the family, including his partner, 'always' ignored him whenever he had something to say. Gillian used this technique to challenge this rule that he applied to himself and his family.

Gillian asked Aaron to give her a specific example of when he thought he was being ignored. Aaron described an evening when his partner had returned from her new job and had excitedly told him all about her day but ignored his experience of being frustrated and lonely that day. Gillian asked Aaron what had been so upsetting to him that his partner had been speaking about her new job when she came in and not asking about him? Aaron described how he thought this meant that she had not thought of him all day and that she valued him very little. Gillian then asked him, 'Suppose she had not thought of you all day, what would this mean to you?' Aaron replied that it would mean he was worthless. Again Gillian followed his train of thought and asked him, 'Suppose you were worthless, what would this mean to you?' Aaron responded that it would mean no one would like him or take the time to get to know him. Gillian replied, 'Supposing this was true, what would that mean to you?' Aaron described how he would be forever lonely with no friends or family who would make time for him. He added that he thought it would mean that he was unlovable and that life would not be worth living.

Gillian stopped this by summarising, 'Does this suggest that you believe that unless people do not talk about their own experiences, that you are worthless and that your life is not worth living?' Aaron corrected Gillian by stating that he thought it was okay for people to talk to him about their own experiences sometimes and that he liked the idea of being a good listener. Aaron, through participating in this exercise, had challenged his own beliefs about what had happened that day. He began to change his perception of his partner's excitement about her first day at her new job and how she had wanted to share it with him *because* he was important to her, rather than because he was not.

Social Work Application

Many service users who become known to social workers have had many negative experiences or have been subject to oppressive societal forces that leave people marginalised and disempowered. In these circumstances, it is likely that most people would attribute some general rules that are negative and unhelpful and do not fit with other people's accounts. Unhelpful general rules can interfere with service user engagement with services and with their motivation for change. These general rules that tend to be wholly applied to life and experience can seriously inhibit an individual's participation in society and in meaningful relationships. In turn, these patterns of thought can lead to chronic problems of worrying about the future and of low mood.

Using this technique to challenge general rules could be perceived to be dangerous in that we would be following an individual's train of thought and taking it to an extreme position. To effectively use the technique, we need to develop a confidence based on judgement that we are not pushing an individual to perceive our questions as feedback that they really are 'unlovable and unworthy'. Using this technique with someone who has suicidal thoughts would not be recommended. Rather, an individual requires some degree of resilience in order to challenge the extreme position as not fitting with their own feelings, beliefs and desires. As with all therapeutic techniques, there is an inherent risk that intrusive and challenging questioning could shake the fragility of vulnerable people's cognitive and affective structures that allow them to survive in difficult circumstances. Before we embark on this or any other technique, we need to be as certain as we can be that a degree of safety is experienced by an individual within their own living environment to allow them to explore unknown or possibly dangerous cognitive and affective territory.

Skills Component

- Use judgement to evaluate whether a person's vulnerability and resilience would allow them to tolerate exploring an extreme position of general rules enough to challenge it.
- Use caution to avoid this technique if not certain of its suitability for an individual.
- Use this technique only after an assessment of the environmental and situational factors to ensure a high enough level of safety for an individual – emotional and physical.
- Consider evidence given in discussions with the service user that indicates that an extreme position is unlikely to fit with their beliefs and desires.
- If in doubt with this fit or a person has suicidal thoughts, avoid this technique.

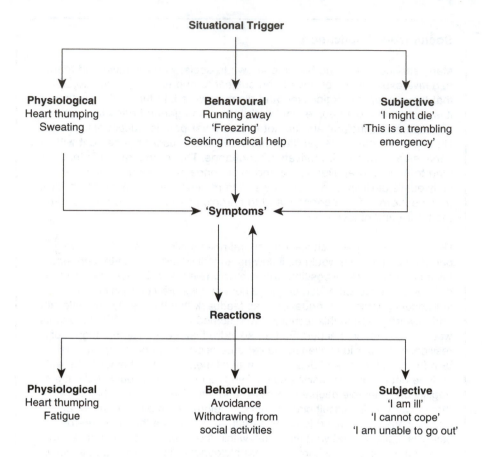

Desensitisation

This technique is primarily used to assist people to confront and change avoidance behaviour due to highly anxious responses to specific situational triggers. This thought/behaviour pattern is often termed a phobia. Hawton and colleagues (1995) provide a model to explain how phobias become a 'vicious circle'.

This model helps us connect the link between thought processes, i.e. the subjective cognitions based on basic beliefs held in the schemata, with behaviours that reinforce beliefs, as they are not challenged. To challenge the beliefs about a phobic reaction, a degree of tolerance of anxious feelings is required. An individual needs to tolerate uncomfortable anxious feelings enough to progress with a desensitisation programme. Thus the first step needs to be an educative role to assist an individual to understand how phobias are being maintained.

Desensitisation techniques are not outlined in detail in this chapter. However, the function of a desensitisation programme is to gradually assist a person to build up exposure to a situational stressor and learn to tolerate anxious feelings in the process. As the programme progresses with 'graded hierarchies' of the problematic situation, a service user begins to challenge beliefs about a stressor and about the causation of automatic thoughts that lead to physiological and psychological distress.

Anthony was a 10-year-old boy who had a generally anxious pattern of seeing his world. He had always been a quiet boy with no observed problems at either home or school. However, his family moved from a rural area to a large town in October. During this time, Anthony and his family had noticed a significant increase in the amount of fireworks that would be set off compared to his previous community. He had always had a fear of fireworks and thunder and had managed to avoid them by staying in the house at times of thundery weather or firework displays. In his new community, the period of time for fireworks to be set off had greatly extended. Anthony managed his anxieties by refusing to leave the house, even for school. Anthony came to the attention of a social worker following several months of school refusal. Anthony worked with his social worker, Mrs Asghar, to develop a graded hierarchy of situations that he feared, and worked with her to learn to tolerate his anxious feelings through gradual desensitisation. Through her work with Anthony and his family, Mrs Asghar noticed that Anthony's mother would also become very anxious when he became upset and would him to avoid certain situations to protect him from his feelings. Mrs Asghar worked with his mother also to assist her to tolerate her own feelings of anxiety to allow Anthony to make progress with the programme.

Social Work Application

'Simple' phobias without the complexity of other social and relational factors are unusual in social work practice. More usual is the development of a phobic form of anxiety as part of a host of other difficulties which mostly require intervention first. For example, an older woman developing a fear of mixing with others after her partner dies might on the surface appear to have a phobia of leaving the house. However, the woman might be struggling with unresolved losses complicated by her recent bereavement. She might have physical impairments that leave her feeling more vulnerable. She might have relied on her partner to assist her to go out, either for physical or emotional support. Many other examples might be offered to indicate how the avoidance of objects, people or places might not be directly related to phobias.

However, once other contributory factors have either been ruled out or addressed, desensitisation programmes can be useful tools for social workers to incorporate as part of intervention.

Skills Component

- Take into account other possible explanations for behaviours and fears
- Address other contributing factors first
- Introduce a desensitisation programme by exploring and formulating a 'graded hierarchy' of the severity of fear in given situations
- Assist a service user to tolerate their feelings of anxiety by starting with exposure to the least fearful trigger
- Introduce relaxation techniques (below) to enable a service user to tolerate their anxiety

Summary of Key Cognitive Behavioural Concepts

- Development of beliefs through experience from infancy and consolidated during adolescence becomes established as **Cognitive Schemata**
- **Automatic Thoughts** occur in response to anticipated events based on assumptions derived from beliefs held within the **Schema**
- Perceptions are filtered by the **Schema** so that we emphasise experience that fits with our beliefs and expectations and dismiss others, leading to **Cognitive Distortion**
- Experiences that generate unhelpful assumptions leading to cognitive, emotional, physiological and behavioural consequences are termed **Critical Incidents**
- **Content-specificity Hypotheses** group together patterns of unhelpful thoughts that lead to anxiety problems and generalised low mood
- The **Therapeutic Relationship** is the necessary context for cognitive behavioural approaches
- Practitioners use **Socratic Dialogue** to track and challenge unhelpful automatic thoughts
- **Reattribution** is used to assist service users to reattribute negative outcomes of events or experience away from perceived self-critical causation to external influence when persistent negative thoughts impair self-control
- Practitioners challenge **General Rules** that are applied to life when views of the world have become narrow and inflexible to the extent that positive events are dismissed
- **Desensitisation** is the technique used to gradually expose a person to anxiety-provoking stimuli in a staged way to address phobias

Conclusion

In social work practice, we regularly meet individuals whose lives are affected by low mood or by anxieties. With our knowledge of societal influences that stigmatise certain groups of people, marginalise others through poverty and deprivation, and oppress people through racism and homophobia among other forms of prejudice and discrimination, we can make sense of some of the reasons why some people might experience low mood and anxieties. Cognitive and behavioural theories do acknowledge the impact of culture and society upon thought processes and behavioural responses, although the focus for change is targeted at individuals rather than the environment.

In social work practice, we can judiciously use these techniques in conjunction with considering societal and environmental factors that can contribute to problems. As social workers, our role is to be mindful of the interconnection between environmental, social and political aspects of life with internal processing of information. When this interconnection is in equilibrium, i.e. the environmental stressors are not overwhelming internal coping mechanisms, an individual can function adequately in the social world. However, when either the coping mechanisms (or core beliefs that shape perceptions) become overwhelmed or the environmental stressors become too high, an individual's social functioning can be compromised. We can integrate cognitive behavioural approaches into our practice while ever we also remain aware of the need to address socio-environmental problems.

With therapeutic techniques comes an inherent danger that social functioning can be improved by 'counselling' or 'therapy' alone. The social model upon which we base the foundation of our practice allows us to avoid this trap by taking into account the environmental elements to thoughts, feelings and behaviours before we focus on internal mechanisms.

Further Reading

- **Wills and Sanders (2002)** offer a concise and 'easy to read' overview of this approach that could be further applied to social work practice. Their use of diagrams to explain key principles and their emphasis upon the therapeutic or collaborative relationship lends itself especially towards compatibility with fundamental social work values.

- **Friedberg and McClure (2002)** also offer a clear overview of the theoretical principles linked with this approach but tailor it specifically to the needs of children and young people.

- **Blackburn and Davidson (1995)** offer a book more specifically directed towards practice with adults with problems with low mood or anxiety.

4

The Application of Psychodynamic and Attachment Theory in Social Work Practice

Key Concepts	Key Theorists and Practitioners
• Unconscious	• Freud
• Transference	• Winnicott
• Counter-transference	• Klein
• Defence	• Fairbairn
• Safe Haven	• Bowlby
• Secure Base	

Introduction

Psychoanalysis is often thought of in terms of Freud, and his initial theories, expanded over time by various theorists and psychoanalytical researchers, provide the theoretical underpinnings of psychoanalytic psychotherapy. This chapter will offer an exploration of how some of the key themes from the psychoanalytic schools can be incorporated into social work practice, without embarking into therapeutic domains that exist outside of the social work qualification (Yelloly, 1980). The psychoanalytic domain is vast, and while this chapter aims to bring some theoretical elements to social work practitioners in a manner that relates directly to social work practice, it is necessarily broad. Further reading of social work and psychoanalytic/ psychodynamic literature is therefore strongly recommended to develop understanding of psychoanalytic concepts in practice further.

This chapter is significant in that many of the barriers to communication that occur that are based on the nature of previous relationships rather than organisational practicalities can be understood using a psychoanalytic perspective. The principal objective for incorporating this model into this book is not for social workers to 'have a go' at psychoanalysis with service users, but to use some elements from the theoretical framework to make sense of some of the ways in which people relate to us in a working relationship. The aim of this chapter, therefore, is to provide readers with a broad understanding of some of the core concepts of psychodynamic theory to assist us to better communicate and engage with service users. Although the terms incorporated and explored in this chapter are used in a very precise, technical manner in psycho-analysis, they are included in a broad manner to enhance social work practitioners' awareness of motivational drives and the wish to free ourselves from psychic pain.

Attachment theories have been integrated into this chapter to assist with the understanding of the nature of a therapeutic relationship. Although attachment theo-ries stand alone from psychoanalytic theory, the theoretical roots are very much con-nected and developed from psychoanalysis and hence are included here. Gaining insight into how personal relationships are formed and sustained, especially during early development where our 'blueprints' for later relationships are established, can illuminate how we can then assist people to form helpful relationships in the future through the use of the working relationship. This chapter aims to offer social work practitioners the foundations of establishing meaningful therapeutic relationships with service users in order that change in the present and for the future might be possible through the medium of communication skills.

The Psychoanalytic Movement

Freud is the founding theorist of psychoanalysis (Freud, 1935, 1937). His work is the basis upon which other theorists have developed ideas and understanding about the nature and development of the self, relations (object relations) with others and of behavioural patterns that emerge as a result of early childhood experiences. An overview of some of the key theoretical positions of psychoanalysis, emanating from Freud's early work, can help social workers to use this theory both to understand some of the roots of their service users' communication styles and to assist in building and maintaining relationships with them, and is therefore offered here.

Gellner (2003) compares psychoanalysis with religion: a set of beliefs and prac-tices with a definite point of creation (Freud, 1935). Gellner offers a history of Freud and his account of the evolution of the movement makes for convincing reading on the fractious validity of the claims psychoanalysis makes. Categorising 'believers' of the movement into committed, resistant and hostile positions does little initially to encourage the reader into embracing psychoanalysis but perseverance with the prin-ciples that form psychoanalysis can be a useful addition to any social worker's 'tool bag'. Empirical research does, however, support the usefulness of psychoanalysis in some instances, although qualitative data is difficult to achieve when outcomes of therapy are largely quantitative (Roth & Fonagy, 1996).

Leiper and Maltby (2004) outline three stages of Freud's work throughout his career that resulted in the evolution of his theory or 'model of the mind'. From 1890–1900, Freud developed theories relating to affect of trauma – that is, the way in which 'the mind' will use defensive processes (see below) to protect an individual from the full emotional affect of traumatic experience (Freud, 1936). His therapeutic intervention aimed to 'uncover' the memory of trauma and so free an individual of intrusive unconscious distortions of the external world.

From 1900–20, Freud was concerned with topographical theory. This theory further developed ideas about the unconscious mind and the instinctive drives that led individuals into action, based on the pursuit of pleasure. As described by Gellner (2003), during this period a group of 'followers' joined forces, resulting in the development of the psychoanalytic 'movement'.

The final period of Freud's work from 1920–39 gave birth to Structural Theory. This theory was concerned with the way in which early relationships become internalised to cope with loss and change. From this developed Object Relations Theory as referred to above (Fairbairn, 1952, 1958) and the introduction of the 'mental structures' of Id, Ego and Superego. In brief, the Id refers to the unconscious, the Ego to the conscious and the Superego to the conscience (Bateman et al., 2000). This is usefully explored in Howe (1992) in context with Freud's stages of development. The aim of psychotherapy is to free an individual from the intrusive nature of the Id and from extreme critical positions of the Superego in order that the conscious mind can operate more objectively. In psychoanalytic psychotherapy, in Freudian times, this was achieved through the therapist adopting a 'neutral' position in the therapeutic relationship. More recently, however, psychoanalysis recognises the subjective nature of therapeutic relationships, although the therapist remaining relatively anonymous and subjecting his or her own needs remains central to the approach (Leiper & Maltby, 2004).

Furthermore, the Structural period also introduced the concept of conflict between internal mental structures. Anxiety thus serves as a threat to the 'governing equilibrium' between these structures and creates internal conflict. This conflict is not necessarily pathological, i.e. a manifestation of mental illness or dysfunction, but one that is inherent to the human organism, albeit in different degrees for different individuals. With this in mind, we can be wary of thinking of vulnerable people who are struggling with their lives as somehow different to ourselves.

Leiper and Maltby (2004) demonstrate the triangle of conflict, representing the dynamic nature of psychoanalytic theory (Freud, 1936). This triangle highlights the dynamic nature of internal relationships between the structures and drives of the mind, as outlined above.

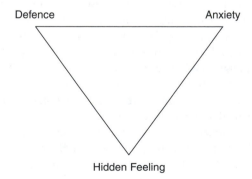

The nature of conflict between our desires located in the Id, our anxieties about these desires from internalised social rules located in the Superego and defence mechanisms that protect the conscious mind from the full effect of this conflict located in the Ego, are constantly at play. By necessity, this is an extremely brief outline of the internal triangular concept that psychoanalytic theorists would argue lead to emotional and behavioural responses within relationships. Object relations theory demonstrates the evolution of these ideas over time that is currently influential in certain fields of psychotherapy (Winnicott, 1951; Fairbairn, 1954), i.e. the motivational force we all have to be attached to someone – the 'object'. For example, an infant will adapt to an incredible degree in order to 'stay in mind' or feel connected to a carer. If a carer is unable to meet the infant's needs in a responsive and safe manner, that infant will adopt ways that might be described as maladaptive to try to get his or her needs met. This can then be perceived as the child having emotional and/or behavioural problems.

Some commonly used terms rooted in psychoanalytic theory that can be useful for social workers to consider in practice are now introduced.

The Unconscious

The Freudian concept of the unconscious is perhaps the most frequently referred-to psychoanalytic term and probably the least understood in the social work field. In short, the unconscious is claimed to exist as a set of beliefs, ideas, feelings and memories that developed over time in early childhood, especially at key developmental stages, and to co-exist alongside the conscious. 'Claimed' is used not to discredit the theory but to acknowledge that, as with all theoretical concepts about the processes of thinking and emotion, it is not a tangible object that can be seen to be proved. The evidence of its existence is experienced as an influence or an effect rather than as a visible object.

The character of the unconscious is disorderly and not constrained to rational proportion (Freud, 1935). It differs from the conscious in that it is subversive, discreet and invisible. It directs the show of life from behind the scenes rather than sitting centre-stage. Most of all, it sits separated from the consciousness and is inaccessible from its reaches – 'hidden'. Contained within the unconscious are thoughts, feelings and memories that could be described as unspeakable – i.e. that are too extreme to be held in the conscious mind; or the experience of them goes beyond the limits of language and rational perception; or that they were formed in early infancy and childhood when we are less able to make 'objective' sense of experience by comparison to other experience (Winnicott, 1945). We might argue, however, that as we filter experience through that which we already 'know', we can never really be 'objective' about anything. This is considered further in Chapter 5.

The importance of the unconscious is that its subtly secretive existence manifests itself largely as the key influencing factor in major decision-making in life beyond childhood. It shapes our interpretation of actions and reactions by others and it underpins our reactive behavioural responses as a result. Unconscious motivation in therapeutic relationships can lead us to seek out and replicate situations in which the 'same old stuff' occurs, i.e. 'someone who depends too much on others seeks a confident advisor; someone who is cut off from their feelings seeks an expert to discuss things with' (Leiper & Maltby, 2004).

Why, then, does the unconscious matter for social workers? If we accept knowledge of the unconscious as positively influencing social work practice, then we might view the key decisions that people make regarding their lives in general and their behaviour within the working relationship as being influenced by the powerful, directing force of the unconscious. We could accept that what might appear irrational behaviour may be founded upon a guiding set of beliefs that were generated out of lived experience and not out of rational logic in keeping with the social norms and expectations of our culture. Some qualified in the field of psychoanalytic psychotherapy claim that only through analysis can the unconscious be accessed and manipulated, and this chapter does not set out to directly challenge this. Rather, we might argue that, in utilising counselling skills within the field of social work, knowledge of the unconscious can assist in both engaging with people and their problems and with making sense of the therapeutic process enough to work towards change. How we might incorporate ideas about the existence of the unconscious into our practice will be explored below, but an example of the unconscious at play can illuminate the theory.

Annique had a history of neglectful parenting until age 8, when she moved to members of her extended family. Her extended family offered her a secure upbringing, but by early adulthood Annique's choices seemed to bemuse her carers. Rather than embrace the lifestyle they had offered her, she chose to return to her mother, believing she was the only person who could offer her the love and nurturing she craved. She cut off her extended family, thinking she must choose one or the other. What followed was a series of troubled experiences leading to the eventual breakdown of that mother–daughter relationship. In later life, Annique was still distressed by the decision made to return to her mother, having been later reunited with her extended family. She knew consciously that she was safe, loved and cared for but she had been driven by a 'maladaptive' unconscious drive to be with her mother as the only way of achieving psychic stability, i.e. inner calm as opposed to physical safety. The strength of the unconscious mind had overruled her logic and driven her to make choices that she no longer believes were in her best interests.

Social Work Application

In childcare services, social workers are often placed in a situation where assessment and decision-making regarding children's needs in respect of their home circumstances are required. Social workers by law must listen to the views of children and young people (HMSO, 1994; McK.Norrie, 1998). Dilemmas in social work practice occur when the views of young people conflict with their needs and who and what can meet them adequately.

(Continued)

(Continued)

Resource issues aside, using only listening skills to acknowledge Annique's communication, i.e. regarding her desire to return to her mother's care, can place both parties in an impasse with regard to any decision-making. Should Annique's mother's care be deemed 'not good enough' and if a return were prevented, Annique's view would not feel heard. This could result in Annique developing mental health problems, including low mood and despondency, in part because she is unable to emotionally use the positive caring offered to her in another environment. Conversely, allowing her to return to a neglectful situation would mean her need for 'good enough' parenting would not be met.

Holding an awareness of the unconscious could help with such dilemmas. Annique needs to be carefully listened to and then helped to see the incongruity in her answer, i.e. she wants to return to her mother's care. That is, a practitioner can raise a curiosity about how she seems to want this which is uncomfortable rather than to be with carers, which would seem better from an outside point of view. The unconscious would never be directly questioned, but recognised through incongruities. Helping someone understand how the unconscious seems to be influencing them can be both relieving and frightening. To manage the frightening aspect, anxiety needs to be managed by providing further safety in the relationship. Without this safety (see attachment theories below), further trauma could be created by pushing someone to explore their feelings further than they feel ready to go.

For example, Annique might be communicating in a non-verbal way that she wishes to return to the care of her mother by running away from her extended family and going to her mother's house. As a young person, Annique might not be able to verbalise that she believes her mother can offer her unconditional love, although she has never actually experienced it. Neither might she be able to verbalise that the care she receives from her extended family does not *feel* like unconditional love, albeit that they have accepted her and her behaviour consistently and without rejection for a longer period than she lived with her mother. Her irrational but firmly held unconscious belief about the nature of love and who can provide it, i.e. mothers only, formed in her early years, had driven her to behave accordingly. Thus an understanding of the unconscious at play can highlight to us as social workers that what appears to be irrational decision-making might be driven by unconscious beliefs.

On a cautionary note, as social workers we can only be aware of the unconscious, if we accept psychoanalytic theory as valid and helpful. We can use it to point us towards understanding and exploration of individuals' behaviour and their choices but we should not be carried on an inflated sense of enthusiasm with regard to its uses in our field. Psychoanalysis in practice uses the therapeutic relationship in strictly defined terms to assist individuals

(Continued)

(Continued)

to allow unconscious influences to surface and thus be explored. For us to make assumptions about possible unconscious processes could be neglectful practice, if not potentially dangerous, if we rely only upon what we see and hear. Through careful listening, reflecting upon theory and exploration of ideas over time, knowledge of the unconscious can be one tool of many that we might consider in trying to make sense of behaviours and decision-making processes. Therefore in social work practice we can become enabled to communicate effectively with service users about them by considering how lives in general might be both directed and constrained by unconscious processes.

Another case example might illuminate the workings of the unconscious further:

Gerald found that every time his key worker in the residential unit came to speak to him, either for a general chat or to discuss specific matters that were arising within the unit, he went quiet and was unable to share his views. Most of the time he was angry and irritable with other residents, especially with those who were more mobile than him. His key worker suspected that his anger was linked to his disability following major surgery and his increasing frailty, but was wary of making assumptions. Gerald had had little experience of talking out problems. His experience of family life and the communication style inherent to his relationships was to act out his frustrations by aggression. When he was a child he had been punished for trying to tell his parents he felt upset, being firmly encouraged to 'be brave' and not cry. His deeply held but uncommunicated belief was that to show any sign of 'upset', especially to someone in the role of a carer, would expose him as 'cowardly'. He held unconscious fantasies that weak people are victimised and punished. He thought that his physical disability impaired his image of someone strong and in control and was unable to compound this by allowing himself to be upset, adding to his feelings of weakness. Unfortunately for Gerald, his key worker and social worker were unable to make sense of his 'stubbornness', which led to a misinterpretation that he was being deliberately awkward and refusing to talk.

Had Gerald's key worker and social worker in this instance been able to recognise that there seemed to be a link to his communication style and his unconscious beliefs about sharing concerns, they might have been able to empower him by acknowledging how difficult he found purposeful discussion, and by focusing more on the meaning of sharing worries rather than the problems themselves. This could have freed Gerald up enough to have at least recognised the influence of previous experiences on his current communication style and the impact it was therefore having on him and others within the unit. The focus here would have been on a much slower pace of engagement rather than quickly coming to the view that Gerald was non-compliant.

Skills Component

- Accept and acknowledge surface communication, verbal and non-verbal.
- Understand that unconscious beliefs can shape surface communication.
- Reflect with people regarding their beliefs and the meanings attributed to experience.
- Affirm the importance of these beliefs, allowing individuals to be heard without being dismissed.
- Offer alternatives without dismissing beliefs.

Realism

In psychoanalytic terms, this relates to the way in which the mind makes sense of 'objects' (people or things) with which it comes into contact. The unconscious mind acts as a type of filter, which alters the perception of each object as it is encountered by the conscious mind. In psychoanalytic theory, it is a type of obstacle that distorts perception and prevents the 'true' nature of an object being experienced by individuals. We might question whether 'true' nature exists. This is debated more fully in Chapter 5, looking at narrative approaches. For this model, however, the psychoanalytic perspective accepts that realism shapes the way in which people process events and the dynamics of relationships. It is born out of the unconscious and shapes what is experienced in the here and now, resulting in emotional and behavioural responses.

The practice of psychoanalysis seeks to remove these obstacles seated within the unconscious, to allow the free-flow interpretation of experiences and events to occur (Freud, 1935; Fairbairn, 1958). Howe (1992) suggests that 'talking about your thoughts and feelings brings them to the surface, into consciousness and out into the open'. Accepting that social work practice does not constitute psychoanalysis, developing awareness of possible obstacles that hinder change and progress for service users – such as ways in which people or situations are viewed that do not reflect how they are viewed or experienced by others – can broaden our understanding of social functioning. This can further improve our ability as social workers to engage with people and work towards change in a meaningful way. As above, Annique's story can help us make sense of this principle.

Annique had chosen to return to live with her mother, believing the surface expression made by her mother to care for Annique and compensate for her troubled past. Annique at this time knew that her mother was both using and selling drugs and had seen no evidence that her mother's lifestyle or negative attitude towards her had changed since she had left. However, she filtered

(Continued)

(Continued)

these experiences out and believed only what she heard, i.e. that she was wanted by her mother and would receive care and nurturance. She also filtered out the lived experience of the recent years of positive and nurturing care by her extended family and saw only her fantasised perception of her mother, whom she believed would offer her that much-desired love.

Social Work Application

When looking at problems from a psychoanalytic position, we might accept that the unconscious shapes our perception through conditioned realism. It might be startlingly obvious to a social worker that an individual or an environment does not offer 'good enough' care for an individual. However, if beliefs held in the unconscious mind of that individual persuade him or her that it does, the 'true' nature of that environment will be filtered out by that person and the experience will be perceived as potentially more positive. It is the potential rather than the actual experience that holds the power – the fantasy of what might be, rather than the reality of what is.

Again, our domain is not analysis. We exist in a world where decisions regarding risks and care arrangements need to be made and our task is often to assess (or provide our own 'filtered' view of) relationships and environments for vulnerable individuals. We use our counselling skills both to gather information for these assessments and to assist people to share their distress with us, hoping to alleviate an emotional burden and improve an individual's capacity for social functioning. Awareness of conditioned realism can allow us to make sense of what can appear to be an irrational reaction to a situation.

Annique was filtering out her experiences of responsive nurturance from her extended family, choosing to reject this in favour of her beliefs that only her mother could offer her unconditional love. She accepted her mother's assurance of a different experience, without any 'true' evidence to support this belief. To engage with Annique, it is essential that any social worker positions themselves alongside her, accepting her view of her situation.

It is all too tempting to launch into challenging views of individuals, even doing so gently, when to us in our supposedly objective position we can see that these views do not equate with our own interpretation of reality. Unless people *feel* heard and their views taken seriously, engagement does not occur and as social workers we will either be avoided or told what people think we want to hear. From this theoretical position we see that our interpretations of reality are conditioned out of the beliefs held in our unconscious and we explore with individuals the factors upon which these beliefs are built. Dismissing beliefs as either faulty or irrelevant will almost certainly guarantee engagement failure.

Gerald's position highlights some of the pitfalls of communication:

Gerald's key worker and social worker were both experienced people with a reputation for being very skilled. If they could not elicit his views, who could? The problem being missed was the meaning of the communication process for Gerald. His experience of this communication process, a one-to-one interview by a carer with him in a relatively powerless position, was for him not dissimilar to a one-to-one encounter with one or another of his parents when he had tried as a young child to share his distress. He had clearly absorbed and internalised the feedback received that he was being cowardly and so should not repeat the behaviour. He then was processing the current 'chats' and perceiving them in the same vein, as a result of his own conditioned reality. Gerald's key worker tried every way known to her to try to persuade him to express what was troubling him – write it down, tell another resident, tell his social worker, offer 'educated guesses' – all to no avail. The aspect of the communication being missed was the *meaning* for Gerald of sharing distress with another, which would open him up to feeling vulnerable and 'weak', a feeling he believed he was unable to tolerate.

Skills Component

- Position ourselves, metaphorically speaking, alongside our service users to gain a sense of what beliefs are held about people and relationships and how they shape their reactions to events.
- Accept and acknowledge an individual's communicated experience of reality, even if this differs from the 'true' picture, as we, or others see it.
- Being aware of the existence of unconscious beliefs frees us to name them and question them with our service users.
- Explore their validity with people without dismissing their own perceptions.
- Challenging conditioned realism in a confronting manner leads to people feeling dismissed, unheard and disengaging with services, either literally or emotionally, and should be avoided.
- In risk assessment and management, a more challenging approach to behaviour and protection is often required, but communication should include acknowledgement of a service user's own position.

Inner Reality

Psychoanalysis is primarily concerned with the inner self as opposed to the external world and socio-political systems (Klein, 1959). Psychoanalytic theory holds that our desires and impulses are crystallised in childhood and that conflict with our inner reality leads to distress. The psychoanalytic movement also asserts that acceptance of our inner reality and the desires we experience that are born out of it, albeit allowing for minor modification, is important to achieve conflict resolution within ourselves (Freud, 1935).

As social workers, we *are* concerned with the interaction between the external world and the inner self (BASW, 2001). Knowledge of the principle of inner reality and how theorists (Klein, 1921; Winnicott, 1945) have come to explain how that inner reality develops in early childhood through interaction with the external world can greatly assist us in practice. This is so in two fundamental ways: firstly, we can use this theoretical foundation to understand how childhood experiences can affect child and adult functioning; and secondly, we can come to accept and explore, rather than criticise and dismiss, beliefs and ideas that underlie behaviours made by service users in and beyond childhood. The counselling skills component within social work that enables us to achieve this end can thus, in part, be derived from the psychoanalytic movement. Annique helps us understand this.

During Annique's early years of neglect and feelings of abandonment, she would fantasise about being loved and cared for. This fantasy was a preoccupation of hers for many years, even when she was safe and cared for by her extended family. She would withdraw into her fantasy rather than fully embrace the love and nurturing offered by her carers in the 'here and now'. This was safer for her than to risk further rejection, abuse and abandonment. Even as a mature adult, Annique remains preoccupied with 'love', caring and nurturance. She still doubts people's ability to provide this and overcompensates by lavishing caring and affection on others. She has learned to channel this doubt about people's ability to nurture her by giving nurturance to her own partner and family. To some extent she accepts caring behaviours from her partner. However, those early desires remain as dominant a preoccupation now as they did in her early childhood, having been crystallised there. These do not inhibit her social functioning in dramatic ways but her desire in life first and foremost is to give and receive 'love'. This overriding desire does reduce her ability to lose herself in other activities whereby she might develop her life skills and knowledge in a broader manner and widen her circle of social contacts. As she does not perceive this as a problem, we need to accept that, but remain aware of the source of such a strong desire.

Social Work Application

There are many instances where unresolved inner conflict leads people in adolescence and adult life to struggle with their identity. These struggles can result in mental health problems, drug misuse, abuse of other people and an overall low level of social functioning and positive participation in society. Experiencing abandonment in her early childhood heightened Annique's

(Continued)

(Continued)

unconscious awareness of the need for loving support and protection. As an adult, her deeply formed inner beliefs about the importance of this influenced her life in subtle forms. She chooses not to work or pursue a career so that she can devote as much of her waking time as possible to caring for her children. Even though her children can attend school and she is both intelligent and feeling personally unfulfilled, she struggles to deviate from these choices, unconsciously anxious about catastrophic consequences of her children being neglected.

Annique struggles with anxiety and depression, lowering her ability to be responsive to her children and inadvertently bringing about some of what she is desperately trying to avoid. While her inner reality about the high priority of giving and receiving love is widely accepted in society, and on the surface does not generate conflict, unresolved experiences of her own history of neglect lead this to be over-heightened and result in a reduction in her overall social functioning and ability to care for her children.

As social workers we can accept an individual's desires as having roots in early experiences, and acknowledge them as having been important at the time they were formed. However, we are often faced with situations where an individual's needs and desires do not meet the needs of others around them. A child's needs cannot be put aside while an adult acts on impulsive desires to live in accordance with their inner reality; a woman does not have to accept a violent relationship because her partner learned that physical aggression is the only way to maintain power within relationships.

Social workers do not have to complacently accept a person acting in keeping with their inner reality as the only way they can function in society, especially if that inner reality impairs others' development or harms someone. However, as above, an awareness of these concepts can enable us to make a connection with our service users, not dismiss their drives and reasoning, and respectfully explore ways of creating change. We can seek acceptance of inner reality through this exploration, while considering in parallel the impact of resultant behaviours on all involved.

Aggression had been the manner in which Gerald had communicated his needs and frustrations over his lifetime. This only came to light as a problem when he moved into a residential unit, where his aggressive tendencies became harmful to other residents.

Staff within the unit became exasperated very quickly when Gerald exhibited violent behaviours. He would push plates and cups at other residents at mealtimes, on one occasion hitting a woman on the arm and she requiring treatment. The level of concern was such that Gerald's placement was being questioned. As he would not discuss his worries, the staff group found

(Continued)

(Continued)

themselves lost as to the root of the problem and he was being ostracised by others as a result of his aggression. Gerald's inner reality was shaped by his view of what he believed was required to be 'good enough' as an adult and as a man. He desired above all else to be seen as a strong individual who could cope with his life. He believed that this was the requirement of a man, to overcome all problems and show no weakness. He found that needing help to eat was a confirmation that he was not 'good enough' as a man, and a lifetime of fears about this culminated around mealtimes, when his vulnerability and level of need was so publicly apparent. Gerald's behaviour was harmful to others and so could not be tolerated. His inner reality of his view of himself as a male adult and his level of competency (or perceived incompetency) in social settings, coupled with his inner reality that violent communication results in being heard, without exposing vulnerability, served to maintain the behaviours, even though significant problems were generated in consequence. Gerald became segregated at mealtimes, eating alone with a carer. The levels of aggression around mealtimes decreased but Gerald's inner reality remained unchanged and his view of his own social competence and masculinity continued to diminish until he plummeted into a depressive state.

Gerald's behaviour could not have been tolerated while it was causing physical and emotional harm to others. However, had Gerald the opportunity to explore the meaning of his behaviours in terms of what it requires to be heard by others without being perceived as socially incompetent and 'weak', and what is required to be 'good enough' as a man and an adult, while in the unit, segregation on a long-term basis at mealtimes might have been avoided. The nature of masculinity and the function of violence for Gerald were later discussed by him with an occupational therapist during a hospital admission close to the end of his life.

Skills Component

- Understand that desires and impulses formed in childhood can drive behaviour and choices.
- Overtly acknowledge both the desires and impulses and the experiences which have generated them to allow a person to be heard.
- Use respectful acknowledgement by verbalising observations and making tentative attempts at making connections between desires, behaviours and early experiences to 'free up' the conversation to discuss the impact on the self and others.

Defence

Again an often quoted and more often misunderstood term, defence reactions occur as an impulsive protection against perceived anxiety within ourselves and operate at an unconscious level to influence actual behaviour (Freud, 1936). They are not unique to service users – we all use them. Anna Freud (1936), Sigmund Freud's daughter, listed nine mechanisms of defence, which were later developed by Melanie Klein (1952, 1959) to demonstrate how defences are generated during the separation process between infant and carer in early development. Defences are generally functional, in that they allow us to tolerate distress and uncertainty on a day-to-day basis. Traumatic experience can result in defences becoming problematic: when leading to extreme emotional or behavioural reactions or when they inhibit social interaction in 'safe' environments, i.e. environments perceived to be safe where there is no actual risk of harm.

Thus defences serve to avoid perceived catastrophic consequences of an anticipated event in the external world. This concept is linked very closely to the cognitive behavioural model (see Chapter 3). The event may or may not be likely to occur in reality but through development a personalised 'lens' (Hoffman, 1990) through which an event is experienced and if catastrophe is envisaged, established impulsive defences manifest themselves in behavioural forms. These defences (or reactions to hidden feelings) can take the form of repression, i.e. suppressing inner feelings; denial, including 'forgetting'; projection (see below); reaction formation, i.e. going to an opposite extreme; rationalisation; psychosomatic reactions, i.e. where unacceptable feelings are converted into physical symptoms such as stomach pains, headaches etc.; phobic avoidance; displacement, i.e. deflecting feelings to a 'safe' source, often inwards; regression to childlike behaviour; de-personalisation, i.e. a sense of feeling unreal and separated from emotions; idealisation of a lost person ('object') or attack of an 'object', i.e. splitting (Freud, 1936; Klein, 1959).

Returning to Annique, defences played an important part in her emotional survival as a young child. She cut herself off from the abuse and neglect by withdrawing into a fantasy about being loved. In doing so, she preserved some part of her that was not directly affected by her environment. She had split off her distress to allow her to live on a day-to-day basis. Without these defences, she would have been overwhelmed by anxiety and unable to function in school, with peers and in other social situations. The abuse and neglect was harmful, but Annique defended herself against the anxiety of the situation by utilising these defences. The defence mechanisms were still in place with her carers, leading her to remain emotionally 'cut off' and reject the care offered. Only in adult life was Annique emotionally ready to lower these defences enough to explore the horror of her early life. To force Annique to lower her defences before she was ready, i.e. when she moved to her carers and was

(Continued)

(Continued)

safe, would have been to subject her to high levels of anxiety with which she was neither emotionally nor cognitively mature enough to cope. For Annique, her defences served a function; they kept her emotionally 'together' until she was ready and able to 'fall apart' in a safe and controlled way in later life.

Social Work Application

Social workers encounter service users in distress on a daily basis. To engage with them and relate to them, an understanding of defences against anxiety and how they can create a barrier to change could be argued to be extremely important in any form of therapeutic work. It is also important to remember that defences are functional in that they arise from perceptions of anxiety-provoking stimuli formed out of lived experience. Inappropriate attempts to break down individuals' defences when environmental stimuli that provoke anxiety still are part of that person's lived experience expose people to the full effect of that which caused the defence against anxiety initially. This misuse of counselling skills in social work, albeit with good intentions, can lead to a significant rise in emotional distress for a service user and therefore caution in this respect is suggested.

Gerald was exhibiting various forms of defence when placed in the residential unit.

The violence exhibited served to defend Gerald against extreme feelings of anxiety about his perceived lack of social competence. He attacked those people he believed would view him as not 'good enough' by pushing plates and cups at them. He also denied any problems when discussing his behaviour with his key worker, out of a fear that he would also view him as a male who was 'not good enough'. These defences initially protected him from being overwhelmed by the anxiety of being in a residential unit, having physical problems for which he needed practical assistance and from his growing awareness of the life stage he had reached and the temporary nature of his existence.

Acknowledging these behaviours and the underlying feelings or fear and anxiety is different from attempting to break them down. Gerald's defences were in place for a reason: they served the function of protecting his fragile sense of self. He was placed in a unit away from his home of many years and was inevitably frightened for his future. It would have been highly unethical to attempt to 'break down' these defences in the interests of harmony within a unit or to 'help' Gerald. However, it would not be unethical to recognise that the surface behaviours have a function for him and to hypothesise about what the function of the behaviours might be. It can then be possible to attempt to reduce the environmental stressors in a way that does not stigmatise individuals but minimises the arousal of anxieties.

There are no easy solutions as to what would work for whom: individuals and our inner realities are as unique as the set of experiences we have. The common factor that does permeate all is that of acknowledging that defences exist, that they have a function and that they are driven by a desire to protect against situations that are perceived as dangerous and are likely to provoke anxiety. Adaptive defences, such as sublimation, also serve to provide outlets for repressed feelings, such as repressed oedipal sexual feelings channelled into creativity.

Skills Component

- Recognise that defences serve a function.
- Attempting to 'break down' an individual's defences, especially if they remain in a harmful or stressful situation, is almost always detrimental to that individual's mental health.
- Accept the defensive behaviour and acknowledge it with the individual.
- Explore the benefits of the behaviours and the detrimental aspects if those behaviours are causing the individual himself or others distress or harm.

Transference and Counter-transference

Transference is an objective of psychoanalytic psychotherapy, within the 'optimal conditions' of the 'consulting room' (Clarkson, 1995). Awareness of the process can be useful for social workers engaging in a counselling relationship with a service user (Freud, 1912; Strachey, 1934). When people are in distress or they are struggling to cope with the demands that society places on them, models of psychoanalysis would explain this as the inner world having become a closed system of feelings and beliefs that directly affect relationships and the interpretation of the meanings of others within those relationships, i.e., that person has become 'stuck' and different external events are not eliciting change.

Transference in working relationships is a process whereby, in the safety and regularity of meetings with a psychoanalytic psychotherapist, a person will attribute feelings held relating to significant people, most often carers/parents, from previous earlier relationships onto the therapist. The defining feature of transference is the link with relationships and experiences that belong to the past but that are brought into the present within the therapeutic relationship: 'Infantile prototypes re-emerge and are experienced with a strong sensation of immediacy' within the context of a therapeutic relationship (Laplanche & Pontalis, 1988). Further, transference will be repeated in differing contexts, will be idiosyncratic and will not fit with the present context in that it will be emotionally charged and fantasy-laden. Projection of strong feelings onto others is also a form of defence, whereby unwanted emotional responses are externalised and attributed to another (Bateman et al., 2000). These two concepts are linked and can often be confused.

The skill of the therapist is crucial here, in that these projected feelings are then recognised as part of the transference process, interpreted and explored by both the service user and the therapist in terms of context and meaning. It is a highly specialised task and not one which this chapter is advocating social workers freely embark on. However, holding awareness in this respect can enable us to recognise where feelings may be attributed to us that do not appear to fit the situation but are more understandable as part of transference. We can then accept the transference process rather than react to the surface behaviour that is presented. Insight into and reflection upon our own feelings within the working relationship are also key to understanding this process. Incongruence between the context of the working relationship and the emotional and behavioural reactions that are expressed by the service user towards us can indicate transference at play.

The feelings that workers have towards service users in response to the transference process is termed counter-transference (Winnicott, 1975). Affective responses are generated within the therapeutic relationship that can be both useful and a hindrance. Empathy would not be possible without an emotional response from the worker. However, a worker's own reactions to a service user's projections can potentially be intrusive and block effective therapeutic engagement, particularly when these responses lead to prejudice and discrimination. This links closely with the person-centred approach, where congruence and genuineness could potentially compromise positive regard where prejudices are held (see Chapter 2). Psychoanalytic psychotherapists make use of supervision to explore personal feelings generated by service users, with a view to preventing these feelings interfering with the therapeutic process. In social work practice, we can equally make use of reflection through peer and line-management supervision to limit the extent to which our own feelings could hinder the change process.

As a child, Annique accepted her carers and accepted various workers from numerous disciplines within the caring professions into her life. However, she remained withdrawn and refused to discuss either her feelings or her experiences in any instance. She was projecting her views of adults, based on what she had witnessed, onto all of these new adults that came into her life. She was both afraid of her feelings, for example overwhelming anxiety, and afraid of being rejected and abandoned again. Transference was at play. Had this been recognised, the adults (workers) involved might not have withdrawn from attempting to engage with Annique, which reinforced her belief that adults came along and then abandoned her.

Social Work Application

It is not unusual to meet with vulnerable service users who greet us with suspicion, hostility or ambivalence. We execute all of our engagement skills with patience and hopeful anticipation of a working relationship being formed. Yet at times we continue to be met with trepidation. Putting the power dynamic of the social worker–service user relationship aside, when attempting to engage with service users, holding in mind the concept of transference can allow us to accept that responses to our attempts at reaching out to people might be born out of earlier significant relationships. An awareness of this can assist us in our continual attempts to be respectful, open and accepting of that person, regardless of response feedback from that individual. From this perspective, it is useful to keep in mind that all individuals use transference within relationships and that it is not reserved only for those in vulnerable positions.

Annique was transferring the feelings that belonged with the caregivers who abandoned her onto the various workers who tried to engage with her. Their attempts to form a relationship with her were not in vain – she spoke positively of how, over time, the modelling of nurturing, respectful behaviour by the adults in her life did allow her to reduce her suspicion of adults and their motivation for speaking with her. However, the feedback she gave those adults during her childhood and youth was that of rejection and dismissal. From Annique we can learn that accepting the transference and responding in a nurturing way regardless can offer longer-term change for individuals, even though the fruits of this are not always evident in the here and now.

One-to-one meetings with his key worker left Gerald projecting his experience of his parents' reactions to any demonstrated distress onto the worker. He viewed him in the same light, that he would also be critical, dismissive and leave Gerald feeling under-valued if he were to share his troubles with him. The key worker noticed Gerald's feelings of hostility and could not understand what might have triggered them. He questioned his own practice over and over but missed the concept that Gerald was projecting fears about earlier relationships, where he was dependent, onto the current situation.

Understanding the concept of transference can free us from the inhibiting pressures of accepting behaviours that are directed at us as social workers that originate from earlier relationships. This is not to advocate that we do not need to constantly critique our practice to improve and develop. Rather, if there is no other obvious explanation for an individual's response to us, it is always worth considering whether transference might be at play.

Skills Component

- Individuals often transfer feelings held towards early significant caregivers onto other adults, including social workers.
- Using effective communication skills does not always equate to a positive engagement with service users due to negative transference.
- Offer reliability, consistency and respectfulness regardless of response feedback, to maximise potential for improved engagement and longer-term change.

Summary of Key Psychoanalytic Concepts

- The **Psychoanalytic Movement** is a set of beliefs founded on research into emotional development
- The **Unconscious** is a discrete set of feelings, memories and beliefs based on early childhood experience and inaccessible to the conscious mind that shapes future behaviour
- **Conditional Realism** is the way in which people or objects are experienced, viewed through the filter of the unconscious mind
- **Inner Reality** is the crystallisation of desires and impulses in early childhood that cause emotional conflict if denied in later life
- **Defences** are behaviours and reactions that protect individuals from anxiety of both real and perceived danger
- **Transference** is the process in which feelings and beliefs held about significant people (usually carers) are projected onto another, even in extremely different circumstances

---

Bowlby and Attachment

From psychoanalytic roots emerged theories relating to the attachment of children to their primary carers. While this in itself is an expansive area of theoretical research and debate that is not the direct concern of this chapter, elements of the theory are crucial for the notion of relationship development when thinking about using counselling skills in social work.

Bowlby's work grew out of his psychoanalytic background, with a slant towards Kleinian thought, but he developed this further by moving from thinking about individuals' internal worlds to how the external world directly influenced the internal world's formation.

Bowlby (1969) drew upon Winnicott (1960) to emphasise that infants develop a sense of self as a result of the quality relationship with the caregiver. The infant moves from a disintegrated state of self to a state of individuation over time, depending on the quality of that relationship. For the purpose of this chapter, the important theme is the knowledge that relationships play a key part in emotional development over time, although further reading on this subject is highly recommended.

Melanie Klein (1959) theorised that infants project their own anxiety onto their caregivers. She developed this by highlighting the need for caregivers to tolerate and accept this anxiety for emotional development to occur unhindered. A caregiver briefly mirrors an infant's emotional state by following the infant's lead and then amplifying the emotion by exaggerated facial expression and sounds in a soothing manner (Holmes, 2001). Winnicott (1960) had termed this the holding relationship, where the caregiver acts as a container for the infant's anxieties through providing the infant with numerous, often subtle responses (Bion, 1962). Physical holding has been shown to be an innate need of primates, while mirroring helps to develop the bond between a carer and a child. Mirroring elaborates on interactions which stimulate the child. This is supportive of development by providing opportunities for more complex interactions and also helps an infant cope with more anxious moments. The child's repertoire of responses is increased. The focus is thus on the two-way relationship between caregiver and child and forms the basis of Bowlby's later research.

For Bowlby (1988), a child's internal or emotional and cognitive world is directly related to the child's primary caregiver, this relationship progressing within the first year of a child's life. Bowlby studied the level of responsiveness and nurturance given to babies and children by their primary caregiver. He then formulated categories for the level of experienced security likely to be internalised by the infant into an 'internal working model' of that relationship (Bowlby, 1973), which would then serve as an internalised template for how other relationships would be experienced in later life. This links closely with the work of Mary Ainsworth (Ainsworth et al., 1978) and the 'Strange Situation Test' that serves to determine levels of secure/insecure attachment between toddlers and their caregivers. The stability over time of internalised templates relating to secure and insecure relationship patterns – i.e. can they change with different experiences? – has long been debated (Fonagy, 2001). However, the stance taken within this chapter is that internal working models of relationships are at least open to some change with experience that differs from that of infancy: reflective function (Fonagy et al., 2002).

Thus, relationships with others are viewed through the 'lens' (Hoffman, 1990) of early relationships. Emotional and behavioural reactions to events occur accordingly. If the internal working model of the early relationship is secure as a result of responsive nurturing coupled with non-intrusive, child-led time for exploration, then future relationships will be perceived as desirable, safe and with a flexible level of support and separation. Difficulties in future relationships will not be tolerated and an individual will leave that relationship, or negative relationship experience will be viewed as an exception rather than a norm. Likewise, if the internal model of relationships has been founded on inconsistent, absent or intrusive/abusive responsiveness, an individual is likely to perceive future relationships with trepidation, generating defences to anxiety as a protection against abandonment, neglect or intrusion/abuse (Howe, 1995; Levy, 2000).

For social workers forming relationships with service users, the quality of our own internal model of relationships will directly impact upon the quality of the working relationship with that person. For many of us who engage in therapeutic relationships with vulnerable people, 'therapy' for ourselves to address unresolved conflicts is often helpful. While the therapeutic relationship is important for service users, however, it cannot substitute for adequate nurturing by caregivers for infants, children and adolescents.

As stated above, primary caregivers, when nurturing infants in a responsive manner, provide containment for the infant's projected anxieties through what is termed a 'holding relationship' (Winnicott, 1960; Bion, 1962). The child is both physically held but, importantly for this discussion, emotionally held (Fonagy, 2001). That is, the child is safe to express and project their anxieties onto (and into) the caregiver, and the caregiver receives and absorbs the child's distress, offering acknowledgement and comfort in return. 'A good enough external holding environment becomes an internalised holding environment' (Barnes et al., 1999). The child in time is therefore able to internalise this model of responding to distress and learns to soothe him/herself, recruiting the caregiver when required by tears or verbal expressions of anxiety when distress becomes overwhelming (Miller et al., 1989). In future relationships, the individual is able to self-manage some distress and recruit significant people to offer containment of distress when it reaches a high level in response to challenging external events. The individual who has experienced containment as a child will seek out and expect it in other relationships, because an established internal working model has been constructed.

The individual who has not experienced sufficient containment via a consistent, responsive holding relationship is likely to have a more problematic response. This individual is likely to struggle to soothe him/herself and might resort to extremes of behaviour to alert distress to what could appear as only a minor event. This internal model will be of relationships that do not absorb distress, and so anxiety remains unsoothed. In early and future relationships, this person is likely to have highly developed defences to resist the impact of perceived abandonment, and of being left with anxieties with which they are unable to cope (Levy, 2000).

Pepe was seen weekly by his social worker in a community mental health team. He had experienced low moods for some time and had recently attempted suicide by jumping from a building. He survived injuries but had been resistant to sharing his worries with anyone. Pepe's mother had had post-natal depression when he was a young baby and throughout his toddler years. His father worked away from home and saw Pepe only occasionally. Pepe had always had his physical needs met but had developed an avoidant pattern of relating to people, believing his worries would either not be heard or ignored. Over time, he internalised his worries rather than sharing them. After having been made redundant, he felt overwhelmed and attempted suicide. His social worker was able to recognise that he struggled to rely on others for emotional

(Continued)

(Continued)

assistance, viewing his sporadic attendance at appointments as a manifestation of this. However, the social worker remained consistent and reliable, offering the time agreed, and eventually Pepe started to make a relationship and use the time to offload his anxieties.

Social Work Application

Observations of service users' responses to our efforts to engage with them can often give an indication of the level of security experienced in early relationships. Regardless of the response feedback we observe, as workers we need to model a temporary relationship that offers the nurturing and containing qualities that are provided by an appropriately responsive caregiver. That is not to say that we treat our service users like babies or children! However, we need to respond consistently to distress in a timely fashion without being intrusive beyond the duties we are engaged in. We need to develop the capacity to listen to and absorb distress and anxiety without giving it back and, most fundamentally, we need to offer this in a reliable way. Unreliable services feed the notion that the worker cannot be trusted, and therefore is not a safe person on whom either to temporarily depend or to trust. Unreliability increases insecure patterns of relating to others.

Skills Component

- Reliability and consistency are the keys to modelling a temporary secure relationship for a service user.
- This includes time-keeping and following through on agreements.
- Unreliability and inconsistency are likely to result in a failed engagement with service users.

As part of attachment theory, several other key concepts are important factors in the development of effective counselling skills used in the forming of relationships with service users, and in the process of working towards change.

Safe Haven

A safe haven (Levy, 2000) is a place or person who is familiar enough to offer a degree of safety and security when anxieties are running extremely high as a result of an external event or transition: a crisis. In attachment theory, a safe haven would be a person who is relatively responsive and can offer some degree of containment at a period of high distress. This is not necessarily a safe or a secure situation and is characteristic of the types of temporary relationships sought when individuals with insecure attachment patterns and poor communication styles who respond only to 'emergency feelings', i.e. extreme feelings of fear and anger.

Secure Base

A secure base (Bowlby, 1988) differs from a safe haven in that it develops over time. A secure base in relationship terms refers to an individual who offers a degree of consistency, reliability and responsiveness to another so that the other comes to believe and expect that person to be available in times of difficulty. The context of this secure base is 'a background of safety', i.e. a safe environment (Sandler, 1987). The level of security of that relationship will ultimately depend of the level of responsiveness, containment and non-intrusiveness given. With a secure base, an individual is able to tolerate separation, knowing that the person acting as a secure base will be available when required to provide comfort and soothing. With this separation, a person is freed up to explore life, develop their personal competence and skill, and build a repertoire of experience from which confidence in life skills can emerge.

With insecure secure base, that person will either cling to the person acting as secure base for fear of abandonment or become extremely self-reliant, resisting support from all sources.

Social Work Application

If we as social workers wish to engage with service users who might well have an insecure working model of relationships, it is crucial that we offer as secure a base as possible by being reliable, consistent and responsively nurturing as the situation requires without being intrusive. We become a temporary secure base with the hope that some of what we offer by way of the therapeutic relationship will become internalised as a template for a working model of relationships in the future.

This chapter recommends further exploration of the intricacies of attachment theory and the nature of developing internal models of human relationships. However, in coming to any therapeutic encounter, we all bring our own internal working model of relationships, and service users do likewise. To successfully use counselling skills in social work, we can be mindful of the internal working model that may influence the behaviour of a service user in attempting to engage with us, and of how our internal working model influences us. We can then attempt to model a relationship that is responsively nurturing to a distressed individual, without being intrusive, and in a manner that fits with our agency role and responsibilities. It is the fine balance between these factors that adds to the complexity of the working relationship.

Skills Component

- Social workers can offer a temporary secure base by using a therapeutic relationship which is reliable, consistent and as non-intrusive as the legal context allows.
- This temporary secure base can allow individuals to change their internal working model of relationships, albeit incrementally and over time.

Summary of Attachment Theory and Concepts Relating to Counselling Skills

- **Attachment Theory** is concerned with the quality of the relationship between an infant and his/her primary caregiver
- Infants **Project** anxiety, which requires acceptance and tolerance by the caregiver. This is later mirrored in childhood, adolescent and adult relationships
- The emotional **Security** of the relationship is dependent on the level of responsive nurturance by the caregiver
- A **Holding Relationship** allows anxiety to be expressed
- Children develop an **Internal Working Model** of relationships based on their experience of nurturing by the caregiver that shapes their view of later relationships
- A **Safe Haven** is often a person who offers some familiarity and to whom a person will turn in times of distress
- A **Secure Base** develops as children (and adults) learn that someone is a reliable object who is both available and responsive in times of distress but non-intrusive, allowing that person room to explore and grow
- Social workers can offer a **Temporary Secure Base** for service users when using counselling skills
- This is achieved by providing basic nurturing in accordance with attachment theory, including **Responsiveness, Reliability, Acceptance of Anxiety** and **Non-Intrusion**
- Social workers experience communication and behaviour from service users indicative of the nature of earlier relationships, demonstrating the process of **Transference**
- Social workers can accept that dismissive, avoiding or rejecting patterns might be a repetition of earlier relationship patterns or **Defences**
- Social workers can model a more **Secure** relationship style, with a view to influencing the adaptation of that person's **Internal Working Model**

Conclusion

The above offers an extremely brief outline of what is argued to be some key concepts of the psychoanalytic movement that relate to counselling skills for social workers. As the use of counselling skills in a social work context varies according to the many roles practitioners undertake, we need to adapt the theoretical concepts to the individual needs of our service users and the agencies in which we work. We are not psychoanalysts and do not embark on attempts at a form of pseudo-psychotherapy. However, although using psychoanalytic theory holds limitations for social workers due to the nature of the role and the training required, opportunities do exist to use this model to enhance our communication skills in our working relationships with service users. Above is an argument for what I believe is the extremely useful integration of psychoanalytic thinking and social work practice.

Further Reading

- **Elliott (2002)** provides a narrative of the psychoanalytic movement as it has evolved since Sigmund Freud, including the theories of Melanie Klein and object relations. The book incorporates a chapter on 'Psychoanalytic feminism' and critiques the post-modern position in relation to psychoanalysis, both of which are theoretically useful for social workers.

- **Leiper and Maltby (2004)** overview a process account of therapeutic change drawing on a psychodynamic approach. This book is especially useful for social workers to make sense of how working relationships can be a catalyst for change, although readers will need to apply the techniques to a social work context to be more directly relevant to social work practice.

- **Howe (2005)** provides a detailed application of attachment theory to the occurrence of child abuse and neglect that is directly relevant to social work practice.

- **Holmes (2001)** explores attachment theory in therapeutic relationships.

- **Levy (2000)** applies attachment theory to a variety of social problems that are often encountered in social work practice, including relationship problems and violence.

- **Kenny and Kenny (2000)** include a useful chapter on psychodynamic theory in social work.

5
Using Narrative Therapy in Social Work Practice

Key Concepts	Key Theorists and Practitioners
• Dominant Narratives	• White
• Exceptions to Problems	• Epston
• Use of Metaphor	• Byng-Hall
• Externalising	(Scripting Theory)

Introduction

Narratives or stories are linguistic means of communication between individuals, communities and cultures. Whether these stories are articulated in Braille, the spoken word or sign language, the essence is the same. We relate our lived experience in story form; we fantasise about our futures, anticipate our dreams and relay our horrors of life through this very mode. Stories are powerful representations of our values, thinking styles and aspirations (or lack of them). As social work is inextricably linked to people and their lived experience, past, present and future, a narrative approach to skills used in the counselling of, and communication with, others seems vital to the nature of the profession.

Using counselling skills from a narrative tradition requires at least a basic understanding of the history and philosophy of the model. Key figures at the heart of the development of narrative therapeutic approaches are Michael White and David Epston (1990). Their work challenges the notion that any therapeutic encounter can be truly objective, but that all workers using counselling skills are inevitably caught up in narratives both of their agency and of the political system that shapes the way in which workers' posts are created and developed, especially relating to workers funded by public monies. We act out roles in accordance with the political agenda of the time, within an organisation or from wider society, and these roles impact on the way in which we view problems, categorise them and attempt to find solutions.

Social work practice is entwined with the constant need to make reference to and reflect upon our value base. We can immediately link elements of social work practice with a narrative approach. Our charge is not to benignly act out the political narrative of the time but constantly to challenge our style of relating to others, questioning our value-base and the assumptions we might make as a result of it.

The objective of this chapter is to provide those involved in social work practice an overview of the narrative perspective and how it might be applied in the direct work that we do with people. Counselling skills drawing on narrative techniques can be broadened to offer us a wider range of linguistic and practical inroads to problem exploration and resolution. This model is not a framework for assessment, but techniques gained can be woven into the assessment process as a skills medium to this end, as well as being used to underpin intervention. This can facilitate the generation of overt recognition of the impact of the intricacies of relationships and, importantly, of social structures that oppress and marginalise people and their choices. Belief systems and their formulation are dominant in this model. Our pivotal link to values and ethics in social work practice sits very comfortably with aspects of this model, whereby we seek to counter oppression and recognise and build upon individuals' strengths.

We are concerned with the nature of oppression and its structural roots, but often practitioners struggle to move beyond practical assistance in relation to accessing housing and social security benefits to facilitate the enlightenment of the impact of deprivation, discrimination and social exclusion and thus empowerment towards change. Using counselling skills in this way is a vehicle to forward the enlightenment process for those of us who experience oppression as a result of our social standing, our gender, race or sexuality among many other 'groupings', but often do not realise it. That is not to argue that social workers should use counselling skills alone as a means by which oppression might be tackled. Ethically we might argue that responsibility for structural oppression should not be placed upon individuals for change, especially upon service users, who are often the most vulnerable and disempowered members of society. This chapter does not set out to advocate this in any way. However, using a narrative approach to problem exploration is one means to the end of countering oppression through recognising its existence and impact upon life.

It is my hope that this chapter will serve two principal functions: firstly, it aims to provide a skill-base for holding conversations with people using narrative techniques that can separate the person from the problem; and secondly, it aims to offer a means by which the political impact of social structures can be explored with people on an individual rather than an abstract theoretical level.

A brief overview of the history and philosophy of narrative approaches to therapeutic encounters will set the scene for an examination of how it can be incorporated into the social worker's tool-bag.

History and Philosophy of the Narrative Approach

The narrative approach to therapeutic or counselling practices has its roots in socio-logical thinking. That is, social structures, such as the beliefs and values upon which society has developed and continues to function, and the elements that create these structures, are born out of the repetition and re-enactment of dominant themes and objectives (Goffman, 1961). Society does not just exist. In myriad cultures, societies have developed over time based on dominant stories that have been held and accepted as the norm, and social systems develop around these narratives as the medium through which they function. For example, a dominant story might be that women are somehow predisposed to be carers and thus expectations held by society of women as they grow into adulthood are much different from those held of men. When men or fathers leave the family home it is not often viewed as shocking, whereas a mother leaving her children would likely elicit a very different response. As individuals are socialised into beliefs and behaviours, the repetition of these over time reinforce the existence of the social structures by re-enacting and repeating social norms. Social controls exist to regulate behaviours that deviate from the norms of that society and so the dominant narrative of a culture continues.

The narrative approach to counselling is a direct recognition of the power and sub-sequent influence held by these dominant narratives, both in society at large and within the micro-system of families. The societal power around gender issues and their influence on individuals and the course of their lives is far from new and can be explored further with Dominelli (1997), among other established texts on the subject. As in society, families also develop and adopt dominant themes over time, and members of families take on roles and repeat behaviours fitting with those roles. Systems theory and its influence in family life is widely covered in Chapter 7, where a more detailed exploration of dominant roles is made. These dominant roles, such as a mother taking primary responsibility for the caring of her children, are gener-ally reinforced by family members socialised into certain ways of thinking. Some are societal, some traditionally familial and most are therefore very difficult to change. This chapter will explore how aspects of the theoretical elements to narra-tive counselling skills can be embraced by social workers in a variety of settings, either wholeheartedly or selectively as part of an intervention package.

Story Development and its Influence

Lived Experience and Story Development

All individuals, by virtue of our existence, have a plentiful repertoire of lived expe-rience. However, when giving an account of that experience, or reflecting on aspects of life lived so far, we are all selective in what we recall most readily and what we do not. From the narrative perspective, this is not an argument for the influence of the conscious mind versus the unconscious mind on how we view experiences, as with the psychoanalytical perspective, outlined in Chapter 4. Rather, the premise is that we actively select, then hold on to, dominant themes permeating our lived experience over a lifetime. These themes develop into a dominant narrative that we repeat and replay. We actively filter out exceptions to this dominant story of who we are – exceptions that may challenge the 'script' we use to author our lives (Byng-Hall, 1995). This authoring both re-enacts and recreates the dominant themes so they are repeated in patterns that become entrenched behavioural and emotional responses, while the exceptions can barely even be recognised, so attuned are we to excluding them from our recognition. As our lived experience will always be deeper and broader than what we describe in discourse, there will always be a wealth of experience that lies dormant for every individual.

Andrew welcomed Sandra into his house, as he was used to social workers and other health and welfare professionals being part of his life since he was a child. She was the third social worker he had met during the previous year and he was well accustomed to the first visit of a new worker assigned to him. He invited her to sit down and listened as she gave a brief account of her role and the reasons she had called to see him. Andrew had been homeless, had recently been allocated housing after a long period of hostel accommodation. He was vulnerable due to prolonged problems with alcohol resulting in regular hospital admissions, including Andrew presenting at Accident and Emergency (A&E) with somatic complaints of various kinds.

Andrew had been referred to the hospital social work team following another acute admission and recent discharge. He had presented at A&E with severe abdominal pains, which were deemed to be of a non-organic cause. Hospital staff had ongoing concerns about Andrew's level of self-neglect and the chronic nature of the problems with alcohol. Andrew recounted to Sandra what he had recounted with many other workers he had met. He told her that he had never been able to work due to missing so much of his schooling and struggling with reading and writing. He explained that money was a constant problem and that he cheered himself up with 'drink'. As he had so many aches and pains, he found it hard to keep on top of things and this resulted in complaints by housing authorities and neighbours about the state of his home and his lifestyle. This left him feeling even worse and so having drinking parties with his pals made him feel better at the time, even though afterwards he felt ill, the pains increased, and he needed to go to the hospital as he believed they should look after him.

Andrew did not mention that, as a young person, he had excelled in sports and had a talent for art that he had not developed. Nor did he describe how he had taken a parental role within his family of origin and had taken great care to

(Continued)

(Continued)

look out for his younger siblings when he thought they were vulnerable. He explained how his family had forgotten him at age 16 when he left the family home to find his own way in life, but missed out the caring aspects to his character that had emerged as he constantly put his siblings' needs before his own. Andrew described how the only people who had not forgotten him were his drinking pals. Andrew clearly did not feel either very skilled or very important as a person and held on to alcohol and the lifestyle it brought him as a comfort and a companion.

Social Work Application

The social work task is first and foremost concerned with engagement with service users. However, often agency pressure pushes us towards a speedy execution of 'assessment' and then some form of intervention that will bring about change. Under this pressure, or perceived pressure, we can fall into the trap of meeting an individual, having a clear agenda of what information we want to glean by the end of the first appointment, and then bombarding that person with a series of what might be well-articulated questions to meet our end. What is wrong with this, we might question, when a vague, directionless conversation is largely unhelpful to vulnerable people in distress? What is lost in such a bombardment is the art of making a genuine link between one individual and another, in a professional capacity, by the generation and mutual understanding of an element of shared meaning.

Strengths inherent in the narrative approach within a social work context are that it holds tightly to the notion of art and creativity when forging relationships with people; it pulls us sharply back to focusing on engagement and on the individual's own story to illuminate the patterns around which their lives have been constructed and are played out; and it dilutes the need for an agenda that sets us apart from people as being 'professional' and therefore perceived by service users as 'better' in some way. We are not 'better' – we might have had a greater array of opportunities to allow our own life story to take us to a position of social comfort and of power with service users by virtue of our role, and we might use developed skills with people to empower them in return. However, we must remember that power relations are socially constructed and that social and political narratives serve to assist in the construction of vulnerable people's stories. This is inherent in the social work task and woven into the social work value system and is crucial to applying a narrative approach in social work.

The role of social worker does take us into authoritarian positions, especially in relation to child protection and within the adult mental health arena. The narrative approach could be seen to be at odds with this and in this respect

(Continued)

(Continued)

would be used in conjunction rather than instead of a more directive approach. However, the essence of using narrative within social work is to allow people, as Sandra did with Andrew, to share their own stories but to listen to the way in which they are described, to seek out patterns and to explore the meaning given to experience with people.

Using a narrative approach in social work tasks opens up a greater opportunity than with many other approaches to explore experiences both of relationships and of societal influences and of how these have impacted upon life and the beliefs about life that are thus generated. We do this by tracking key elements of a dominant story and noticing what might be being excluded. We search for meaning within these stories and, in doing so, strengthen our link with an individual by a genuine attempt at understanding the nature of a problem to a service user and the way in which it affects their lives.

Skills Component

- Use a narrative approach to refocus on the art of engaging with people.
- Accept that stories that people tell and live by are influenced by social and political constructs as well as by relationships.
- Listen both to the content of the story and to the meaning given to it.
- Acknowledge the power imbalance in the worker–service user relationship generated through socio-political narratives that have created the social work role.
- Emancipate the service user's voice through careful listening to their dominant story.
- Set the scene for an individual to change the course of events in their life through a process of enlightenment and empowerment, beginning with identification of key themes in their dominant narrative.

Problem-saturated Stories

When the dominant themes we re-enact in our lives lead us to emotional or behavioural problems, then the narrative perspective would argue that this is a direct result of our dominant story becoming problem-saturated. That is, the dominant themes that we selectively hold as an accurate account of our lives and of our lived experience are largely negative. They are invariably based on perceptions of powerlessness and belief in a distinct lack of 'luck' – a mysterious notion that puts the control over our lives firmly in the hands of others, be it people, social structures or 'fate'. This chapter does not intend to criticise religion or spiritualism in any form, only to highlight the manner in which control over life can often be handed over to others, albeit inadvertently; where regaining elements of personal control over life can assist in problem resolution. From an anti-oppressive stance, we can justifiably argue that, through prejudice and discrimination, people and social structures do limit individuals' power and control over their own lives and the narrative perspective does not negate this. However, this model of therapeutic contact or counselling does actively seek those exceptions that would counterbalance problem-saturated themes and open up the opportunity for exploration of alternative stories to the dominant narrative.

Andrew's story, as told to Sandra and recounted many times to others, had become problem-saturated. He selected negative aspects of his life – the rejection by his family as a young man, his lack of success with employment and his underachievement with academic skills – as a reflection of his overall ability as a person. Alcohol was his friend and with it came people who seemed to value his company. This became his dominant story and the script he was to live by for another 20 years. The problems that were created by Andrew following this script were numerous and yet his sense of helplessness about the situation prevailed. He developed entrenched beliefs that he was powerless to bring about change and he authored his life around his problem-saturated story of rejection and failure by not trying any different ways of living, and selectively rejecting events or attributes that did not fit with the dominant theme. Andrew screened out exceptions to this story over the years, so that any acts by him or to him with others that did not fit with the dominant narrative were not acknowledged. Small successes went unseen by him; times when he had not turned to alcohol to 'cheer him up' were dismissed; periods where he had had temporary employment and maintained a housing contract were ignored; regular attempts by hospital staff to dissuade him from using them for basic nurturing rather than for emergency treatment were perceived as staff 'not doing their job' and him having 'failed' to elicit their support; and nurturing and offers of friendship from non-drinking neighbours and relations who had tried to build a relationship with him over the years were not recognised as 'real'. Andrew had become so lost in his own story that any positive elements of his life were not even noticed. He continued to repeat the scenes, albeit with different players, over and over, until he met Sandra.

Social Work Application

A problem-saturated story of failure and despondency can be daunting to a social worker who might often be at a loss as to where to start. The narrative approach advocates starting with listening to the story and acknowledging its impact. Andrew's dominant narrative only told a small element of what was 36 years of lived experience during which he had survived, and was still able to reflect and use his intellect to make sense of his world. This already was an

(Continued)

(Continued)

exception to his belief about his own life being 100 per cent failure. Many circumstances in which social workers find themselves leaves us faced with people struggling with their lives, which have become problem-saturated. We should be concerned with hearing the dominant story – for example, Andrew's belief of social failure, worthlessness and lack of competence – and then look for experiences that counter the dominant script that is being replayed by the service user. As we help people to seek additional elements to the plot of their lives through disregarded experience of success, the problem-saturated story – a narrow plot with little deviation from a theme – becomes one with sub-plots and counter-themes that offer variation and difference. We are not looking for new information, merely unstoried experiences that are given less or no weight in the influencing course of an individual's life script.

Caution is given to embarking on this approach when the client does not believe that he or she has problems, but that referrers do, for example the criminal justice system with someone involved in offending behaviour, or a health visitor concerned about the parenting skills of a couple with a young baby. The individual in each respect might firmly believe that their behaviours are acceptable within society, their community or group of peers and thus the dominant narrative is not problem-saturated. In such instances it is important to discuss the concerns held by others and attempt to establish whether a narrative approach would be one that could be adapted or would be mismatched with the type of concerns and the beliefs held by clients about them.

Skills Component

- Seek for exceptions to the dominant narrative without negating the themes implicit and explicit within the recounted story.
- Assist the service user to add unstoried experience to their narrative of life to provide a broader repertoire of experience by which they can re-evaluate their own personal competence.
- Use caution with this approach if the referrer believes there are problems and the service user does not – theirs might not be a problem-saturated story.

This is examined more fully, in the case of Andrew, below.

Alternative Narratives

If the dominant narrative governing an individual's current life experience has become problem-saturated as above, a narrative approach would be primarily concerned with the exceptions that are not problem-laden. Searching for exceptions and exploring alternative themes does not require a dismissal of the problems. Individuals who approach services for assistance are often highly sensitised to feeling unheard. Any perceived dismissal of the level of problems and the impact they have on a person's life will almost certainly result in the disengagement of that individual. This might be very explicit (for example, non-attendance at meetings) or an emotional disengagement by remaining closed to exploration of presenting difficulties and experimenting with change.

The search for alternative narratives is a crucial element of this perspective. To be successful in coming to a position in which an individual is ready to explore exceptions, timing is absolutely paramount. It is not a question of a tight structure for this undertaking; for example, session two would always be the right time. Rather, it is a question of judgement by the worker as to when the individual seems to think and feel that they have been heard and their problems taken seriously. This therefore requires a high level of skill in the engagement process, drawing very firmly on listening and communication skills as a foundation for the process. It is covered in more detail in Chapter 2.

Seeking alternative narratives needs to be a process undertaken between the client and the practitioner. If a client could construct an alternative story away from a problem-saturated one, it is unlikely that they would require intervention from a social worker. If a practitioner was to construct an alternative story for a client, it would be the social worker's story and not that of the client: there would be no ownership and complete disempowerment of that individual. Co-construction is the process whereby new meanings and solutions are jointly generated by two or more parties, in this instance the service user and the social worker. In a narrative approach, this is a central theme of seeking alternatives: a way of regenerating the essence of the problem-saturated life story into an alternative one that is more positive and upon which both parties agree.

In order to co-construct an alternative story, the problem-saturated one needs to be deconstructed (or taken apart, bit by bit, in order that understanding can be gained of what and who influences what, whom, and where and when!). That is, component parts of a person's problem-saturated story need to be questioned and challenged in such a way that assumptions and patterns of behaving are not simply accepted as being 'the way it is'. Included in this deconstruction process is questioning the societal discourses of power relations that support the problem-saturated story. Not only are individual influences on behaviour and forms of communication questioned, but also the influence of societal beliefs. General societal beliefs that a woman is somehow predisposed to be a carer, as described above, and therefore spends her time looking after others' needs while neglecting her own, would be a societal discourse. This discourse influences social structures, such as the distinct lack of childcare opportunities outside of the family and thus the life of an individual. The narrative approach would sanction challenging such a discourse through deconstruction of a person's story and by expanding awareness, and therefore knowledge, of how society can affect an individual's day-to-day living.

An assumption is immediately generated by this approach. To successfully embark upon the deconstruction process, knowledge of power and oppression and its function within society is required. The explicit purpose is to redirect the internalised problem held at an individual level, often loaded with blame and guilt serving as an obstacle to problem resolution, to an externalised status. Here it can be more objectively considered in conjunction with the structural influences and beliefs about its creation and maintenance.

Sandra listened carefully to Andrew for several minutes, and then reflected that she noticed that Andrew had not mentioned any positive attributes about himself or his life. In searching for meaning in Andrew's dominant story, Sandra invited him to share with her what it was like for him, living on social security benefits and struggling to make ends meet. He was able to describe the impact of deprivation; his sense of futility in trying to leave the area in which he lived, even for a day, due to poor access to transport within his rural community and the high cost, being out of his budget. He felt trapped but used to wish he could go into the city more often and 'do things'. She observed that Andrew had the TV on and was watching athletics. She enquired as to whether this was an interest of his and he started to describe in some depth who was running well this year and who was not doing so well. Sandra recognised that Andrew's insight into current affairs within the athletics arena was beyond that which people without a specific interest would have. She followed up her enquiry by further exploration into his insight. Andrew began to share a little about his early talents and his fantasy that he could have been 'good' but had had no opportunity to compete. He quickly dismissed the conversation, returning to discourse around his stomach pains and the recent complaints from neighbours. Sandra had been using elements from a narrative approach to search for alternative themes from Andrew's dominant story. She had not imposed it on Andrew, but had used her observational skills and respectful enquiry to explore this further. She had not ignored or rejected his dominant story, which might have left him feeling that he had not been heard. Rather, she gently sought out an alternative story whereby briefly Andrew had been able to recognise a talent, albeit underdeveloped and lost to him.

Social Work Application

Social work theory is concerned with sociological and political concepts that enable us to make sense of social structures, decision-making processes and the manner in which these impact at an individual and community level. Our task, in various forms, is to make links between the individual functioning of people within the social circumstances they experience. These social circumstances can only be understood in terms of socio-political thinking, and out of which socio-political narratives that impact on individual functioning can be explicitly illuminated. This requires the social worker to have a foundation of knowledge about such matters, especially in relation to oppression and deprivation.

(Continued)

(Continued)

For alternative stories to be sought, insight into the impact of the dominant story must be generated by a collaborative effort by the worker and service user. Sandra helped Andrew deconstruct the meaning of poverty and of deprivation by questioning the impact it had on him. He had become trapped within a cycle of events and the socio-political climate had restricted options to assist him out of that trap. Societal barriers were being explored on an individual level. This form of problem exploration immediately separated Andrew from some elements of the problem, seeking to reduce any possible feelings of blame he might have been feeling. This reduction in blame – an outcome of the deconstruction process – freed Andrew to begin, with Sandra, to co-construct an alternative story about his life, including forgotten but important positive personal attributes.

As dominant stories are so well rehearsed over years of re-enactment of the 'life' script, there is little room to add alternatives without unpacking the meaning of elements of the dominant narrative. A woman who has spent all her life caring for others, who then presents at mental health services with problems of low mood would first need to deconstruct the meaning of being a woman. This would necessarily include the societal expectations that come with gender stereotypes, how these have been adopted and translated in her family and how this has impacted upon her life. Only then can a social worker start to co-construct alternative scripts with her, having opened up space for her to think and feel as part of the process. The woman is likely to have many attributes and successes that to her have gone unnoticed, and deconstructing the meaning of gender is one way of allowing her the opportunity to notice them.

Skills Component

- Deconstruct the nature and impact of problems in relation to socio-political factors by taking apart each influencing factor and examining its impact.
- Assist individuals to resist accepting personal blame for the impact of social policy.
- Consider in detail with service users who does what, when, where and with whom in relation to the problem.
- Facilitate the service user to explore the meaning of events and interactions.
- Begin to co-construct alternative stories to problem-saturated ones by observation of service user strengths, interests and successes.
- Enhance skill development in this area by becoming familiar with the nature and impact of poverty, oppression and deprivation.

Metaphors

A metaphor is a noun that is used in place of a given name for an object that symbolically embraces that object's characteristics as experienced by an individual. For example, volatile family relations might be described as 'fireworks', embodying the explosive and dangerous nature of the object to illuminate our understanding of the situation in mind. Use of metaphor in the therapeutic process with clients is not a new concept. It is inclusive within the counselling techniques of drama and art, both of which draw upon the symbolic use of metaphor to bring to life and explore aspects of an individual's existence, of which it would be otherwise difficult for that person to comprehend.

Metaphors are seen in abundance in children's fairy tales with monsters and heroes in different forms. Gardner and Harper (1997) offer an overview of how core anxieties in childhood, such as fear, grief and loss, are recreated in stories that, through 'formulaic repetition', govern emotions such as terror and violence in predictable ways. Stories repeated over time allow children to reflect on extreme events that have inherent endings and solutions. These stories are fictitious and therefore do not pose a direct threat, while they allow most children to experience an emotional response in a relatively safe environment that has a certain end point. (A cautionary note: highly anxious children in an environment that is unsafe might not be able to tolerate such fairy tales without distress.) The use of metaphor, such as a monster being outwitted by a hero, brings anxiety-provoking experiences under an element of control, reducing the impact of that anxiety and serving to open the metaphorical door to ways around a difficulty. The message given by such tales is that problems can be resolved. In the fairy tales, the repeated happy ending puts a boundary around childhood distress and brings fear and anxiety under control. Use of metaphor in the narrative approach to counselling has the same objective.

Metaphors are symbolic representations in object form that have characteristics that can be compared with and are easily identifiable with the nature of the problem. To use metaphors to work with people experiencing difficulty, it is imperative to draw upon creative flair. There is a high requirement to make full use of the imagination to develop a metaphorical object with a client that both has meaning for them and relates to the dominant narrative, which is shaping their lives. Metaphors used without direct relation to the subject matter or ones that are so abstract that a client cannot make useful links with the problem will not be successful. The object of symbolic representation must be meaningful for the client. Individuals who think in very concrete and literal terms, such as those categorised under the Autistic Spectrum, would not fare well with this approach, it being reliant upon the application of abstract concepts. If we as social workers struggle to tap into our imagination, then we might also run into snags along the way, the end result being clients started on a process of engagement and change and then finding themselves lost without direction. Individuals in these circumstances are likely to resort to what they know best to provide an element of safety in unsure ground – the dominant narrative, which might include beliefs about their capacity for success being insufficient. The end result could be a reinforcement of previously held beliefs that serve to sustain a problem-saturated narrative.

Sandra's second visit to Andrew was a repetition of her first: he recounted a tale of problems with the neighbours and of struggles with money. Sandra had undertaken to provide Andrew with assistance and advocacy in relation to housing problems and income maximisation but was left with a gap in the facilitation of the change process. Andrew was held fast in a cycle of repeated behaviours that compounded his belief in his personal incompetence in life. Sandra introduced the idea of alcohol in metaphorical terms, drawing upon words that Andrew had used. He referred to alcohol as 'Drink' and she capitalised his use of language to offer a metaphor to which he could easily relate. Sandra started to refer to alcohol as 'Drink', a phrase that Andrew quickly picked up and embraced. During the next few meetings, they would use this term when speaking about any aspect of their work where alcohol use became a factor.

Social Work Application

Sandra's role was much wider than providing Andrew with counselling. Her remit involved practical assistance at times, which is often argued to be a barrier to any therapeutic process for social workers. However, she was able to bring in elements of a narrative perspective to the work to assist in problem resolution where problems had been entrenched over many years. The use of counselling skills was intrinsic to the overall assessment and intervention. It did not require a separate time in a clinic or other specialised facility to focus on the nature of the problem. Instead, a more subtle inclusion of metaphor was incorporated that seamlessly allowed a transition in the use of language to be made by both parties involved in the work.

The metaphor used was not one that Sandra had thought up and possibly was not a term she would have chosen for herself. However, the term had meaning for Andrew, being part of a phrase he had used and therefore had validity with him. The use of metaphor was introduced in a low-key manner that did not draw attention to it directly. Nevertheless, the power of the use of the phrase was immense. The phrase allowed the personification of alcohol as a separate and distinct entity having influence in its own right. It was accepted in open discussion where there had been no need to use stigmatising labels such as 'alcoholic' to describe Andrew's relationship with the substance.

Skills Component

- Co-construct metaphorical representations of a core problem by using a noun that embodies the nature of the problem but does not link the individual directly to it.
- Ensure the metaphor both relates to the problem and has meaning for the service user.
- Establish the metaphor in conversation by direct and personified references to it.

Externalising Narratives

As outlined above, the narrative approach to counselling relies upon lived experience that is recounted in story form and generates the script from which we live out our day-to-day existence. The stories developed around our experience consist of sets of beliefs to which meaning for each experience is ascribed and processed through our thoughts and then our feelings. So entangled are we in that complex web of our own dominant narrative that it can be extremely difficult to separate out what of our stories is helpful to our lives and what is not.

For a narrative approach, the initial concern, after listening to the dominant narrative and opening up channels for the possibility of alternative stories, is to explore a means to externalise the major theme that either creates a problem or blocks progress towards change. This is done using a metaphor. Externalising problems in this way, the person is not the problem but 'something else' is. That something might be 'exhaustion' experienced by a carer with financial problems through inability to work due to responsibilities and inadequate benefits to cover the cost of living; it might be 'anger' at the lack of voice a young man believes he has within his family and within society. As Russell and Carey (2003) explain, a person might easily be labelled with a diagnosis such as depression, which is then internalised by that person and who then takes full responsibility for its cause. With an externalising approach through narrative, 'exhaustion' or 'temper' become the problem, not the person, allowing a freer exploration of the impact of various social structures and relationships that led to the problem. 'Temper' is used instead of 'anger' so that an otherwise healthy emotional response is not misperceived as a problem in its own right.

The function of externalising a problem is to objectify it. By objectifying some cause for concern, the unhelpful feelings of guilt and blame can be removed and the individuals involved in the counselling process can be freed up to explore the impact of a problem, its course through its lifetime and what strengthens and weakens its power. It is rarely possible for most people to be able to map the course of problems over a period of time without doing it in a problem-saturated story. Externalising the problem allows its various components to be analysed. This might include the impact of gender oppression in a woman diagnosed with depression; or the impact of social constructions around age for a previously socially active man who finds that through retirement his opinions about his areas of knowledge are less valued by others. Objectifying a problem then separates the individual from it and allows room within an alternative story to discover other aspects of life and of relationships. This method aims to generate the possibility of problem resolution by considering to escape the influence of problems in future lived experience and take more notice of strengths and supports that might have been inadvertently neglected. Externalising problems facilitates the deconstruction and co-construction process through conversations between practitioner and service user (White, 2002).

Using this approach, most importantly is the opportunity given for flexibility in the development of an externalised metaphor representing a problem over the period of intervention. The retaining of flexibility offers a model for clients that stories can change and that alternative stories might be more helpful to individuals as time progresses. Also, it allows for the adaptability of the approach to accommodate changing demands that clients might experience during the course of the work. Key to the success of externalising problems is evolution and fluidity, according to White and Epston (1990). Thus the course of the development of 'exhaustion' over a period of time might be gender-related but mapping the problem will involve unique variables from individual to individual. We need to be comfortable with the co-construction of alternative stories that might not go where we expect or want them to, and our fluidity here is vital.

Russell and Carey (2003) demonstrate how 'externalising conversations' is based on several important dimensions. The practitioner needs to assist the client to identify the problem as separate from them; the problem then requires location in history and in a story-line; and finally the effects of the problem on life and relationships need to be traced. Using a metaphor for naming the problem allows the maintenance of the conversation to be directed away from the individual who might revert to internalising it in a problem-saturated way. A further key aspect of the externalisation process is to look for unique outcomes or exceptions, where the client has 'resisted the influence of the problem'.

'Drink' became a more regular topic of conversation for Sandra and Andrew. Sandra introduced the that was to become the subject for externalisation in a gentle way that did not overtly challenge Andrew's own reference to alcohol. Rather she personified it in a way that could then be examined as having a 'life of its own': its own history and elements from Andrew's life that maintained its influence on him. Over several meetings, Sandra encouraged Andrew to share the life of 'Drink' with her. He expressed in great detail how 'Drink' had once been a friend and an ally that had given him comfort when he had been alone when he first left his family home. 'Drink' had dulled his awareness of fears he had about his future and overwhelming feelings of being alone and unsupported. He pointed out how he had been deceived by 'Drink', who had betrayed him by leaving him ill, forgetful and even more alone when its effects had worn off. Together they also uncovered 'Drink's' influence over him and how it still managed to deceive him. 'Drink' was everywhere he looked – shops, bars, on TV, with 'friends' … When he tried to ignore it, he found himself listening to beliefs he had that the dull feelings were good and better than the ill feelings and the lonely feelings.

The influence of 'Drink' was strong and consistently persuasive. By externalising the problem, Andrew was not being labelled as an alcoholic during the conversation, nor was he being criticised in any way. He was given an opportunity to separate himself from alcohol problems in a manner that preserved his dignity and reinforced where his control over events had been jeopardised. Further discussions included the lack of training and employment opportunities that had been available for him as an adult and how poverty

(Continued)

(Continued)

through living on state benefits meant that he could not both adequately nourish himself with food and purchase 'Drink', and so food was neglected most of the time. Oppression in various forms was explored at an individual level. Sandra remained interested in exceptions, as when Andrew had withstood efforts by 'the Drink' to influence him. He was able to identify several occasions where he had fought against drinking for several days and instead had bought food. She was introducing the concept that he had strengths that allowed him to control his use of alcohol, although 'Drink' had managed to persuade him otherwise most of the time.

Social Work Application

In day-to-day terms, we are often faced with opportunities to externalise problems with service users to effect change. This technique does not require a clinic base. It does require the creative use of language by the social worker, the time and commitment to see the story through with a person, and the patience to assist in the mapping of the problem in specific terms. The technique is unhelpful in a crisis situation when, first and foremost, specific tasks need attention, often in practical ways. Intervention post-crisis would be the most helpful time to use externalising as a means to tracing the development of the problem that led to a crisis. Simplistic use of narrative techniques often is most effective, whereas becoming too complicated can be confusing.

In a situation where a child has been injured by a stressed and distraught parent, a narrative approach might be used post-investigation when the worker and the service user are considering what preceded events leading to the incident. Externalising problems such as 'fatigue', 'frustration', 'behaviour' or others that could be the primary factor, could be co-constructed into metaphor that can be used to map the course of the problem and discover the beliefs that have become attached to it. For example, exploring frustration as an object might facilitate how it has led to violent reactions by a parent, then lead to an exploration of beliefs about how violence might be seen to be acceptable by that person when 'frustration' is around. Caution is required again here so that responsibility for actions that have harmed another is not diminished. Instead, the problem 'frustration' becomes separated from the individual (not the assault) to map its influence, highlight belief systems that lead to action and seek alternative stories. It is these alternative stories that enhance an individual to regain control over what could be believed by them to be situations where they have no control over actions born out of frustration. Crucial to the validity and success of a narrative approach is timing.

Skills Component

- Timing of when a narrative approach is useful in a social work context is crucial.
- Retain a flexible position in relation to where the deconstruction and co-construction of a problem that has been externalised will go.
- Map the course of the problem with a service user in historical terms, its influence and what and who maintains and reduces that influence.
- Seek times when the service user has resisted its influence and the factors that have allowed this.
- Reinforce those times with service users to assist them to co-construct an alternative story about themselves.

Maintaining Alternative Narratives

Once alternative stories to the dominant narrative are established, certain skill is required to enable people to develop and strengthen these stories to become more, and then most, dominant. A period of time is required that is variable according to individuals, the nature of the problem and how entrenched it has become. Individuals must test out alternative stories and then receive feedback in some form that will validate them as being worthwhile or 'true'. The nature of truth, from a social constructionist position, is debatable but for alternative stories to carry influence in a person's life it must have meaning to them and contain elements that are believable. The key to success on a long-term basis in achieving change is the gradual nature of the work with feedback to reinforce behaviours and beliefs; how gradual, again will depend on the individual and their problem.

The theoretical basis of reinforcement by feedback fits closely with cognitive behavioural approaches covered in Chapter 3, but the emphasis here is on a person's dominant story rather than on his or her thinking patterns. Feedback can be received in different forms, but this model would argue that raising awareness of already existing feedback that supports an alternative story that has been filtered out by the dominant narrative is sufficient to generate the essence of change. A belief in the validity of an alternative story and that an individual is neither powerless to the influence of problems, nor ignorant of their impact, enables this process.

Byng-Hall (1995) provides an elaboration of how narratives exist in the form of scripts and explores how they are replicated within family environments through generations. Social workers in all fields can have an interest in the family of an individual. It is difficult to explore the social circumstances in which a client finds him- or herself without making at least some reference to the family history and the nature of family relationships. (Counselling skills in a family context are considered in greater depth in Chapter 7.) Including consideration of family relationships in developing and maintaining alternative, improvised scripts seems vital; even family members are not directly present during the work.

If we accept that our perceptions of ourselves and of our potential for social action are at least partly founded upon feedback from others over a lifetime, then including significant others, even implicitly, in the search for alternative narratives becomes important. Byng-Hall makes clear links between attachment theories (Chapter 4) and the emergence of family, and therefore individual, scripts, played out to form roles that become entrenched and extremely difficult to shift.

To construct changes in lifestyle and thinking patterns, an individual must feel secure enough to explore alternative narratives, test them out and eventually accept them on their own terms. Without a form of security provided to test out alternatives, it is very difficult for individuals to release their often extremely tight grip on familiarity to launch into something that seems new. The type of security to which Byng-Hall refers is also covered in Chapter 4. A social worker attempting to assist people to make changes in lives that have become problem-saturated needs to offer an emotionally holding environment first, before a client is likely to feel safe enough to metaphorically dip his or her toes into unknown waters. Once safe enough to consider alternatives, these can be repeatedly tested until a less problem-saturated narrative can emerge.

No miracles occurred with Andrew's alcohol use but gradually he started to have fewer hospital admissions and his somatic symptoms lessened. He did spend more of his income on food and was starting to acknowledge more positive attributes about himself than he had previously. Discussions with Sandra about his family allowed Andrew to identify beliefs he had about his lack of value as an individual following his parents' 'rejection' of him at age 16. He had found himself living alone without adequate life skills and thus had judged himself to be incompetent as a person in general as a result of his struggles. He was able to make connections between his life experience and the development of his dominant story that him in a wholly negative light. In the continued search for exceptions and for alternative stories, Andrew had found that he had attributes that warranted his self-respect and so did develop a renewed interest in his self-care and a consequential reduction in his alcohol use. The genesis of an alternative narrative for Andrew was the shift in his beliefs that became the foundation of significant, if not total, change. Sandra's regularity and reliability alongside her acceptance of him provided Andrew with a secure-enough holding environment in which he could experiment with change that started to become an established pattern for living.

Social Work Application

Facilitating change requires feedback for the alternative story to be tested out, and to enable this requires a time commitment from social workers embarking

(Continued)

(Continued)

on this as a form of intervention. The length of time will vary, be it short follow-up appointments to reinforce progress, or a series of meetings that slowly aim to facilitate change. A social worker's judgement is required to assess the progress of each individual and their capacity for change over a period of time. Without considering how an emotional temporary secure base can be provided throughout the work, our efforts are likely to have little success. Fundamental elements to the communication process recur here, such as reliability, focus on the individual and conviction of a sense of that individual's own importance as a person in their own right. Careful consideration of closure is also necessary so as to be a positive experience and not one that is perceived as rejection, or important enough to continue, and would result in a reversion to a previous dominant narrative, i.e. that all relationships end in rejection and abandonment.

Skills Component

- Provide an emotional temporary secure base through focus and reliability.
- Offer enough time for alternative stories to be tested, and feedback received and processed into an alternative story.
- Pay careful attention to how endings occur, being planned and with the service user retaining an element of control.

Summary of Key Narrative Concepts

- Life stories are constructed through **Dominant Themes** that have a socio-political foundation
- We actively select experiences that are replayed and recreated and become our **Dominant Narrative**
- People often develop **Problem-saturated Narratives** that exclude positive experience
- Narrative approaches seek for **Exceptions** to develop **Alternative Narratives** for future life stories
- **Metaphors** are used to bring descriptive character to problems that are then **Externalised** to relieve an individual of blame
- **Alternative Narratives** are maintained through experimentation and feedback over time

ıclusion

A narrative approach to using counselling skills fits well within a social work context for various reasons. The values underpinning the approach ally themselves with social work values in our commitment to counter oppression and deprivation. The narrative method of raising awareness of these values can be easily integrated into a social worker's approach to engagement with service users and with intervention to bring about change. It is only useful as an approach when it timeously fits with our role and task, governed by the type of problem faced and the agency remit held by us and when we have some degree of flexibility in terms of length of involvement and opportunities for reliable contact.

Further Reading

- **White and Epston's (1990)** classic text on the use of narrative approaches gives the socio-political context of the theory as well as techniques to develop practice when people have problems that appear to be stuck.

- **Dwividi (1997)** provides a collection of papers that explore narrative approaches broadly in therapeutic work. This includes work with children as well as adults.

- **Byng-Hall (1995)** offers an exploration of trans-generational scripts with families where roles become prescribed and entrenched. He interweaves attachment theory with narrative theory and highlights difficulties that families face when trying to make change.

6
Solution-focused Therapy in Social Work Practice

Key Concepts	Key Theorists and Practitioners
• Developed from Brief Therapy • Emphasis on Change • Outcome- and Goal-orientated • Specific Solution-focused Language	• Erickson • De Shazer

Introduction

Solution-focused approaches to counselling skills rely on a shift away from a problem-focused approach towards seeking positive change with individuals or families. Problem-resolution is put aside in favour of seeking desirable outcomes. The desired outcomes need not equate to the resolution of the problem for this approach to be successful. Thus the successful outcome might co-exist with the problem but the shift in focus away from the problem towards the desired outcome brings this approach into future-orientation rather than reinforcing past preoccupations.

While there are critics of this approach, drawing on elements of solution-focused therapy can help social workers to broaden our skills in communicating with individuals and groups through widening our repertoire of language and therapeutic options. This chapter offers an overview of the foundations of solution-focused therapy and details the manner in which some of the techniques can be incorporated into social work practice to achieve change.

The 'Miracle Question' (de Shazer, 1988) has deliberately been excluded from this chapter, because of the high level of skill required to integrate it successfully into practice.

An Overview of the Solution-focused Approach

Solution-focused therapy relies on a radically different orientation from many of the other counselling approaches. Many other counselling models require problems to be understood by both the service user and the practitioner in some form of collaborative alliance termed the working relationship. While collaboration within a working relationship remains essential, solution-focused therapy does not require a link to be made between the problems experienced by a service user and the outcomes or solutions they wish to achieve in their lives. Thus the emphasis of conversations between service users and practitioners is less on trying to understand the cause of problems in depth and reduce their impact, and more about exploring what is required to bring about change. Problem-resolution and desired outcomes of therapeutic intervention are not therefore synonymous.

De Shazer (1985) is the principal author and practitioner associated with this approach, although Milton Erickson's innovatory work was initially influential (Erikson, 1980). Although brief and solution-focused approaches are not totally interchangeable (solution-focused therapy is a type of brief therapy), elements in practice of how problems are acknowledged, understood and then solutions sought for change to occur bring the two models closely together.

Theoretical Underpinnings of a Solution-focused Approach

Born out of a shift from psychoanalysis and its requirement for intensive therapeutic contact over a significant period of time for problems in life to be understood and resolved, brief and then solution-focused therapy challenged this requirement for change to occur. Extensive research over the 1960s and 1970s (Bateson, 1972) indicated positive outcomes for short-term intervention (Street & Downey, 1996). Steve de Shazer (1985) and colleagues from the Brief Family Therapy Centre, Milwaukee, discovered that those attending therapeutic sessions were at least as able to bring about change by talking about the future, as by gaining insight into problems in the past. Examination of problems seated in past experience was not an absolute requirement for positive change in the future.

Brief therapies are those that are short-term, with minimal intervention and a determined shift away from practitioner-led goals towards those identified by a service user. Immediately we recognise that social workers in statutory services are often bound to work towards service-led and legal objectives, which sits in contrast to the stance of brief therapies. As research has indicated strong links between meeting service user expectations and their resultant perceptions of 'better' outcomes (Street & Downey, 1996), to successfully embrace elements of a brief or solution-focused approach, a resolution to this dilemma in practice needs to be found. This is explored further below. Nevertheless, the expectation of a brief approach is that of short-term as opposed to long-term intervention.

Social Constructivism as a Foundation

Brief and solution-focused therapies are seated within the post-modern genre of social constructivism, whereby objective meaning of reality does not exist. Rather, experience is interpreted as a result of an individual's social context and culture. Social constructivism serves as the foundation for solution-focused therapy, that is, 'we can never really "know" the reality of the world of another' (Hoffman, 2002). The crucial aspect of social constructivism is the inclusion of social context to the development of perception, beliefs and behaviour.

Language, the Development of Social Structures and Individual Experience

Social constructivist ideas linked to language are important in understanding the theoretical basis of solution-focused therapy. According to our lived experience within a social context, we interact with each other through language that is mostly construed from dominant discourse. Thus social structures such as those determined by social policy form the basis of social interaction: of our beliefs about who we are and how we should be living our lives. However, while interpretation of events is made as a result of our socialisation within these contexts and although is influenced hence, meaning of experience remains unique to every individual. It is the interpretation of the meaning of events that cannot easily be accounted for from the perspective of the dominant discourse in society – the dominant social group where 'expertise' is believed to be located. For example, a white male 'expert' is unlikely to be able fully to make sense of the lived experience of a black woman. Any 'expertise' in this respect becomes invalid. Taking the stance of 'expert', from this perspective, inadvertently leads us to make assumptions that might not be part of an individual's own experience. Thus the stance of 'expert' is largely rejected, notwithstanding legal requirements such as legal and ethical matters that cannot be abandoned by practitioners.

Social constructivism therefore rejects the modernist scientific position that a certain set of variables would result in a certain outcome for individuals, and is unconcerned with scientific validity (von Glasersfeld, 1987). While this is not an argument for an 'anything goes' approach, the diminishing role of the expert, with an exclusive hold on 'truth', is put aside for individual accounts of experience. Personal accounts of experience are given weight since they contain both personal knowledge derived from social encounters and individual meaning given as a result of interpretation through a social context. In this respect, there are some similarities between solution-focused approaches to counselling and narrative approaches, since they share a post-modern foundation and acknowledge the importance of the social context in shaping meaning given to experience.

Solutions and Outcomes in Social Work

Committed practitioners of other models of counselling might highly criticise this model for ignoring 'underlying' factors that often result in problem repetition.

However, research (de Shazer & Berg, 1997) does support the efficacy of emphasis on solutions in therapeutic encounters rather than on problems for short- and long-term change. While this does not account for change within a social work context, it offers some validity for inclusion of the approach in therapeutic practice.

It is argued that the motivation for assessment and intervention when embarking on forms of counselling is often different for the service user and for the practitioner. Service users, assuming that there is no statutory requirement for engagement to which they object, are more likely to be motivated to want to find a solution to problems and ease distress. The practitioner, however, is more likely to be interested in understanding causal factors to problems before making a progression towards problem resolution.

Certainly in social work, if we accept a process model of engagement, assessment and intervention, we could easily fall into this 'typical' practitioner's frame of reference. We attempt to engage with people, we use theoretical concepts alongside data collection to formulate an analytical assessment of the problems experienced, and then move towards intervention based on our findings (Compton & Galaway, 1999).

Although social work actively embraces social constructivist ideas in that we recognise and value the uniqueness of individuals, we also rely on a level of 'expertise' (for example, knowledge about the legal framework, psychological theories and research findings) to inform our practice. For the most part, the social work role does not fit with a pure solution-focused approach, although the strong emphasis on engagement and developing a working relationship puts this approach into our domain. As with other counselling models offered in this book, a solution-focused approach can be integrated into social work practice, albeit selectively, as a form of intervention and as a way to shape intervention, acknowledging the dilemma that occurs between the role of 'expert' and the 'not knowing' position of solution-focused therapy (de Shazer & Berg, 1992). This is discussed throughout this chapter.

Techniques for Practice

Several key principles are intrinsic to the solution-focused approach. An understanding of the use of language and the way we frame experience is of overriding importance. The approach uses the setting of goals with service users, seeking exceptions, searching for evidence of individual competence, and incorporation of scaling questions to work with a person towards a desired outcome. The manner and context in which these skills can be incorporated into social work practice are examined further.

Solution-focused Talk

De Shazer (1994) outlines the importance of language in problem definition and exploration of future outcomes. Solution-focused language moves away from statements which are stable, permanent, internal and global (O'Connell & Palmer, 2003). For example, 'I am naturally shy, which means I have never been able to make friends. I am always lonely'. This is parallel to the cognitive behavioural approach (see Chapter 3). The assumptions that can be made from such statements are various.

The position of such a person is assumed to be a result of biological or genetic factors that are out of the control of the person to change. The stability of the problem over time, the all-encompassing nature of the description and the internal orientation of the problem immediately limit the possibility for change. Solution-focused language would lead a practitioner to enable a service user to see a problem as 'unstable … occasion-specific … external … [and] transient' (O'Connell & Palmer, 2003). To redefine the problem described requires deconstruction by the worker and the service user – that is, to examine the components of the problem in relation to space, time and impact. The example above could be deconstructed and reframed as 'When meeting new people I find it hard to talk so it limits me making friends. When I am not sure what to say and others are talking I feel very alone. Not having friends gets to me and I get lonely when I want to share my thoughts with someone else.' The shift in language and the specificity of having deconstructed and reframed the statement provides an opening for exploring future hoped outcomes of the work, for example, 'What I want is to be able to talk to other people and share activities with them.'

Arriving at a position where future hoped outcomes could be explored requires some acknowledgement of the problem, otherwise a person might feel unheard. Drawing on listening skills outlined in previous chapters is essential, as is offering a temporary secure base, referred to in Chapter 4, for change to occur. The attributes of offering positive regard, warmth and empathy as explored in Chapter 2 are also absolutely relevant. However, it is the language used and the stance of 'not knowing' another's position that are integral to a solution-focused approach, as is the reinforcement that the service user has 'expertise' to define how their situation would feel 'better'.

In many of the helping professions, the language used to describe and formulate problems often groups and labels people into broad categories that leave little room for individual accounts of experience. Individual descriptions might not entirely fit with the broad groupings and therefore labels are viewed as unhelpful by the solution-focused approach. Social work has long been committed to challenging oppressive language. This model therefore fits well in this respect with social work values. Diagnostic 'mental health' labels are especially limiting when seeking positive outcomes with people. They can generate assumptions that problems are internally located and are therefore insurmountable and influential over all of life experience. Employing a solution-focused approach requires the abandonment of using labels for people with problems: for example, 'a depressive', 'conduct-disordered', 'anxious personality'.

Carol sought social work assistance when, as a carer for her mother, Joyce, a woman in her eighties with poor physical health and early-onset dementia, she believed she could no longer cope with her responsibilities and required help. Carol had attended her GP on several occasions a few years previously feeling fatigued and had been prescribed anti-depressants. Carol

(Continued)

(Continued)

thought of herself as a 'depressive person' and believed her 'emotional weakness' was the cause of her lack of coping. She had struggled with her feelings for several months before she decided to ask for practical help. Carol's social life had been declining in quantity and quality over the seven years that she had been caring for Joyce on a full-time basis. She had retired from a busy profession where she had experienced companionship and status, and hoped to travel and see the world. Her plans had been cut short when her father had died six months after her retiring and she took on the caring responsibilities that had been her father's.

As Carol's social activities had been declining, so had her mood. She had long since lost sight of her plans to travel and on one occasion had felt so frustrated that she hit Joyce. Carol was horrified by her actions, which prompted her referral to social services to request support. Carol at that time did not know what kind of help she wanted, only that the situation could somehow 'feel better'. Carol was certain that she did not want Joyce to move out of her home into any form of residential care.

While Joyce was the named service user, her needs were being met primarily by Carol and, therefore, any future consideration of social services support also needed to take into consideration Carol's needs and capacity for caring.

There are several features of Carol's story that could be reframed using a solution-focused approach. Her beliefs about herself, as indicated by the language she used, 'a depressive person' with 'emotional weakness', are located as an internal problem, i.e. as if some biological or genetic tendency were the reason for her feelings, leaving no obvious scope for change. The terms also appear to be all-encompassing or global, as if every minute of every day, in every situation, life is a struggle. This globalisation of feelings or problems limits any opportunity to recognise strengths or small achievements. Carol believes she has 'emotional weakness', yet for seven years has put the needs of her mother above her own life plans and coped without any other practical help. Deconstructing the situation allows these areas of success to be acknowledged.

Using internal and global frames of reference for feelings and problems leads to them appearing to be stable over time. Carol's life story, however, indicates that she held a responsible position throughout her career and was once optimistic and excited about her future. Over seven years, her love of life has eroded to the point where she resorted to violence as an outlet for her frustration. Deconstructing her descriptions reveals that her low mood has not been stable over a lifetime but in fact has been situation-specific.

While Carol had already considered her role as a carer and her own and Joyce's needs before referring to social services, i.e. that they required practical assistance in order that Joyce could remain living with her, Carol was caught up with unhelpful feelings of blame and guilt. These feelings, if left unresolved, might have continued to impact on her relationship with Joyce and on other more separate aspects of her life.

Using a solution-focused approach to deconstruct Carol's story, Anne Marie worked with Carol over three sessions.

Anne Marie listened carefully to Carol's statements. She noticed that Carol was describing herself in globally negative terms and seemed to be locating the source of her struggles to some kind of internal emotional problem, rather than situational. While Anne Marie did not halt the flow of Carol's descriptions, she enquired how she had managed to keep going. Further discussion of the various strategies Carol had employed and how she had adapted them as Joyce's condition worsened revealed to Carol her strengths and successes over the course of the previous few years. Carol did not appear to have noticed these before, including her determination and endurance required to continue caring for her mother, even though she felt exhausted. This compounded her belief that she was somehow inadequate for her role.

To ensure that Carol did not feel unheard, Anne Marie did not dismiss her descriptions of the problems she was currently experiencing, but allowed her some time to share this. Once confident that Carol had shared what she had hoped to share with her, Anne Marie led the discussion into exploring the outcomes of the contact that Carol had hoped to achieve. Carol articulated that she did not know what could be done but that she needed help to continue to care for her mother and to ensure that she did not arrive at a point of frustration where she would assault her mother again. Carol was deeply regretful about this incident.

When Carol had started to discuss her problems, Anne Marie helped her to identify times when the problems impacted upon her life less and when she seemed to be coping better. Carol recognised the least stressful times being late evenings when Joyce was asleep and when Carol could read or watch TV.

Anne Marie encouraged the flow of conversation to touch on Carol's interests. While her involvement in leisure pursuits had gradually declined over the years, they were able to identify that Carol enjoyed history and archaeology, and especially visiting old buildings of historical interest. Her membership in a club had lapsed but Carol did still read about archaeological discoveries from time to time. Anne Marie noted how Carol became more animated as she spoke of this.

Using the three sessions to this end, Anne Marie and Carol explored ways in which Carol could work towards her preferred outcomes, including obtaining practical support to assist her to care for Joyce and increase her leisure activities again.

Social Work Application

While the referral of Joyce was a request for practical assistance from social services, another risk inherent in Carol's and Joyce's situation was the potential for further violence to Joyce. Using a solution-focused approach, Anne Marie was able to offer minimal intervention to enable Carol to deconstruct her own personal account of her situation and allow Carol to seek solutions that would both improve the quality of her life and reduce her stress. This approach opened an avenue to explore strengths and interests that had been overlooked by Carol as a result of feeling overwhelmed and powerless regarding her life circumstances. The focus here is on Carol, as the solution-focused component of the care plan was undertaken directly with Carol, although it led to protecting Joyce.

Anne Marie had used questions that generated discussion about Carol's competence and reinforced to Carol that she did have many positive attributes and strengths. If Anne Marie had made this observation herself, it is unlikely that Carol would have accepted it. As it was Carol's own personal account that provided the affirmation of ability, it was accepted as having validity. Competence-seeking as a mode of communication skills can be incorporated into most areas of social work practice.

This approach would not advocate exploring the decisions made around the time of the death of Carol's father, nor the impact or reasoning of choices that culminated in her isolated position. This would result in a problem-focused rather than a solution-focused approach. Instead, the focus was on exceptions to the problems and the outcomes that Carol wished to achieve to 'feel better'. Carol 'feeling better' would protect Joyce from future harm by preventing an escalation of Carol's frustration. What Carol would need now does not require to be directly linked to experiences in the past or the causal factors that led to feelings of low mood for this approach to be successful.

The opportunity for a pure solution-focused approach rarely presents itself in most social work settings. However, the language of the approach can be incorporated into our work as a means to empower people to share their own account of their experience and to find outcomes that are favourable to them. At times these outcomes might not include those required by the agency and this is a factor that social workers need constantly to question. In Carol's case, her favoured outcomes, to reduce the quantity of her care responsibilities and increase the quality of her life, would result in a reduction of risk towards Joyce and thus was in keeping with agency objectives.

Skills Component

- Develop a working alliance by being clear about role, nature of agency and any agency constraints.
- Use communication skills such as being attentive, reliable, and showing genuine warmth and positive regard.
- Encourage service users to give their own account of experience rather than what they believe is the cause of their problems.
- Ask questions that affirm competence, e.g., 'How did you accomplish this?'.
- Listen for exceptions, when someone is coping more or the problems seem less.
- Introduce the concept of different choices in the manner in which experience might be perceived, i.e. a reaction to high stress rather than an internal 'breakdown'.
- Facilitate the exploration of what specific outcomes a service user would most hope for following contact with the service: 'What do they want?'.
- Resist placing the emphasis of the work on seeking causal explanations to problems or trying to link problems with potential outcomes.
- Engage in 'problem-free' talk: for example, 'What are your interests?'.

Goal Setting

Once the beginnings of a working alliance or working relationship are formed, and after the service user feels they have heard enough to explore desired outcomes for the work, specific goals can be agreed upon by the two parties, i.e. social worker and service user. The purpose of goal setting is to assist motivation for change through incentives and to keep a focus on the work, which facilitates the brief nature of the approach. To set goals using this approach, an emphasis is made upon the language of questions used. Goals need to be achievable, specific and well-defined. They need to be generated from the ideas of the service user and not the worker to be successful. This requires workers to have a belief in the abilities of the service user and an acceptance of their definition of what needs to change.

Some examples of goal-setting questions that can be incorporated into a first meeting with a service user are taken from O'Connell and Palmer (2003).

- How will you know that coming here has been worthwhile for you?
- What are your best hopes for this session?
- How do you think coming here might help you?
- How will you know when things are getting better?
- What is the first sign for you?
- What is your main concern?

- Where do you want to make a start?
- If you were able to make some changes soon, which would be the most helpful to you?

During their first session, Carol and Anne Marie discussed in detail what Carol had hoped to achieve by coming to the service. She was able to explicitly share her wish to continue to care for Joyce but with help so that she could 'get her life back'. Carol's immediate preferred outcome was for social services to start some regular practical help. Anne Marie arranged for a home care assessment for Joyce after their first meeting. Carol articulated that she would recognise the reduction of stress as she started to rediscover her interest in life. To some extent this had already begun by her request for services. She had identified that some aspect of life needed to change and made steps to bring this about by seeking help.

Social Work Application

Formulating a care plan and goal setting are closely linked, albeit that a care plan might include areas for change which are neither desired nor motivated by the service user. Goal setting from a solution-focused perspective includes the outcomes that a service user wishes to achieve in order to 'feel better', in whatever form that might mean for the service user in distress.

If this is not possible due to conflicting objectives of the service user and the agency, then a solution-focused approach might not be the most applicable for the piece of work being undertaken.

Carol and Anne Marie had ascertained a general outcome that Carol wished to achieve: to receive practical assistance for Joyce and to improve the quality of Carol's life. Anne Marie then assisted Carol to articulate them in specific terms. Carol thought that, between the first and second meeting, she would be able to set aside an hour during the day when she would usually be preoccupied with household chores. She would use this time to attempt to re-establish contact with two friends, with whom meetings and phone calls had gradually declined over the last few years.

Skills Component

- Separate out solution-focused goal setting from a more comprehensive care plan.
- Accept the service user's position on what goals are to be worked on.

(Continued)

(Continued)

- Acknowledge the service user strengths and abilities required to achieve goals.
- Assist a service user to select goals that are attainable, specifically defined and measurable.
- Prioritise specific goals with the service user.

Consolidating and Reviewing Progress

Following goal setting during the first solution-focused session, further meetings are to consolidate any progress made and renegotiate goals if necessary towards a successful outcome. Various techniques are employed with this approach to facilitate this. O'Connell (1998) uses the analogy of a 'client' being like a 'scientist' who is experimenting with their own life – testing out different experiences to accomplish the outcome desired. This is only possible if the goals are service-user-led and if a temporarily secure working relationship has been formed. The need for a temporary secure base (see Chapter 4) in all therapeutic relationships is integral to their success and cannot be overstated.

This temporary secure base offers a show of commitment to the process, reliability and unconditional positive regard. However, for a solution-focused approach, this is not enough to elicit change. There is a requirement that the worker demonstrates an explicit commitment to assisting a service user to achieve a desired outcome. The skill required at this point is to be able to accept failure as well as success, without which it is unlikely that a service user would feel open to discuss the whole experience and could disengage from the service.

Therefore, from the temporary safety of the working relationship, a worker, at some early point in the second session, will enquire about the progress made on specific goals set previously. One of the principal purposes of such discussions is to elicit how the service user managed to achieve what they achieved. From a social constructivist perspective, these conversations assist the service user to construct their own meanings in relation to their achievements, which is infinitely more powerful and more consolidating of success than meanings offered by workers. High-toned congratulations for small successes could easily be perceived as patronising and thus undermine the work.

Service users struggling with experimenting with making changes, however small, require recognition for the efforts they are making in relation to their goals, even if this has only been contemplation. Failures can be reframed by deconstructing the effort made and the progress achieved towards being wholly successful. 'Scaling questions' are most useful in this respect. An example of a scaling question might be, 'If 0 is how things were at the start of our work and 10 is where things are just right, where are things now?' Using this form of questioning, which can be adapted to suit any area of enquiry, moves away from an 'all-or-nothing' response to change. Often it can be difficult for people to notice small changes and this facilitates a change in perception regarding successes. A solution-focused approach will draw on scaling questions to measure progress and to set further small goals, i.e. to move from 3 to 4 might be the difference for Carol between having an hour for herself during the day or not. The principle is that small, incremental changes lead to the overall desired outcome.

Carol returned to the second meeting with some optimism for change but was clearly still very weary. She had managed to phone one friend, Clare, and practical assistance had started for Joyce, which freed her physically from some of the tasks she was previously undertaking. Carol remained racked with guilt, however, for assaulting Joyce some months earlier. Thoughts of 'being bad', coupled with the continued belief that she had some form of emotional weakness that led her to these actions, inhibited her progress towards her goal.

Anne Marie spent time with Carol assisting her to deconstruct these beliefs, by exploring the social circumstances leading up to the event and all of the times when she had felt frustrated with caring for Joyce but had not been violent. During this session, Carol was able to reframe the event in the context of time and circumstance, rather than locating it as an internal deficit.

By recognising the efforts she had made between the sessions, Anne Marie encouraged Carol to explore how she had managed to make the time to phone her friend and how difficult this must have been, given it had been several years of no contact. Carol recognised her achievement and set herself the goal of contacting her other previously close friend during the next week.

Anne Marie used a scaling question to both measure and consolidate the progress Carol had made, and to encourage her to continue to try. 'If 0 was how you felt when we first met and 10 is how it would feel if everything was perfect, how do you feel now?' Carol gave '3' as her answer. Anne Marie responded, 'What would need to be happening for you to move to 4?' Carol replied that she would feel better if she thought she could go out and socialise once in a while. Anne Marie then asked, 'What would you need to do to make that happen?' Carol stated, 'I will call Clare and ask her if she would like to meet for a meal.'

Social Work Application

To communicate effectively with people in social work, we use techniques borrowed from various forms of counselling, often in eclectic form. Using scaling questions taken from solution-focused therapy can be an effective mode of enabling a service user to communicate to us the level of their distress and the rate of progress they believe they are making. Using these

(Continued)

(Continued)

questions facilitates focus on both the nature of the work and specificity, i.e. moving away from broad generalisations as to whether change is under way.

This approach does not directly account for the obstructive nature of social structures in putting a barrier between goal attainment. In using scaling questions, the onus for success lies with the service user to make changes. We do, however, need to keep sight of the socio-political factors that could stand in the way of even small successes, such as poverty limiting use of the phone for communicating with friends, poor local transport impeding travel possibilities, etc.

Where possible, the role of the social worker is to access resources to reduce the impact of poverty and social exclusion. This would need to be part of a care plan for any work undertaken, rather than identified as a solution-focused goal to direct the onus of responsibility away from the service user.

Skills Component

- Maintain a working relationship through reliability and commitment to the success of the therapeutic encounter.
- Enquire about progress on goals, reframing 'failure' in terms of effort made towards success.
- Assist the service user to construct their own meaning of achievements.
- Use scaling questions to work towards goals in incremental and measurably definable steps.
- Retain an awareness of the social barriers of poverty and deprivation.

Further Consolidating Progress and Endings

In brief and solution-focused approaches, endings are introduced at the beginning of the working relationship. The nature of the approach is to assist people to take control of their own lives as much as possible. In this respect, the working alliance needs to specifically make firm acknowledgement of the temporary nature of the relationship. One question is often asked that can help in defining endings: 'How will you know that you no longer require assistance from meeting with me?' This introduces the end of the work in an empowering manner without rejection. The temporary nature of the relationship is established and the expectation for progress is set.

Regular use of scaling questions and seeking and affirming competence as the work progresses serves to empower the individual to taking ownership for any achievements, rather than becoming dependent on the practitioner. An agreed end-point, negotiated at the beginning and reviewed as required, promotes the possibility of an ending with the service user having an element of control.

Anne Marie assisted Carol to consolidate these goals by seeking evidence of competence with Carol and using scaling questions to quantify her progress. After three sessions, Carol thought she could continue to rebuild her social life without social work assistance and, with practical support, had significantly reduced the negative impact on her life of caring for Joyce. Her relationship with Joyce had improved markedly. Carol had been able to take ownership of her success and had not attributed this to Anne Marie alone, enabling her to continue with progress without ongoing therapeutic sessions.

Social Work Application

Effective endings are an important but often neglected aspect of social work practice. The solution-focused model of defining endings offers an approach that can be incorporated into most areas of social work practice, in that endings are agreed and acknowledged at the beginning of any work. There are always exceptions, but facilitating endings in this way reduces the possibility for service users to view endings as a form of rejection, which could then sabotage the achievements made during the intervention. Managing endings as a positive conclusion to the work can assist in the consolidation of changes that have been made by the service user.

Skills Component

- Consolidate progress by assisting service users to affirm competence.
- Use scaling questions to quantify progress.
- Give attention to the management of endings at the beginning of a working relationship.
- Allow the service user an element of control in the management of endings wherever possible.

Summary of Key Concepts from a Solution-focused Perspective

- **Social Constructivist** ideas underpin the solution-focused approach
- Goal-orientated **Outcomes** are explored rather than underlying contributory factors to problems

(Continued)

> *(Continued)*
>
> - **Solutions** are not necessarily the result of the resolution of problems, i.e. a problem does not need to be resolved for an acceptable outcome to be reached
> - **Solution-focused Language** is used to create opportunities for change
> - Practitioners use **Goal Setting** to assist service users to make staged progress towards outcomes
> - **Rating Scales** allow service users to track small increments of change that can assist in motivation
> - The **Therapeutic Relationship** can provide service users with a **Temporary Secure Base** so that change can be tested out
> - Progress is **Reviewed** and goals adjusted accordingly
> - **Endings** are introduced at the beginning of the work and progress is measured with a view to ending the work.

Conclusion

The solution-focused approach offers some extremely useful techniques that can be incorporated into practice when working towards change. It allows the service user to identify and set goals to which they are likely to be motivated to work towards. It embraces the value of empowerment, so central to social work practice, based on its social constructivist foundations. As the nature of the work using this approach is to move away from problem-talk into solution-talk, this often introduces dilemmas for those whose theoretical and therapeutic preference is towards seeking causal explanations for problems. As this approach does not require the understanding of problems in order to attain solutions, it sits uncomfortably with many.

From a social work perspective, when objectives for change are defined by the agency or the legal system, this approach would conflict with the role of a social worker. For situations in child protection work, criminal justice and youth justice, where the legal and social policy system has a part to play in defining desired outcomes, the solution-focused approach is not well suited. However, for defined areas of work within an overall care plan, techniques used in solution-focused therapy can be extremely effective in quantifying and making progress towards change.

Further Reading

- **De Shazer (1985, 1988)**, well known for driving this approach forward, incorporates detailed guidance on how to use solution-focused techniques in a therapeutic setting. This requires adaptation for use in a social work role.

- **O'Connell (1998)** offers a clear foundation for the principles of solution-focused therapy and how it can be used in practice, with examples of dialogue. The language of a solution-focused approach is made explicit.

- **O'Connell and Palmer (2003)** include chapters by practitioners in a wide variety of fields, including social work, in a broader examination of solution-focused therapy. These chapters give a flavour of the model in action rather than depth to the techniques of the approach.

7
Systemic and Family Approaches to Social Work Practice

<table>
<tr><td>

Key Concepts

- Homeostasis
- Feedback within Systems
- Circular Causality
- Lifecycle Transitions
- Societal Influence

</td><td>

Key Theorists and Practitioners

- Bateson
- Haley
- Minuchin
- Cecchin
- Hoffman
- Carr

</td></tr>
</table>

Introduction

Service users are fundamental to social work and all service users will have either a present-day and/or a historical family context upon which many of the behavioural and communication patterns used throughout life will be based. Whether working with families as a whole group, some family members or with an individual, concepts taken from systems theory and family therapy can be invariably useful for incorporating counselling skills into social work practice.

There are several schools of family therapy, which will not be detailed here. However, all of these schools have one common thread: the use of systems theory to understand the reciprocal nature of behaviour within groups of people with emotional ties (Jones, 1994; Hoffman, 2002). Family ties need not be positive ones or ones that have links to present-day interactions. Cultural influences place importance on the role of 'family' in western society (Gorell Barnes, 1998).

The principal objective of this chapter is to introduce the use of systemic theory and techniques to assist social workers to view individual presenting problems in the context of family functioning. This shift from an individual to a systemic perspective offers an alternative blueprint for practice in understanding presenting problems and moving towards facilitating change. The aims of this chapter thus include introducing theoretical foundations to systemic family counselling by providing an overview of key aspects of systems theory, set within a social constructionist context. Factors relating to lifecycle are also considered.

The chapter will then clarify some of the fundamental concepts that allow us to view communication and behaviour within families as part of a system rather than being wholly attributable to the needs and desires of an individual. The chapter aims to build upon these theoretical concepts of systemic family functioning to offer some techniques that can be usefully incorporated into a social worker's skill base.

An Overview of the Approach

Social workers, by the nature of the title, are interested in the social context in which a person lives and conducts their life. Implicit is our concern with society and its impact upon people and their problems. Chapter 5 outlines social constructionist ideas: the theory that beliefs are given meaning through the discourse of dominant members of society over time. Chapter 6 touches on social constructivist ideas: that the experience of reality and the meaning attributed to experience is unique to each individual. Beliefs about age, gender, race, among others, become accepted and perpetuated through language in society that can oppress groups of people who do not fit within the 'ideal' norms. For example, a 'marathon athlete' generates a mental stereotype; a marathon athlete who uses a wheelchair does not always fit with the dominant societal image.

Family therapy is interested in the interpretation of meaning by more than one individual in a family group. Roles and stereotypes defined and held by family members do not always fit with the needs of an individual. Thus understanding social constructionist and social constructivist ideas (Hoffman, 2002) allows an exploration of how individuals find themselves in roles that generate internal or interpersonal conflict. This conflict often results in one or more members of a family presenting with an emotional or behavioural problem.

We are able to understand the impact of social structures and of the creation of oppression through social constructions – commonly held beliefs that become established as 'truths' over time. Families will react to the impact of social policy, such as state benefits, employment policies or housing opportunities, in that the availability of resources will determine the form and level of social participation (Adams et al., 2002). A family struggling with poverty will be unable to access the same level of social clubs, for example, for their children, as will a family with greater financial resources; changes in the employment market, such as the closing down of coal mines, can leave some families rurally situated without access to regular transport to commute to areas where employment might be more readily available. When we view a family's problems, we can take into account the impact of social policy and its outcomes. We can then explore the impact of social factors on families as part of a systemic approach to understanding emotional and behavioural functioning.

As people living in twenty-first-century Britain, we come to view life in ways typical of our culture. With advanced conventional medicine, we are used to having cures to physical problems found for us by specialists in their field. Our human organisms are examined and the 'faulty part' is identified and treated. Just like a motorcar, we can be fixed and return to the road to metaphorically run on for another few thousand miles. When we think of social and emotional problems, often the cultural pattern laid out for us leads us to a similar pattern of problem-exploration.

This can be especially so when working with the extremely vulnerable group of children and young people whom we describe as 'looked after and accommodated'. Children and young people who are or who have been separated from their family of origin and have had to adapt to one or more 'new' family situations, including experience of residential care, often do not have a willing or able family of origin with whom they could explore the systemic nature of their problems. Despite our knowledge of troubled or traumatic histories, it is often tempting to view surface or visible behaviour that is difficult or challenging as a form of individual/intrinsic mental health problem that can be 'treated' like a broken leg.

We are often concerned with the presenting problems of the individual, be it situational or emotional. However, we can overlook the reactionary nature of problems as they occur as a result of the environmental context in which they are experienced. As a society in general, we can find that we are often immersed in the beliefs of a 'medical model' of life. That is, when problems arise we look at the 'symptoms' of problems, i.e. how they manifest, and then look for some pathological failing within the human organism to explain the apparent 'breakdown' or 'illness'. In other words, we often look for an explanation that is located within the individual to explain what might be the expression of thoughts and feelings through behaviour. This can be especially apparent with behavioural problems and with problems relating to mental health.

Using a systemic approach to understanding problems, and then communicating effectively to assist the change process, moves us firmly away from this traditional 'medical model' form of thinking. Instead, we become concerned with a person's social and political context on a macro-level and with the subtleties of current or historical family functioning that influence beliefs and behaviour on a micro-level. We direct our interest away from seeking causal factors internal to the individual for problems and re-focus on external influences that co-exist with difficulties. This approach sits firmly and comfortably with social work values, where diversity is embraced and oppression is to be understood systemically and to be challenged.

Fundamental Concepts in Systemic Family Work

Family and systemic therapies, like other counselling models, have evolved from several schools. Early family therapy models include strategic therapies (Haley, 1976; Madanes, 1984), structural therapies (Minuchin, 1974), and the Milan School (Boscolo et al., 1987) where most of the concepts and techniques outlined below originated. Later therapies are more closely linked to the post-modern era of social constructionist ideas. They weave some of the narrative and solution-focused ideas (see Chapters 5 and 6) through systemic counselling ideas. Rather than give a description of these schools in more detail, as can be found in other texts (Carr, 2000; Dallos & Draper, 2000), this chapter will take some elements from these models to provide a broad framework when engaging therapeutically with families in social work practice.

Introducing concepts inherent to family work immediately raises the question of what defines a family (Barnes et al., 1999). We make assumptions about the constitution of families according to our own experiences and cultural upbringing. Beliefs about gender and sexuality immediately come to the fore when exploring the nature of family. Geographical factors such as location of extended family and roles ascribed to individuals according to age and status can vary immensely from one family to another. The legal status of couples, such as those who are 'married' and those who are not, does not in western society indicate the composition of a family group. Some families include relatives from older generations, some might be composed of single parents and children and some will have no children at all. In referring to 'the family' in this chapter, the term is intended as a broad description with no one clear definition, other than that it is held together with varying sets of emotional ties that exist between individuals.

Therapeutic family work of all types draws upon an understanding of the functioning of systems in general. The manner in which all systems operate, including mechanical and computerised systems, to maintain certain patterns of 'behaving' and to modify these patterns according to new information obtained is fundamental to this approach. The early research into systems theory often referred to systems in families as cybernetics, the science of self-regulating systems (Bateson, 1972).

Cybernetics

Cybernetics identified several features of an intelligent system that enabled it to regulate itself and adapt its behaviour to become most efficient. Dallos and Draper (2000) use the example of missile systems in World War II to illuminate the comparison between mechanical/computerised systems and those of groups of people in the form of families. Several characteristics, such as functional patterns and adaptation to external stimuli, observed in these missile systems, could be compared to the way in which families were believed to operate to maintain conformity to family beliefs and values and to adapt to new information and circumstances.

> The Kurz family had moved to the west of Scotland in the early 1950s. They had arrived in the social aftermath of World War II and had become accustomed to discriminatory comments regarding their Bavarian roots. Their organisation of family life, their behavioural patterns and communication style, were centred on their cultural history as well as on their present-day experience. While they enjoyed life in Scotland, the parents of the four children (one of whom later shared their experiences with a social worker) had perpetuated a belief that the only way they could remain safe in their community was to have
>
> *(Continued)*

(Continued)

no social contact with others. The children incorporated this belief and functioned in school with a fear of bringing others into the family. Throughout childhood, they did not mix socially outside school with their peers. If they tried, their mother would become distraught. Her fear of reprisals, both from her and from others, prevented the children being free to fully explore their world. While the children did receive new information – through school experience they learned that local children were accepting of them and did not present a threat – it was not until early adulthood that the children within this family system were able to fully integrate socialising into their lives. The family system, based on cultural context and beliefs, had regulated to serve a function, i.e. to protect children from parentally perceived external threats.

Social Work Application

When we meet with service users in any field of social work, we can consider the family context in which they live and/or grew up. Individual behaviour can most often be linked into family context, whether it be that patterns are repeated over generations or that people make extreme shifts to function in very different ways from those of their family of origin (Byng-Hall, 1995). Successfully integrated experience of the family of origin experience allows individuals to evaluate what worked well, and what not so well, about life with parents/carers and/or siblings. This can facilitate selectivity and openness as to whether behavioural patterns wish to be repeated or rejected from the previous generation in adult life. Where these experiences have not been fully integrated in adulthood, rigid patterns of behaviour often occur, resulting either in repeating or rejecting certain ways of relating. With the Kurz family, it seems that the parents adopted a rigid pattern of organising family life, from the basis that their primary function was to keep children safe from harm that was perceived to be a threat outside of the family home. This rigid pattern did not allow flexibility to accommodate new experience that the local community was a safe enough place to be.

With knowledge of systems theory and how family systems self-regulate, we can begin to be curious about the various factors that influence this regulation. This curiosity can lead us to ask the family questions about parental family experience, cultural context and history. This is a shift from asking only questions that relate directly to the individual who is presented as having a problem. The theoretical basis for asking these questions is drawn in part from psychoanalytic ideas (Chapter 4), where unconscious and uncommunicated beliefs that influence surface behaviour (or behaviour that is seen and acted out) can be explored and integrated into a greater understanding of the self.

Skills Component

- Take into account generational influences on family functioning.
- Allow individuals with presenting problems the opportunity of exploring their family context.
- Gain insight through conversations with families as to how they adapt to new information relating to beliefs held about life and society (or how they do not).
- Facilitate individuals and families to explore their cultural history and how this influences their beliefs and behaviour.

Feedback

Intelligent systems of all forms rely upon feedback from internal and external sources to ensure efficiency in the task being undertaken (Bateson, 1972). Underlying this is the assumption that a system has some 'understanding' of its purpose and function, be that through computer programming or through some form of conscious awareness, such as is collectively held by a group of individuals.

In a family system, internal feedback might be from a parent who does not approve of a child's behaviour in some way, based on their belief system. For example, a parent might discourage a child from eating sweets before meals, believing that this is not a way to good physical health, by verbal feedback or through practical means, such as not making them available. The child will receive the feedback and, if it is clear and consistent, will adapt to this information (Beck, 1970). The values and beliefs held by parents influence children's functioning, and patterns of behaving evolve as 'the norm' within family units. This simplified example of how behaviour is learned draws to some extent on social learning theories that are not directly covered in this book. However, broader notions of the regulation of behaviour within families are explored below.

A further example of feedback that can occur can lead to emotional and behavioural problems in children also demonstrates how families can explicitly and inexplicitly regulate communication patterns in keeping with a set of values or beliefs. An 8-year-old child experiences a form of emotion about an experience that has occurred within the family; for example, a child feels frightened when a father explodes into a rage and is verbally abusive to the child's mother. The child then expresses that fear to the mother, who, not wanting the child to have an unhappy experience of childhood, persuades the child that 'Daddy did not mean it' and states that the child is not really frightened. What has happened is that the child, still at a very formative age developmentally, has had her feelings negated by the mother. The feedback received has invalidated the child's sense of the world. As the child continues to experience life, confidence will have been lost as to the meaning or even the reality of felt emotions, and emotional and behavioural problems in the future become more and more likely. Although this example is of a 'one-off' experience, it is typical that communication styles that offer forms of feedback such as this indicate patterns that are replicated over and over to regulate individuals' behaviours within the family system.

Within the Kurz family, a pattern of feedback was regularly occurring. Anderl, the eldest of the four children, described how as a 7-year-old boy, he had brought home a friend from school. His father had been frostily polite to the child but then left the house. Anderl knew that something was really wrong but did not fully understand what was happening. His mother had seemed agitated and hovered close as the children played outside the family home. When the child left, Anderl's mother broke down in tears and his father did not speak to him all that night. He was told not to bring people back again but not told why. However, he had clearly heard and felt the feedback given to him by his parents and this prevented him from sharing any of his friendships with his family as he grew up. His example to his younger siblings, although not a direct communication to them, also prevented them bringing schoolfriends home. Feedback regulated the family system for almost 20 years until the youngest child had left home. The four siblings knew of each other's friendships at school but a pattern of secrecy developed that functioned to allow them to share friendships but keep them away from the family home.

Social Work Application

As we come to understand the role of feedback, explicit or implicit within families, we begin to develop a greater understanding of how an individual's behaviour and feelings are directly influenced by others. Anderl had received both implicit and explicit feedback that bringing friends back to the house caused his father to withdraw and appear angry, and caused his mother to become frightened and distressed. This also influenced his younger siblings, who learned implicitly that it was not acceptable to bring friends into the house. Moreover, from other forms of feedback not known, we could speculate that discussions regarding friendships would have generated a disapproving response from both parents, confirming to the children that this was not acceptable within this household. Feedback in school would have given the children a different experience of others outside the family and probably generated some confusion for them. Anderl and his siblings formed a sub-system that was closed to his parents regarding friendships. Closed sub-groups within families can often occur when a rigid system that does not respond to external feedback prevents successful integration of holistic life experience. When feedback from external sources overrides any family patterns, such as

(Continued)

(Continued)

with very chaotic families, the system also struggles to function well. The constant behavioural shifts undermine family cohesion and, again, confusion for individuals, especially children, often develops.

When meeting with individuals and with family groups, we can be curious about the feedback that is given to regulate behaviour. This can lead us to enquire about how others respond to a situation in a family and how others might be feeling/what others do (see circular questions below). Exploring how each family member reacts to an event will often illuminate the feedback that individuals in families give other individuals. This then can open a door to seeking understanding of meaning within families that can then lead back to the underlying beliefs and values that shape each person's behaviour. With Anderl, we might be curious as to what happened the next time he thought about bringing a friend home, or what happened if a schoolfriend asked him to his/her home. It is likely that some of the feedback that Anderl received when he brought home his friend at age 7 would have been internalised to serve as a form of map that would guide him with what to do if the opportunity to meet with friends out of school occurred again. This internal map would then remind Anderl of the likely response of his parents to friendship and so regulate his behaviour. This would explain why Anderl, or his siblings, never brought home friends again.

Skills Component

- Explore feedback given by family members to an event or behaviour pattern that causes concern by involving all family members in offering their view.
- Enquire about the feelings and behaviour of each individual in the family around a specific event.
- Seek to understand the beliefs regarding the behaviours of each individual regarding a specific event.
- If working with one family member, explore his/her beliefs regarding the reactions of others to an event and his/her understanding of the meaning of that reaction.

Circular Causality

Feedback in family systems is constant and exists in various forms, including verbal statements, body language, tone and facial expression. It can also be found in communication, both explicit and implicit, through observable behaviours and through perception of another's emotional response. Communication can therefore be as much to do with what is not said or who says what to whom, than what is verbally stated. To regulate a family system through feedback, it is necessary that communication flows from more than one direction. It is often therefore circular rather than linear, i.e. communication rarely, if ever, flows from one person to another without any feedback response at all (Jones, 1994). When we act in a certain way towards another person, we perceive their reactions in myriad forms, which help us to evaluate the impact of what we have done or said. All forms of communication generate a response from another, whether it is the desired response or not, and even if the response is to ignore what has been said or done. In turn, the response communicated will be received either consciously or unconsciously as a form of feedback, and a further response will be generated. Responses are based on our belief systems coupled with our emotional reactions to an event.

An example might illuminate the circular manner of communication and feedback further. A child demands of his father that he should be bought a toy in a shop. The father says no, based on his belief that children should not demand gifts and based on his strained finances. The child is not satisfied with this response; he wants the toy and believes he should have it, and so raises the stakes somewhat by screaming. The father, a well-known man in his community, tries to ignore the behaviour, embarrassed at the outburst and believing that others will recognise him and judge him negatively for not having the situation under control. The child screams louder. The father, further embarrassed and wanting to leave the shop to escape the situation, relents, buys the child the toy and leaves. The boy stops screaming, satisfied with the outcome. The father leaves with him, angry and resentful about the boy's behaviour.

Several messages or forms of feedback have been given in this example. The boy has learned that if he screams loud enough and for long enough, the father will concede and retract his 'no'. Either consciously or unconsciously he perceived that his father's resolve was weakening and so persisted with his screaming behaviour, believing that there was a possibility of achieving his desired outcome, i.e. the toy. The father, anxious that continuing with 'no' will escalate and prolong tantrum behaviour, becomes increasingly reluctant to say 'no' in future situations. He starts to believe the boy has behavioural problems. The feedback from the father to the child and from the child to the father has not occurred in a linear form. Rather, the communication has been of a circular nature, each responding to the other's verbal and non-verbal reactions.

Circular causality expands our understanding of interpersonal feedback. The example above could easily be viewed as a linear problem – the child has behavioural problems, the father is doing his best and the child needs some form of individual help that will help him to manage his tempers more easily. With this form of linear thinking, responsibility and even blame becomes wholly attributed to one individual, the child in this instance, even though most forms of behaviour are largely based on interpersonal dynamics. The individual, often a child, becomes vulnerable to labelling with some kind of disorder, if the problems persist and become more extreme. Circular causality instead explains the generation of problems as the outcome of a series of communications between two or more individuals. The problem becomes located in the communication pattern that exists and is perpetuated over time and not wholly within the individual. This does not negate individual responsibility for actions, but instead only highlights that we all react and respond to our environment, including the subtleties of interpersonal relationships.

Where actions of violence and abuse have been perpetrated, it is especially important to retain a perspective where safety and risk minimisation is paramount; albeit interpersonal relationships can be viewed systemically. Circular causality does not preclude individual responsibility for abusive actions (Vetere & Cooper, 2003).

As Anderl came into adolescence, he started to resent the restrictions on socialising only with members of his family. He had learned that this was unacceptable and that somehow his peers presented some kind of threat to his family and so he complied with this rule. His experiences of friendships threatened the myth held within his family that they would be harmed in some way if allowed into the household. However, he had witnessed his parents' reactions to others coming to the door of their home on occasions and had observed the frozen expressions of his parents, indicating their feelings of fear. It was a confusing contradiction for Anderl. He could laugh and discuss his opinions with his friends at school and yet even mentioning a friend would elicit a disapproving reaction from his parents. Anderl harboured rage as he drew closer to adulthood, but had learned not to share his feelings about friendships for fear of reprisals. These rages started to manifest at home. His parents became convinced that this was a result of mixing with others at school and stopped him attending. This fuelled Anderl's anger further. His parents became more reclusive and were anxious about his siblings attending school also. Anderl left home at age 16 and for many years, until a time close to his father's death, had no contact with his family.

Social Work Application

Most often in social work practice we are presented with an individual who is seen to be in need in some way. Through children and family services it is not uncommon to have children and young people presented by their parents/carers with challenging behaviour. In Mental Health Services, it is an individual that is presented with needs. In Criminal Justice Services likewise, individuals who offend attend as the service user. When making sense of problems from a systemic perspective, we would only view the individual with the presenting problems in the context of his or her familial environment. This includes both the physical environment, taking into account levels of deprivation; the cultural context of the family of origin and that of the local community; and the emotional environment, incorporating how families communicate with one another. To successfully communicate with families and with individuals about their families, the concept of circularity is important to understand.

Considering Anderl's presenting problems in the time frame of his early to middle teenage years, these could easily have been pathologised as having

(Continued)

(Continued)

some form of conduct disorder, based on his rages and then his withdrawal from school. Explored from a circular perspective, we can make sense of how Anderl's feelings, his experience and his family's reactions to his experience could result in rages at home. He did respect his parents and their views, which created conflict for him. There was no outlet for the expression of his feelings and for an acceptance of his view of the world, and so these repressed feelings resulted in a build-up of uncontained emotion, frightening his family further. The beliefs held by his parents about the influence of other local young people on Anderl led his parents to interpret his rages as the consequence of victimisation, given that they viewed themselves as kindly and protective parents. While Anderl decided to share these experiences in adulthood, he acknowledged that a facilitator to assist him and his family to make sense of these experiences in his early teens would have helped him not to flee the family, a decision he regretted after the death of his father. Communicating therapeutically with families involves facilitating the members to gain insight into the beliefs and behaviours of others in a respectful way, with a view to co-constructing, i.e. rebuilding together, a different meaning to events and creating opportunities for alternative outcomes.

Skills Component

- View presenting problems in the context of family communication and behaviour, social and cultural context.
- Explore the beliefs of each individual in a family about a problem.
- Explore the meaning ascribed to communication and behaviours by each family member.
- When working systemically with individuals, enquire about family beliefs and *perceived* meaning ascribed by others to events.
- Avoid taking a critical stance regarding any position, risking marginalising one or more family members.

Homeostasis

This term is taken from biological references to the maintenance of equilibrium in a system. The 'status quo' in a family, a term to which we often refer, is maintained by a series of norms generated from patterns of relating and behaving that are both expected and acceptable within a family. Homeostasis, or status quo, is achieved by the regulating aspect of interpersonal relationships in the maintenance of patterns of behaviour and the resistance change (Bateson, 1972). It comes in the form of circular communication: feedback and behaviours that are responsive to the actions of family members. These responses serve as forms of communication to inhibit the introduction of behaviours that fall out of the range of acceptability.

For example, a child breaks an ornament in temper. The child's parents decide that she must pay for the ornament and her pocket money is withheld until the replacement is purchased. The parents respond to the unacceptable behaviour and the child, through this feedback, learns that the behaviour is unacceptable. The behaviour has resulted in undesirable but explicit feedback for the child and so the behaviour is regulated. A non-aggressive status quo within the family is generated and maintained through these means. A less explicit example of homeostatic regulation might be where a boy becomes tearful when watching a sad film with his family. The family might react to his tears by ignoring him but then later making generalised comments that 'boys who show emotion are weak'. The communication could shame the boy into withholding his tears in the future, regulating male affect within the family by implicit means. These examples relate to internal family processes. However, families also interact individually and within a group with others, such as members of the local community.

The level of openness in a family system, i.e. the extent to which external factors influence the patterns of behaviour within a family, will determine the ability of the family to adjust to changes in circumstances and then establish a new form of homeostasis. In families that function well, being able to manage a crisis and then adapt their behaviour to meet the needs of each of the individuals, a balance of openness is achieved. These families can receive new information and react accordingly, while having some boundaries that allow homeostasis, or some form of norm regulation, to be established. Family members then remain aware of expectations and limits of acceptable and desirable behaviour. In contrast, when a family system is either too closed or too open, patterns become either too rigid for adaptation to changes, such as crises or changes through the lifecycle, or too flexible, resulting in chaotic, unpredictable behaviours.

Rigid family patterns might have established homeostasis within the system, but problems occur as individuals are restricted in personal growth (Minuchin, 1974). For example, a child living with two parents might have experienced a secure and loving environment and have had no problems until pubescence. As the child becomes a young person, the parents will need to adapt to biological changes in the lifecycle and the social changes that achieving adolescence brings. If the parents cannot adapt to these changes, behavioural and emotional problems are likely to emerge in the young person as conflict between social roles, such as peer expectations, and familial roles arise. Unless parents can adjust, changes in the young person's needs are likely to be resisted through verbal and behavioural communication, and unconscious rules. Homeostasis is maintained but the family system is no longer functional to meet each member's needs.

Extreme flexibility within families, where the rules of expected conduct either are not present or continually change, equally leads to problems. A level of homeostasis is necessary for a sense of security and identity to be established. However, when patterns of behaviour are in flux, predictability diminishes and distress among family members can occur. For example, a child living with two parents where the household is open to visitors day and night, and where routines are generally not in place, inevitably leaves the child feeling anxious and uncontained (Levy, 2000). The impact of many people influencing daily family life results therefore in a lack of stability that does not fit with the developmental needs of babies, children and young people (Holmes, 2001).

For most of Anderl's childhood, a rigid status quo had been maintained in the family, and 'outsiders' were not allowed to visit the home. The myth held by the parents, that to protect their family they needed to keep a distance from local people who were prejudiced against them, was not open to adaptation from external feedback. Offers of friendship were viewed with suspicion and rejected. The four children had learned not to challenge this family pattern, otherwise the parents would recruit behaviours that would maintain this order: the father would withdraw and become emotionally unavailable and the mother would become distraught. Anderl had found these reactions extremely uncomfortable and so he learned not to push these boundaries, which prevented his parents becoming distressed. Homeostasis had been established and was maintained by parental behavioural responses to non-conformity.

Social Work Application

Social workers in children and family services often meet with families who function in a chaotic manner and where children exhibit behaviour problems that are visibly extreme. Using knowledge of systems theory and of the concept of homeostasis, the target for change would be the parents, who would need to develop a less chaotic system of behavioural controls and a less open environment so that children are not exposed to many different and unregulated influences. Chaotic families are often more easily visible than ones where the regulation of behaviours is rigid. At an extreme, rigid family patterns could be a result of controlling and aggressive parenting, whereby a child might present as timid and fearful of others. Less extreme might be caring and protective parents who struggle to adapt to changes either in circumstance or in needs according to the lifecycle. For example, a child might present with behaviour problems, but, on initial presentation, the family could appear extremely caring and organised people who live without the problems that poverty and deprivation can bring.

Giving thought to homeostatic functioning could reveal that the parents had not been able to adapt to changes in the lifecycle and become rigid and unable to adapt to change, i.e. a young child becoming more independent than during infancy, or a young person maturing towards adulthood. This occurs for

(Continued)

(Continued)

many reasons, often linked to parental fears of separation and loss. The child might be struggling to adapt to changes but restricted from doing so by parents who are also having difficulty with change.

For adults, implicit and masked forms of communication within families of origin are often linked to mental health problems in later life. In adult services, we are often working with individuals as the primary target for change. However, incorporating exploration of earlier family functioning into social work practice can enable a shift in unconscious factors that influence behaviours to more conscious awareness that can facilitate change. Using therapeutic family work is not only useful for children.

With Anderl, his parents had a fixed belief that local people would not accept them and would respond to them with violence and contempt. This belief was based on the atrocities they had witnessed during World War II but it did not apply to their current situation. However, their fear was so great that it led to extreme rigidity in one aspect of life – socialising with others. Although this rigidity applied only to one aspect of life, it was such an important one that it generated anger and resentment for Anderl, to the extent that he fled the family for a different style of life. On the surface, it could have appeared that the problems were located in Anderl, that he had anger problems and that he needed anger management to change his behaviour. However, using a family and systemic approach to communicating with families, we would be more interested in the way in which communication occurs, what it is about and the beliefs that drive these forms of communication.

Skills Component

- View individual presenting problems in the context of family functioning.
- Explore with families the ways in which behaviour is regulated and how they adapt to changes.
- According to the age of the person presenting with a problem, explore lifecycle matters that could be in conflict.
- Track the course of behaviour problems to establish whether patterns emerge in relation to when problems occur, with whom and in relation to what.
- Through tracking problems, encourage families to consider the beliefs and myths they might hold regarding individuals and situations.
- Accept the beliefs of families but, through conversations with family members, gradually introduce curiosity as to how these beliefs fit with lived experience.

Internal and External Influences on Family Systems

To begin to make sense of the various factors that impact upon family life and therefore the nature of family relationships, gaining some insight into contributing social and cultural influences, including lifespan matters, can be useful. Dallos and Draper (2000) separate internal and external influences.

Internal influences on the family include the make-up of the family group and the roles ascribed to each individual, incorporating age, gender and birth order, sibling sub-groups, alliances within the family and attachment relationships. External influences relate to social policy, socio-economic status, cultural beliefs and expectations, extended family members, peers, school, leisure activities, among others. The complexity of potential influences combining to shape family life and, for counselling purposes, the family dynamic is clear.

Given the above wide-ranging influences contributing to the family dynamic and thus to individuals' behaviours, a counselling approach to resolving conflicts requires some understanding of these factors, the combination being unique to each family group. This search for understanding is often referred to as an assessment, in social work terms. However, thought should be given as to who needs to understand what. It is often possible for workers meeting with families to draw together an analysis of the various influencing factors that seem to generate and maintain a problem, referred to as a 'formulation' in family therapy. The more difficult task is to manage the analytical process while engaging and empowering members of a family to come to their own understanding and then move towards change. This task brings us to the heart of using counselling skills with families.

There had been many contributing factors to the genesis and maintenance of the Kurz family system. The family had left Bavaria for the hope of a different life in Scotland. World War II was fresh in people's memories and acceptance of cultural diversity was not a typical topic of conversation. The parents had lost their high hopes of a better life in a different country because of the anxiety that overwhelmed them regarding the enormity of their decision. Their cultural identity had been threatened, in a way that they had not expected, by moving home. Driven by anxieties, the parents had tried to protect their children from imagined harm by others but inadvertently were restricting their social development. Their strongly held beliefs about the atrocities that members of one culture could inflict on another were projected onto a local community that initially had accepted and welcomed them. Their reclusive behaviour had eventually generated suspicion from other community members and had led to a wary distance being kept from them. The children, as Anderl

(Continued)

(Continued)

described, suffered great distress but would not share this with their parents. The parents could not understand Anderl's hostility to them when they believed that they had acted in his best interests. They gave meaning to his behaviour by attributing the blame to his mixing with local people in school and so became more restrictive of him, amplifying his anger and frustration. Later, as an adult, Anderl was able to make sense of the internal and external influences on the family and became more forgiving of his parents' reactions. After his father's death in the late 1990s, Anderl and his mother had a session with a social worker where these factors were more openly discussed.

Social Work Application

As part of communicating with families for assessment and for using counselling techniques with a view to intervention for change, we can assist individuals and their families to track the influence of external factors on their lives. The art of this approach is to be able to seek permission to explore various influences and then to pace any conversation to match that of the family and of their understanding.

With the emphasis on assessment in social work practice, we are often pushed to provide insight into an individual's behaviour for legal purposes, such as for reports required for court and for Children's Hearings in Scotland. If our involvement with an individual or a family is to bring about some form of change, then developing grand hypotheses as to what is influencing whom, without the agreement or understanding of the individual or the family, is unlikely to be successful. There always remains the debate as to whether a situation is 'good enough' to be tolerated while engagement and slow changes occur. In child protection work, in the field of criminal justice, in working with people with severe mental health problems or physical health problems where there are risks to either the individual themselves or to others in the family or community, a therapeutic approach must often be overridden by more direct forms of intervention. This might include the removal of an individual to an environment where harm to self or others can be minimised. However, where the situation is 'good enough' or has become 'good enough' for slow change to be tolerable, helping families to make sense of the influences on their behaviour can bring about long-term adjustments in many instances.

For understanding to be sought regarding problems and how they are maintained and repeated, social workers can draw upon therapeutic pace to match that of families. If we try to impose our understanding of influences on family life, this can meet with resistance and appear as if the family are unwilling to make changes. If we work with a family's pace, such as using the cycle of change to facilitate the contemplation of ideas, the process becomes

(Continued)

(Continued)

less of an external imposition and more of a joining between worker and service user (Prochaska & DiClemente, 1984; see also Chapter 8). A mutual goal of shared understanding can be generated to form the core of a working relationship. Moving from data collection regarding family events and experiences, towards attributing meaning and then outcomes of these experiences can assist families to make sense of their lives and therefore their behaviour within the family. Counselling skills in this instance refers as much to pacing the exploration of ideas as it does to the words that we use.

Anderl and his mother spent time following the death of his father reflecting with a social worker on some of the influences that led to Anderl to leave the family. Both Anderl and his mother would have spent many years contemplating the events of the past, either consciously or unconsciously. At the time of meeting with a social worker, they were ready to openly share their experiences and try to make sense of them. It is possible that had this been available to them when Anderl was a young person, they could have been less ready to take the risk of examining family relationships and the influences of world events at the time. When we meet with families whose level of personal insight is less clear than it was for members of the Kurz family, the need for a paced engagement becomes essential. We can enable people to contemplate some of the influences that contribute to the ways in which a family will function, and support them through the move towards change by offering a reliable and respectful service. This is, however, dependent upon adequate resources. If the circumstances indicate that risks to an individual or to others require a more immediate solution, then this needs to be taken before embarking upon therapeutic family intervention.

Skills Component

- Work with families to explore internal and external influences on life experience at a pace that matches their developing understanding.
- Acknowledge that change can be slow.
- Allow families time to contemplate ideas about factors that influence their lives.
- Allow families to contemplate what changes would mean for them.
- Resist pushing families to make changes before they are ready, which inevitably leads to disengagement or 'going through the motions' of a care plan.

Factors Relating to the Lifecycle

All members of a family will be at varying stages in the lifecycle and these stages bring roles and expectations (Bee & Boyd, 2002). In addition to the various burdens and opportunities that changes in the lifecycle can bring, the matter of social and emotional development requires acknowledgement. While western culture brings certain cultural norms regarding development and change within the lifecycle, such as the expectations of degrees of separation from parents during and after adolescence, other cultures do not always follow these same social patterns. As we take lifecycle factors into account, we need to consider them within the cultural context of the family in question (McGoldrick, 1998).

When considering children in a family group, we need to be mindful of their cognitive and linguistic development, according to their age and experiences. Young children are less likely to understand sophisticated use of language and thus meta-communication, communication about communication, can be extremely confusing for them. For example, adults will often use ambiguities with which children can struggle, such as 'I am unhappy with you doing that', yet smile at the child while speaking. The verbal message is very different to the non-verbal message and meaning can be difficult for the child to determine. Is this disapproval or approval for carrying out an act? As young children make sense of the world in concrete and literal terms initially, children confused in this way tend to act out these blurred forms of communication through behavioural or emotional problems. Understanding the forms of communication, such as meta-communication, in which families engage with one another, can help us to make sense of how emotional and behavioural problems might be generated.

It was during the beginning of adolescence that Anderl started to question the family beliefs about the threat of local people. His experience did not fit with the family story. Changes in adolescence moved him closer to independence of thought and action. Anderl could not make sense of his world and he became angry. He could not communicate this to his parents and became angrier still. Inferences that the local people were not to be trusted conflicted with his confidence in the reliability of his peers, many of whom had been schoolfriends for a significant number of years. The stage of his development and the onset of behavioural problems was not a coincidence. As a younger child he had been more reliant on his parents' view of the world but now his own opinions were growing in importance. Soon he would lead his own life as an independent adult and needed his view of the world to make sense to him. This crucial stage in his development was characterised by confusion.

Social Work Application

Whether we work in social work practice with adults or children, lifecycle factors need consideration. For Anderl, adolescence highlighted his emotional conflict between his experience and the views of his parents. Lifecycle

(Continued)

(Continued)

transitions are relevant to be taken into account across the lifespan. For example, separating from parents in a move towards independence; retiring from a lifelong career, etc. Additionally, sexuality and parenthood for people with learning disabilities has long been debated in social work, as have the experiences of parenthood that coincide with the re-emergence of sexual abuse trauma. Older adults moving towards retirement and the social changes it brings often requires a huge adjustment. In all of these transitions, emotional adjustment or emotional conflict can be played out through behavioural interactions with others but are most often experienced within families. When undertaking a therapeutic role with families, we can be mindful and then curious with families about the impact of lifecycle transitions that might be occurring and the perception of gains or losses as a result.

Skills Component

- Be curious about lifecycle transitions in families, especially in relation to presenting problems.
- Facilitate discussions with families regarding the meaning of transitions.
- Consider the appropriateness of having children present for all discussions, i.e. the details of the impact of sexual abuse trauma on a parent might not be best discussed in full with children present.
- Develop therapeutic conversations that consider the past, present and future to generate a greater understanding of potential losses and gains of lifecycle transitions.

Techniques used in Systemic Family Therapy

This chapter draws upon techniques taken primarily from Carr (2000), Dallos and Draper (2000) and Pote and colleagues (2000). Carr provides a framework for assessment of the circular nature of behaviour and communication that occurs within families. As in social work practice, the emphasis is on taking theoretical concepts and applying them to live family situations through a process called tracking. Families present to social work services either with their own ideas about an identified problem, or following a referral by someone who believes there is a problem within the family. Tracking problems in detail can assist the service users and the worker to gain insight into who does what, and when, in response to problematic behaviour. Formulating problems into hypotheses about causal and maintaining factors within family relationships, i.e. relating theory to practice, is an important technique. However, it is only useful if undertaken in collaboration with the family and not formulated about them separately, if the goal of intervention is to promote change through the therapeutic process. Most families become at least defensive if hypotheses are made non-collaboratively.

Empowerment of families to come to their own understanding of how members of the family relate to one another is a key component of present-day family therapy practice. Although more directive family therapy models were predominant in the early development of practice from the 1950s, the current trend for transparent and empowering practice fits comfortably with social work values. This chapter will not include all techniques used by the various schools of family therapy to engage with and promote change with families. Instead, a selection of skills drawn from different schools of family therapy that seem most suited to using counselling techniques with families in a social work context is offered.

Neutrality

In meeting with families where more than one person is present, each person will have a different perspective on the problem. The skill in eliciting these views is to make enquiries in which each person has the opportunity to speak but where the social worker neither agrees nor disagrees with any of the views. This technique is called neutrality (Jones, 1994). It is based on the systemic assumption that individuals within a family group will have a unique experience of the problem. Although this is an important aspect to communicating with families, we remain subjective beings and absolute neutrality is arguably unachievable. However, in striving for this position, we can monitor our behaviour during practice and reflect upon the level of neutrality that we are offering, to avoid bias for or against a family member as much as possible.

Balwant met the McFarland family in the social services interview room. She invited them to share their concerns with her. The father, Mr McFarland, described his 8-year-old son Rory as a 'monster' and said that Rory's troublesome behaviour was affecting the family so much that he wanted 'something done with him'. Mr McFarland stated that Rory's sister Heather, aged 9, was being affected to the point that her schoolwork was suffering. Heather repeated what her father had said about Rory's difficult behaviour. Mr McFarland was threatening to physically injure Rory if Balwant did not do 'something'.

Balwant needed to acknowledge Mr McFarland's distress but not join him in scapegoating Rory nor in defending Heather's position. She used neutrality to listen to Mr McFarland's views in order to validate his feelings, and then to speak respectfully to Rory to let him know that his view was also important. Balwant acknowledged the importance of Heather's school performance to her but did not collude with her to criticise Rory. Rory was able to engage with Balwant to tell her which school he attended and his teacher's name. He was also able to tell her that he did not like getting into trouble and wanted some help. Balwant reflected back a summary of the three points of view, that

(Continued)

(Continued)

Mr McFarland was really struggling with this, that Rory wanted some help and that the problems were also affecting Heather. At this Mr McFarland agreed that the family needed help and apologised for his aggressive outburst. Balwant had succeeded in initially engaging with each family member without taking sides in areas of conflict.

Social Work Application

Remaining neutral in discussions with families does depend on the role and task of a social worker. In child protection work or working with abuse in other forms, remaining neutral could be viewed as condoning a form of behaviour when it is our duty to protect a child. There are obvious problems also within the arena of criminal justice, where within our role is the expectation that we assist a person to reduce offending behaviour. Again we cannot condone certain forms of behaviour that are unacceptable within our society. However, in social work practice our underlying values direct us to be respectful of individuals and to empower people to have more control over their lives. Within the social work role we can separate, to some extent, neutrality regarding people's feelings, vulnerability and marginalisation from unacceptable behaviour that we cannot condone. That is, we can be clear that we do not give approval to certain forms of behaviour that impact on other individuals or communities, but we can listen to and acknowledge individuals' feelings and experience with respect.

Neutrality requires a high level of reflexivity: the ability to reflect on action in practice while we are practising it (Schön, 1991). It can often be difficult not to sympathise with one view in a family over another, according to our own values and experience. As we become more self-aware through ongoing reflection, we can catch ourselves moving from a neutral to a biased stance with families while we are in the process of practising. Developing reflexivity enables us to critique practice in action and adjust our stance while we are still in the situation. In social work practice, we are encouraged to be reflective.

Skills Component

- Listen and acknowledge the view of each individual in a family without taking sides in areas of conflict.
- Summarise different points of view in one statement to highlight recognition of difference and of acceptance of each position without negating others.
- Draw upon reflection about practice and then increase awareness of the stance being taken and of any emerging bias.
- Recognise the limitations of neutrality when the social work role requires a more directive or investigative stance.

Linear Questions

Linear questions are direct questions to one individual within a family group. They allow the worker to obtain specific information, either regarding data collection, such as age or school attended, or about behavioural responses to problems, i.e. what do you do when that happens? These questions are usually best fitting with a counselling approach when they are open rather than closed questions. For example, 'which school do you attend?' is an open question; 'do you go to XY school?' is not. Open questions allow people to provide their own information; closed questions generally generate a yes/no response.

When Balwant tried to empower Rory to participate in a discussion rather than remain marginalised as the family member with the problem, she used open linear questions directed at only him. As these questions regarding more benign topics such as school and friends were only for him to answer and not open to all of the family, Rory was heard. This was timed so that Mr McFarland had not been dismissed in his anger and distress but not left so long that Rory was being ignored. Too soon and Mr McFarland might have left, believing Balwant was not listening to him, and too late might have closed the door to Rory being able to have a voice in the meeting.

Social Work Application

Practitioners in social work will be familiar with using linear questions, open and closed. Moving into useful therapeutic communications generally requires a shift from closed to open questions in order that we are not 'leading' individuals in their opinions or descriptions of events. The skill required to use linear questions in a family-based therapeutic encounter is to time them to meet the needs of an individual, i.e. to directly engage a person in discussion. In families who present with problems, often one family member will be more vocal than others and at times one or more family members will appear to be marginalised. Linear questions in this respect can assist more marginalised family members to contribute to the conversation. There are no rules as to exactly when they should be used. Experience accrued over time and judgement effectively executed, based on practice reflection, provides social workers with greater efficiency in these skills. However, the more structured an interview, the more likely linear questions are to fit with the purpose of the interview. The less structured and the greater the emphasis on deconstructing and co-constructing meanings for families, the more linear questions would be mixed with circular ones, as below.

Skills Component

- Become more aware of the type of questions used in practice through reflection.
- Develop greater use of open questions.
- Use linear questions to gather specific information.
- Empower marginalised family members by directing timely linear questions to an individual to include him/her in discussions.
- Be cautious about overloading an interview with a family with questions, at the expense of effective listening and tolerating silences.

Circular Questions

In contrast to linear questions, circular questions join families in connecting meaning and responses between more than one individual. Pote et al. (2000) provide several examples, categorised into six broad themes of questions: those about another's beliefs or behaviour; those enquiring about alternative perspectives; those about relationships; those that generate definitions; those about possible futures; and those that rank responses. Examples of these offer further insight.

A circular question regarding another's beliefs or behaviour might be 'How do you think Jenny feels when Penny shouts?' or 'What might Jenny believe about what is happening when Penny shouts?' A circular question regarding an alternative perspective could include 'What does Peter think about how Paul gets on at college?' One about relationships might be 'How do the children react when their father leaves home?' A circular question relating to the generation of definitions could be 'When Penny starts crying after she has shouted at Jenny, what does Jenny do next?' Using a circular question to enquire about possible futures could include 'What do you believe Jenny will think about this two years from now?' Circular questions to rank thoughts and feelings might be 'Who becomes most upset when Penny shouts?' or 'Who is most worried about this problem?'

The use of circular questions allows different viewpoints to be obtained about a problem that, on the surface, appears to affect only one or two family members. For example, a parent might assume that one child misbehaving and the parent shouting at her might only impact on the parent, i.e. raise stress levels. Directly asking the child involved for an opinion can often appear to the parent that the worker is siding with the child against her. However, asking other family members can often allow difficult problems to be tracked in a neutral manner, raising awareness of the impact of a form of behaviour on others. The worker can more freely discuss incidents without using a confrontational stance. Clearly in social work practice there are exceptions to this being acceptable, the most obvious being in child protection work. Interviews in this respect would need a more directive approach and the worker, being involved in an investigative process, cannot remain neutral when matters of significant harm are raised.

Circular questions tend to be most successful when used some but not all of the time when meeting with families, and when they are relatively uncomplicated in their nature. Using jargon is rarely, if ever, facilitative for families, and where children are involved, language must be especially simple.

As the interview with the McFarland family progressed, and as Balwant gained a sense that Mr McFarland's high emotional affect was decreasing and engagement with her was increasing, Balwant introduced several circular questions. She asked the family who was most affected by Rory's behaviour. Heather responded that her father was. Balwant asked Heather how she thought her father felt when Rory refused to go to bed. Heather said that her father would think that Rory missed his mother and this would make her father sad. Balwant checked this out with Mr McFarland who appeared surprised by Heather's hypothesis. Balwant then asked Mr McFarland what Heather did when Rory refused to go to bed. He stated that 'She interferes and tries to be a mother to him when she should be doing her homework. Rory gets angry with her and starts to kick out at her. Heather should leave it to me. Rory is bound to miss his mother at bedtime. She used to read him stories, didn't she, Rory?' Rory started to cry and sat on his father's knee. His father responded to him by patting him on his back. Balwant noted the shift from criticising Rory to having some compassion for him, then to including him in the discussion and finally to showing some emotional warmth.

Social Work Application

Using circular questions allowed Balwant some insight into some of the dynamic that occurs within the family. It also gave her some insight into an absent family member, Mrs McFarland, who had died. The family introduced a reference to her without Balwant having asked direct and possibly intrusive questions. Most importantly, it freed up family members to name a significant event that had hugely impacted on each individual, i.e. their loss and their sadness. Circular questions can also free workers to explore a family's way of relating to each other without bombarding an individual with threatening questions, including who reacts to what, when and how. These questions can also enable a conversation to develop between two or more family members in the safety of a meeting, that might not have occurred away from the interview setting.

Thus, using circular questions is a useful technique for social work practice as it allows people the opportunity of seeing and hearing accounts of experience involving their behaviour as others experience it. Circular questions provide feedback from important people with whom there is some emotional connection, which can be infinitely more powerful than feedback from a worker, which is often perceived as critical. This form of

(Continued)

(Continued)

communicating with families requires practice and judgement about timing to be effective. As above, reflection about practice and reflection in action regarding the judicious use of these questions can enable us to develop this skill.

Skills Component

- Use circular questions to explore each individual's reactions to behavioural events in a family.
- Facilitate the use of these questions to enable one family member to interpret the actions and feelings of another regarding a specific behavioural event.
- Incorporate circular questions to empower quieter family members to add their experience of an event to the discussion.

Clarifying Statements

As with other models of counselling, working with families requires the use of clarifying statements to ensure that the worker has understood what the family member(s) were describing. This is most useful when summarising and checking out the meaning of an important point, rather than over-using the technique, where it can become repetitive and appear to the family that the worker is not listening. An example of a clarifying statement includes 'So, after Penny has shouted at Jenny for not doing her homework, Peter shouts at Penny, Penny starts crying and Jenny comes over to comfort Penny. Have I understood what happens?' A further example could be to verbalise the emotional impact of an event, 'It sounds like this is very distressing for all of you'. To be effective, these clarifying statements need to be short enough for each of the family members to follow and should not consist only of the worker's own ideas without reference to significant events that have been discussed or enacted within the room. Also, these statements need to be open to reinterpretation by the family if they do not agree with all of what has been said.

Balwant was immediately struck by the impact that bereavement must have had on the McFarland family. She used clarifying statements to acknowledge their loss but also to make a general link to what appeared to have been a factor in Rory's difficult experience of evening times, his fatigue and irritability during the day and his father's loss of confidence as a lone parent: 'Losing Mrs McFarland seems to be still having a huge effect on all of your family'; 'All of you must miss her very much.' These statements freed up an outpouring of tears. Again Balwant used a clarifying statement: 'You are all still very sad'.

Social Work Application

Balwant used clarifying statements to provide an emotionally holding environment where the family could acknowledge their grief. She provided a temporary secure base (see Chapter 4) for hidden emotions to be given expression. Rory's position within the family quickly shifted from troublemaker to a vulnerable child in need of comfort.

Clarifying statements can be incorporated into any interview to affirm unspoken feelings that seem to be in the room or to check out whether a statement has been understood. In all areas of social work practice, and whether an interview is highly structured or not, clarifying statements can be used. However, in investigative work, these would be limited to checking out that what a worker heard was actually said, rather than including interpretation of meaning, that could be inaccurate.

Skills Component

- Summarise statements and presentation of affect and offer them back to the family in question form.
- Use clarifying statements to check out whether meaning understood from a family/individual's descriptions fits with their intended communication.
- Be aware of the role and nature of the interview before including summarisations of meaning in clarifying statements.

Externalising Problems

Taken from narrative therapy (Chapter 5), externalising techniques can be incorporated into working with families in a low-key manner. This allows a problem to be discussed without attributing blame to an individual. An example of this, following on from Jenny, Penny and Peter above, could be, 'It seems that temper causes problems for all of the family around homework time.' This statement does not criticise behaviour, but only draws attention to the impact of it on the family group. 'Temper' becomes the problem, not Penny or Peter. This technique allows Penny and Peter to retain some dignity while discussing the high level of frustration and anger that occurs around certain times of the day.

Balwant met with the family a second time, where she referred to 'sadness' in an externalised form. She encouraged the family to share with her some of the

(Continued)

(Continued)

ways in which 'sadness' had affected them. Heather told her that sometimes she could not concentrate at school because she would keep remembering things about her mother. Balwant externalised this statement: 'So sadness gets in the way of your school work'. Heather agreed with this. Rory told Balwant that he hated going to bed as he got too upset. Again Balwant externalised this as, 'So sadness gets in the way of your sleep as well.' Mr McFarland started to add to these statements, engaging with this narrative technique: 'Sadness gets in the way of me seeing you to bed sometimes, Rory', and, 'Sadness has made our lives miserable for some time now.' As Mr McFarland and his children shared their feelings in this way, the emphasis on Rory's 'misbehaviour' lessened and 'sadness' seemed to be making way for shared understanding.

Social Work Application

As social workers we are concerned with reducing stigma for individuals in all aspects. Using externalising descriptions can remove stigma from conversations and enable a freer discussion of the impact of either feelings or behaviour on family functioning. Using this technique does not require narrative therapy to be embraced as a model in its entirety. Rather, it can be used selectively to reduce emotional affect in discussions and to enable marginalised members of families to be valued as individuals and not scapegoated as 'problems'. However, this might conflict with a social work role if the aim of the work is to help an individual within a family to take responsibility for a form of behaviour: for example, in working with perpetrators of sexual abuse. In this instance, externalising techniques would not be recommended.

Skills Component

- Selectively name and personify a problem as an object rather than as an intrinsic part of an individual, i.e. temper upsets family life rather than an angry girl upsets the family.
- Work with the family to engage with this idea and then build up a description of its impact on each individual.
- Avoid using externalising problems if the role and task is to assist a person to take responsibility for their actions.

Genograms

Genograms (De Maria et al., 1999) are pictorial representations of family relationships across several generations. They use a system of symbols to depict, for example, male, female, twins and the nature of relationships. They are extremely useful for

The MacDonald Family, 25 December 2004

making sense of cross-generational patterns of problems, such as relating to attachments, gender etc. Genograms should be dated as they only represent a snapshot of generational family patterns for the time at which they were made. Relationships might change over time, children are born and family members pass away. All of these factors would alter the appearance of a genogram. Illustrated above is a simple four-generational genogram where males are represented by squares, females by circles and the family of origin begins at the top with great grandparents, down to the children at the bottom. Close relationships link two persons with a single line, distant relationships with a broken line. Conflictual relationships can be marked with zigzag lines. Parental separation is marked by a break in the connecting line between the parents.

To be most effective as a therapeutic tool, these are best compiled with families, rather than about them retrospectively.

Social Work Application

Using this tool with families can be an effective way of considering who is in the family network and who is close to or in conflict with whom. As the influence of family members for either support or contributing to social isolation permeates all aspects of social work practice, using this tool can allow us to explore the nature of family relationships in greater depth than verbal accounts. It allows each family member to be given consideration, rather than 'the family' being described in global or sweeping statements. Although this chapter makes reference to working with families in groups, the genogram can also be part of practice either for assessment or for ongoing therapeutic involvement with an individual.

Skills Component

- Invite the family or individual to participate in the exercise, allowing them to give permission for potentially intrusive questioning about the family.
- Use large paper, e.g. a flip chart, so that what is being written and drawn is clear and visible.
- Allow people time to tell their story about the individuals and relationships within the family history.

Summary of Key Systemic and Family Therapy Concepts

- The science of self-regulating systems, **Cybernetics** underpins this approach
- Verbal and non-verbal **Feedback**, given and received, serves to regulate behaviour within families
- **Circularity** refers to the continuous giving and receiving of feedback within family relationships
- Behaviour regulated within families and functioning as a set of norms is termed **Homeostasis**
- Families are influenced by internal factors, such as those relating to the **Lifecycle**, and external factors, such as **Social Policy**
- Working with families requires **Neutrality** to allow all members to discuss their point of view. Notwithstanding subjective involvement in working relationships is not possible, however
- **Linear Questions** allow information to be obtained and can be less threatening than open questions for quieter family members
- **Circular Questions** facilitate discussion regarding others' experience of an event
- Using **Clarifying Statements** during interviews with families allows individuals to feel heard and to challenge the practitioner's understanding
- Drawing on techniques from other approaches enables a broad use of skill, e.g. **Externalising Techniques** from narrative therapy
- Map multi-generational family relationships using a **Genogram**

Conclusion

The nature of therapeutic work with families immediately draws our attention to the diverse manner in which 'family' can be constituted. Social workers, with our interest in people and their relationships, meet with service users and their families throughout all aspects of practice. A definition of 'the family' has been purposely avoided to raise awareness of the fluid meaning of the concept, according to individual history, i.e. experience of adoption or fostering, gender, race, culture and sexuality. Perhaps more fitting in social work practice is to remain open to shifting definitions of who is and is not included in the family, according to culture and experience.

This chapter has introduced two components of communicating using counselling skills with families. The first has focused on making sense of the impact of communication on surface behaviour that is visible within families. Developing understanding of the systemic nature of communication and behaviour regulated and maintained through feedback, can provide us with some direction in what we might notice within the family dynamic and what we might be curious about. The second component to communicating with families is the techniques themselves. These techniques are not intended to give a step-by-step guide regarding what to ask a family and when. The skill of pacing and judgement in these matters will only come with experience and time. However, some insight into the different style of questions can broaden our ability to assist families to make sense of their own lives and empower them to make their own changes.

Further Reading

- **Barnes et al. (1999)** offer a critical appraisal of the definition of the family, including race and gender factors relevant to service users and to workers. This book addresses the need for developing awareness of the impact of various forms of oppression on the family and on workers who meet with families in a therapeutic context.

- **Carr (2000)** provides a comprehensive framework of the stages of undertaking family therapy, from initial engagement through to analytical assessment of family functioning and managing the intervention process. This book is useful for social workers in that it offers greater detail about the approaches and techniques of the various schools of family therapy. However, unless one is in an area of social work practice that is primarily therapeutic, it might be only partially relevant.

- **De Maria et al. (1999)** provide many examples of how to integrate the creative use of genograms into therapeutic family work. This includes an overview of the theoretical underpinnings to genograms and a helpful guide to the symbolism and questions that might be asked of families while putting them together.

- **Hoffman (2002)** successfully integrates theoretical and historical components of therapeutic family work with a narrative of her experiences, as family therapy has developed, in an entertaining manner.

8
Using Counselling Skills with Groups

Key Concepts	Key Theorists and Practitioners
• Planning and Environment Priorities	• Tuckman
• Leadership Style	• Prochaska
• Phases in the Group Cycle	• DiClemente
• Stages of Change	
• Transtheoretical Model	

Introduction

The previous chapters have offered various therapeutic approaches to engaging and communicating with service users. This chapter differs in that the context of social work practice has shifted from individuals and families to groups. Group work can draw on a range of different therapeutic schools, many of which are referred to in the preceding chapters. This chapter will focus more on the characteristics of groups and how counselling skills from various therapeutic approaches can be brought into the group process. The aim of this chapter is therefore to introduce group counselling skills to social work practitioners in a way which can be expanded in practice by drawing on different counselling approaches.

Why a Group?

Working with individuals within a group setting introduces a social aspect to the context of a working relationship. It is the membership of the group and participation in the group process that becomes the vehicle for change, rather than the working relationship in one-to-one work. Groups often have a dominating theme, e.g. groups for women or social skills groups for young people, whereas working with individuals is more likely to be a broader and more holistic process. What groups might lack in breadth of assessment or intervention, i.e. including a family or systemic overview, they can bring with focus, e.g. social skills, bereavement etc.

Groups, therefore, offer a 'multi-dimensional experience' (Benson, 2001). This occurs at physical, emotional, intellectual and experiential levels. As part of the physical dimension, members of groups meet 'somewhere'. If the environment does not meet the basic needs of safety, warmth and ventilation, adequate facilities and accessibility, the therapeutic skills of the leader and organiser of the group will be lost. Thus the physical experience of a group sets the scene for experience at emotional and intellectual levels. The emotional experience of a group will relate to feelings about the self, members of the group and group leaders. As relationships develop and conflicts are played out, individuals in group settings each experience an emotional journey that can be helpful and cathartic when working towards change. Intellectual dimensions to group experience require some parameters to be set down prior to committing to participation, i.e. the objectives of the group, the level at which responsibility for group decisions lies and with whom; and during the group process, for ideas to be sought and shared. The experiential component to group work involves the medium of the group as a learning and social environment. Through participation, members might become involved in a wider range of activities than would be typical in their day-to-day lives. Experiential learning can assist in the development of skills and social competence in a controlled environment. Of course, the level of control depends from group to group but the existence of a boundary to the group can provide a degree of safety for new experiences to be had.

Group work practice is based on the premise that people are 'in constant interaction and relationships with others' where 'explicit agreements' are made that allow practitioners to use 'conscious, disciplined and systematic use of knowledge about the processes of collective human interaction' (Benson, 2001). Using this as a definition, this chapter will explore some of the complexities to using counselling skills within groups, drawing on group work theory as a foundation.

Group Work Theory

Using counselling skills within groups requires social work practitioners first to draw on leadership and organisational skills. For a group to come into being, it requires parameters that set it apart from everyday life and some boundaries that help to define its function and purpose, as well as providing emotional and physical safety for members. Practitioners therefore need to give thought to the constitution of a group prior to the commencement of any programme, including characteristics of members: for example, young people, people who have experienced ill health; purpose of the group, for example, what is hoped will be achieved; and type of group, i.e. art therapy group, drop-in group. In considering these factors, the way in which the leadership of the group would best facilitate the group process can therefore be usefully linked.

Six young people between the ages of 11 and 12 were brought together to form a short-term group closed to new members after the start. The young people of

(Continued)

(Continued)

mixed gender had several common characteristics. Each of them came from a socially deprived family background and had been referred by a social worker in a Children and Families setting. In addition, each young person was socially isolated and struggled to make relationships with peers. Some of the young people had had a period of non-school attendance. The group ran for a fixed period of one two-hour meeting per week over an eight-week period. A base was used for the first meeting and for the first 15 minutes of each subsequent meeting. The young people were collected from home after school hours in a minibus and dropped off at home likewise by group leaders at the end of the sessions. As all of the young people and two group leaders shared the minibus journey, this added approximately a further hour on to the time the young people spent in the group. Interactions between group members began as they entered the minibus and ended when they left the bus at the end of the meeting. The aim of the group was to work with the young people on social skills through the medium of experiential learning. As such, the group was activity-based with a theme of 'adventure' for the young people running through the programme.

Social Work Application

Social workers have traditionally used groups for many purposes, with both adults and children. While the group work setting as above could not meet all the needs of the members – for example, access to improved housing or help for parental mental health problems – the group setting could offer a unique environment to test out relationships with peers in a relatively safe setting. Clear limits regarding acceptable behaviour, and reliably consistent leadership set the ground for emotional safety within the group. The group was closed to new members joining the programme after the first week. This allowed some stability that would facilitate the exploration of peer relationships within a social setting. In this instance, an open group might have paralysed group members from taking risks with new relationships, given that each young person struggled in this respect.

The duration of groups for potential effectiveness requires consideration of the purpose and desired outcomes against budgetary and other resource concerns. In this instance, the high demand for youth work services and the limited provision of group places shaped the short-term nature of the group. Arguably, a longer programme might have been more effective in consolidating progress for the young people and bringing about more lasting changes for participants. However, too long and the group programme could have lost momentum and thus become stale. These dilemmas face social work practitioners when trying to maximise resources that invariably are scarce.

Approximately 12 to 15 women were meeting on a regular basis through the organisation of a group for women who had recently experienced mastectomy. The two social workers had initially set up the group in response to a request by the hospital ward for assistance for several women who were struggling to come to terms with their experience of cancer and of major surgery. The group had started with four women attending an out-patient clinic setting within the local hospital. The group met weekly for an hour at a regular time. The structure was informal, with refreshments, soft seating and the opportunity for discussion. The session began with introductions but otherwise the direction of any discussion was unplanned. The group ran as a regular, rolling programme with open boundaries to allow new members to join at any point. The social workers organised their annual leave to ensure that one was always present to allow the group to run as often as possible to maintain continuity. The women took the group discussion in many directions, including family experience and the impact of health problems on employment. Gradually, the women began to explore the emotional impact of mastectomy, although this was not always the principal focus of the sessions every week. As new members joined and left the group, the pace and focus of the interactions within the group shifted towards and away from emotionally charged subjects.

Skills Component

- Identify the purpose of the group, the commonalities of potential participants and anticipated outcomes prior to organising the practical aspects of the group.
- Ensure the environment for meeting is comfortable and without hazards.
- Consider the duration of the group to maximise the likelihood of reaching goals in the context of resource concerns.
- Explore the benefits and potential pitfalls of open as opposed to closed groups.

Leadership Style

The extent to which a practitioner aims to control the group or allow the group to control itself (or self-govern) will determine the leadership style adopted. This will also link to the purpose of the group and the intended outcomes. The theory base of the group will also play a significant part in determining the leadership style. Some groups will require more direction than others. For example, psychodrama uses symbolic exploration of the acting out of defence mechanisms and requires a leadership style that can assist members to make sense of experience in a structured and contained environment. This need for structure and emotional containment does not demand that responsiveness is abandoned to provide rigid controls. On the contrary, without responsiveness, a psychodrama group could not function. However, the group is managed in such a way to provide specific direction with the aim of facilitating enactment of internal impulses. 'In psychodrama the client (the protagonist) controls the action and the therapist (the director) uses skill and creativity to facilitate the action' (Bannister, 1991). Thus leadership is a necessary skill in this form of therapeutic group process.

Lang (1972) provides a continuum of leadership to group-member-controlled groups, moving from leader-controlled (allonomous) groups to shared-control (allon-autonomous) groups to member-controlled (autonomous) groups. Leader-controlled groups, as above, does not equate to rigid and unresponsive management, but to a high level of responsibility for and/or structure of the group that is linked to its purpose and function. Brown refers to levels of power and authority that are inherent to the social work role, which by default brings most groups in social work settings under some form of leadership control, if only by virtue of the fact that the group would not exist without social work intervention. The power and authority inherent in the social work role as group leader does not, however, automatically result in the behaviour of members within a group being controlled by the leader. Thus the leadership style chosen by the social work practitioner needs to be matched with the intended outcomes for the group without denying the power and authority of the social work role.

Dixon (2000) explores 'What kind of groups and for whom?' Outlining groups for people involved in the criminal justice system, Dixon makes reference to groups that are structured to offer problem-solving skills, drawing on cognitive behavioural approaches. While this type of group would require a leader-controlled structure, other less prescribed groups constituted for a specific purpose. For example, groups to assist sex offenders with rehabilitation call for a high level of leadership skill in holding 'emotional tensions surrounding the discussion of sexual and violent offending while facilitating the enabling process'. Chapter 4 describes some of the skills required to provide an emotionally holding relationship and these can be applied to the group setting. Leadership style in relation to control exercised within groups and leadership skill are not therefore synonymous. A highly skilled worker able to hold and contain 'emotional tension' might facilitate a largely autonomous group. Equally, a worker might compensate for a lack of confidence in skill by choosing a more controlling leadership position than the function of the group calls for. Fear of losing control is one of many contributing factors that can lead to this occurring (Brown, 1994) and can inhibit the development of ownership and peer relations within a group. A worker might intervene in the group process either prematurely or unnecessarily. To reflect upon the group process sufficiently to make this judgement, however, requires a high level of skill from a practitioner that is not always visible to the untrained eye. To develop this skill, knowledge of group processes and conflict within groups is required.

The social skills group of six young people required the group leaders to take an authoritative stance, emphasised more during the first session and during the 'pick-up' routine in the minibus. This authoritative stance allowed the group leaders to set firm limits for acceptable behaviour – an experience with which, out of the school environment, many of the young people were unfamiliar. However, as the group progressed through the programme and as the young people became more accepting of the boundaries around acceptable behaviour, the young people were encouraged to make more decisions as a group. These decisions included the organisation of the mid-session snacks, choices between activities for the latter two sessions and the form and location of an 'end of group' outing. Other responsibilities were gradually given to the young people, including input into the management of the budget for the group. As these responsibilities were gradually increased, the group members had the opportunity to explore their levels of competence and make 'safe' mistakes without dire consequences. As their confidence and competence increased, so did the level of ownership for the group.

Social Work Application

Leadership style that is effective for groups is determined by the needs of the group, the anticipated outcomes, and the ability of group members to manage their behaviour towards other members and themselves. Ideally, practitioners working with groups in social work practice require a repertoire of skills that allow flexibility to respond to the needs of various types of groups. Flexibility in leadership style refers to the ability to make informed judgements regarding the needs of a particular group and respond accordingly. While some flexibility was used with the social skills group, the leadership style remained firm in respect of setting limits for behaviour and keeping to time, this being appropriate for young people for whom the social workers had a level of responsibility while temporarily in their care. Had the leadership style been so flexible that the young people were denied the experience of consistency, increased ownership of the group by members would not have occurred as the members would have experienced a degree of chaos. This chaos would have inhibited the process of group membership consolidation, leaving group members feeling emotionally unsafe. However, if the group leaders had remained rigid in their leadership style, the group members would have been denied the opportunity to develop responsibility and social competence.

The social workers leading the women's group took responsibility for several matters relating to the group. They ensured that the room was booked and available weekly, they organised their time to both attend as often as possible and arranged for refreshments to be provided. One of the social workers would facilitate introductions and then the time would be metaphorically 'handed over' to the members to use as they wished. Occasionally, members became frustrated with other members and the group process would become 'stuck'.

(Continued)

(Continued)

At these points the leaders would facilitate the exploration of the group process with the members regarding the matter 'in the room'. This required them to take an observational role to track the group process during the hour, including when the group interaction was flowing unhindered. The leadership style was less directive but with enough of an authoritative stance to intervene in the group process when required.

Skills Component

- Leadership style needs to be attuned to the needs of the group.
- Some flexibility towards less directive stances as groups progress can facilitate increased ownership and feelings of confidence for group members.
- Consistency is required for group members to feel emotionally safe.
- Chaotic or overly passive leadership styles can increase feelings of anxiety for group members.
- Social work practitioners have a responsibility to manage the behaviour of group members and thus need to attune their leadership style in groups accordingly.

Group Process and Group Conflict

Members of a group who come together through facilitation at any level by a leader create 'synthesis'. 'Synthesis', or 'the coming together or combining of parts to make a higher-level whole', according to Benson (2001), 'is the primary principle which informs the practice of the creative group worker'. The group leader(s) and members join to create both 'unity and diversity' during the group experience, which is separate from that of non-group members and maintained by tangible boundaries.

Benson (2001) offers three stages to the group process. The first is her vision of the group as 'a place of formation'. The group members bring their identity and self-awareness to the group process. Through participation as a member of the group as 'a place of reformation', identity and self-awareness become challenged as a result of being faced with a new environment. This can result in regressive behaviour, i.e. behaviours that have previously been used either to cope with change or to relate to other people. Leaders need to understand and manage this rather than obstruct the process, unless behaviour becomes dangerous either to the self or to others. By allowing members to work through these regressive responses to situations, the group becomes 'a place of transformation'. Members learn new ways of relating to others, learn new skills and therefore develop their self-awareness and identity. This is facilitated by the group leader providing a nurturing role comparable to a caregiver nurturing an infant by containing and absorbing high levels of anxiety and protecting the group from outside threats (Barnes et al., 1999).

During the first three meetings of the social skills group, Robbie, who had been excited to be invited to join the group at an earlier interview, displayed several episodes of challenging behaviour. He refused to accept the group rules and related to the group leaders in an aggressive manner. The other members of the group shied away from Robbie. A real risk arose that Robbie would find himself alienated from the other group members and could potentially be excluded from the group on grounds of safety. However, the group leaders recognised Robbie's anxieties relating to participating in a group with very clear boundaries for acceptable behaviour. The group leaders also recognised that the other group members were likely to be equally anxious but were demonstrating their anxieties in a different way. By rejecting Robbie they would be rejecting their own feelings of anxiety that had the potential to move them through a new experience of being an acknowledged and important member of a group of peers. The group leaders spent time with the group, recognising the difficulties of coming together and meeting new people and recognising how 'scary' that could be. The leadership style remained firm. As the group members accepted their own apprehensions, the previously growing animosity towards Robbie decreased. As the group progressed over time, Robbie's behaviour became significantly less challenging.

The theoretical stages of development in group functioning are well known in therapeutic literature and will be briefly outlined here (Garvin, 1974). Groups 'form' (Tuckman, 1965) as a collection of individuals who come together or are brought together either for a common purpose or with characteristics in common. This stage is generally accepted to be a period of high levels of anxiety, which the group leader needs to be prepared for and ready to manage. Challenges to the leadership of the group can often occur at this stage, as can a testing out of group boundaries by behaviour that challenges the group process. Barnes and colleagues (1999) highlight the initial stage of the group as a period of transition from attending as an individual to moving towards becoming a group member. As anxieties are acted out, sub-groups can form where dissatisfaction in respect of the leader can be safely expressed. This serves the function of managing anxiety and of attempting to regain a level of control when members feel emotionally challenged.

The leader an understanding of this process and an ability to sit with the discomfort while maintaining the boundaries agreed at the initiation of the group. As the group leader retains his or her position and does not become either overly rigid in an effort to obstruct the process, or overwhelmed by the process that can result in stepping out of the leadership role, this process of 'jostling' serves as the vehicle upon which group cohesion can be developed.

Once each individual has taken a role as group member and a certain level of safety and predictability is established, the group moves into the 'storming' phase (Tuckman, 1965). Brown (1994) describes this as 'a critical stage in the group's development'. Crucial to the role of group facilitator is the ability to tolerate uncertainty during this period. The group structure remains in a fragile state and can appear to be threatened by active expression of conflict. Various relational processes are at play, whereby anxieties, previous behavioural patterns, individual beliefs about people and groups and displacement of anger through defences generally come to the fore. One member might be scapegoated by the other members when anger and other difficult emotions struggle to be freely expressed. Like a boat crossing a stormy sea, the group leader, aware of the turbulence, needs to develop the capacity to tolerate the discomfort and to raise explicit awareness of some of the potential concerns that could be troubling the group, masked by scapegoating and sub-grouping. The group is addressed as a whole and members are not targeted, to ensure that group cohesion is preserved and not irreplaceably fragmented.

As this process is tolerated and managed by continued consistency, greater intimacy and honesty are developed. The members come to know that the group leader and other members can 'accept and contain aggressive and destructive feelings' (Barnes et al., 1999) and a higher level of experienced emotional security is felt. Thus the storming phase is a crucial but difficult aspect of group functioning, without which transformation and change for the group as an entity and for individuals on a personal level would not occur.

Significant changes to the behaviour of Robbie and of the group as a whole were noticed by the mid-point of the group programme. Robbie had moved from the centre-stage position of challenging the leadership of the group to accepting group rules without difficulty. Nina, however, had become increasingly clingy to one of the female group leaders. At every opportunity, she would attach herself to Charmaine's arm and avoid interaction with the other young people. The five other group members joined together to form a sub-group that began to scapegoat Nina. As Nina experienced their frustrations with her, she clung to Charmaine all the more. Again the group leaders recognised the acting-out of behaviours in the group which were likely to be regressive expressions of previous experience. The group leaders hypothesised that Nina's anxieties regarding the lack of emotional and/or physical availability of her carer(s) would lead her towards clingy behaviour. It was likely that she was replaying this within the group. The group leaders also hypothesised that the other group members might perceive her clinginess as restricting their own access to the group leader and were potentially replaying their own early experience of hostility towards siblings. Again the group leaders discussed with the group the importance of each of them being recognised as important members and their individual achievements to date were verbalised within the group. This acknowledgement appeared to reduce the level of hostility towards Nina and she started to cling less.

Brown (1994) identifies the 'norming' stage of group functioning that follows 'forming and storming'. Whitaker (1995) refers to this as the established phase of a group.

As members develop trust in each other, they become more willing to share more of themselves and become more invested in the group. Members begin to take some ownership of the group. This point of individual and collective responsibility leads a group towards the 'performing' stage (Tuckman, 1965). 'Much performing occurs at the norming stage ... Performing is the point at which the group becomes a largely self-sufficient resource, using all the skills and potential of the members to achieve its aims and solve problems' (Brown, 1994). Leadership skills at this point need to remain consistent enough to allow for emotional security and predictability but also need to be responsive enough to enable the group to mature. Leadership styles initially explicitly in place can become more implicit as the group performs within previously established parameters. However, as setbacks and crises occur, explicit use of consistent leadership authority is often required as the group process briefly re-lives the forming, storming and norming stages.

> By the fifth week, the group members were showing signs of establishment and cohesion. Activities became the primary focus of the sessions and the group functioning received less overt attention. Other than minor matters, the behaviour within the group was generally unproblematic and the level of enthusiasm for adventure activities was evident. Robbie and Nina both made links with other young people and humour became a shared experience within the group. Responsibility for managing the group finance for the week was given to the members, who worked together to ensure that the budget figure, the receipts for activities and the change tallied. All of the members took this responsibility seriously and it served to strengthen the cohesion in the group.

As most groups are time-limited, endings become inevitable and potentially difficult for members. Endings generate feelings of loss and members often wish to resist or defer this inevitable outcome; avoiding endings can be a way for members to cope with the loss of the group. During the norming and performing stages of the group process, the leader becomes less central as the group takes collective ownership and responsibility for its function. During the ending stage, the group leader becomes a more central figure again and skills are required to facilitate this. Benson (2001) identifies the leadership role as one of nurturing anxieties and distress during this difficult period, while maintaining physical and emotional safety through the continued maintenance of clear boundaries and limits. It would not be unusual for members to draw on previous defences to cope with the ending, including regression and denial. On the surface, it might appear to the group leader that the previous successes of the group have been sabotaged by the defensive reactions of group members.

However, awareness of the high level of difficulty for many individuals at this point can help the worker to avoid feelings of frustration and despair. We need to be as aware of our own feelings about the ending of a group as we are regarding the feelings of the members. This insight can allow us to resist moving boundaries regarding the time-limited nature of the group that can arise out of our own wish to avoid the sadness experienced in separations in general. By working with the group towards the physical and emotional separation of an ending, members can be enabled to resolve ambivalence and look towards the future. Avoiding endings denies members of groups this opportunity.

The seventh group meeting had been challenging for the group. Although the group activity went ahead, conflict arose between Robbie and Wesley, a young man who had been one of the quietest group members. During the ride home in the minibus, the conflict escalated to the point where Robbie put a lighter to Wesley's head and singed his hair. The group leader sitting in the back of the minibus managed to control the situation by separating the young people and removing the lighter from Robbie. The group members were all extremely distressed. The group leaders reflected at the end of the 'drop-offs' that Robbie especially was probably really struggling with the ending of the group the following week. It was after a discussion about the final 'end-of-group' activity that this incident took place. The leaders recognised that Robbie had again taken the role of expressing anger and disappointment on behalf of himself and the rest of the group, linked to the forthcoming loss of the group (and other unresolved losses that they were likely to have experienced). Robbie's extreme behaviour had to be considered in the light of safety for the group as a whole. With regret, the leaders stopped Robbie from attending the final activity, to facilitate risk management.

As Robbie had known from the beginning of the group that such displays of aggression would lead to exclusion, and as he had coped with group rules for the majority of the sessions, the leaders surmised that his behaviour served to allow him to avoid that which he feared the most, the group ending. He had experienced a level of emotional safety enough to allow him to trust and therefore 'hand over' the leadership responsibility to the group leaders. As the loss of this emotional safety loomed closer, he reverted to previous coping behaviours that allowed him to feel more in control. Understanding this process enabled the leaders to manage their own feelings of disappointment as the once highly successful group came to an end.

Social Work Application

The group process elicits emotional and behavioural responses from leaders and members throughout the duration of a group. Group leaders in social work practice are required to manage the balance between meeting the needs of individuals within a group and manage risk. Working with children and young people introduces further responsibilities for the welfare and protection of

(Continued)

(Continued)

those in our temporary care. To facilitate a group effectively, a broad range of skills are called for, including communication skills to listen in a genuine and congruent manner, as well as an understanding of the group process and likely emotional and behavioural responses that can present as conflict.

In a social work setting, we are generally concerned with the social and emotional development of those with whom we work. Activities to occupy a group are not enough to effect change. The role of the group leader to facilitate the change process is thus crucial to the overall effectiveness of the group in influencing the domains of life that exist for members away from the group setting. It is also difficult to measure the direct impact of the group experience in a qualitative way, as often the core beliefs (see Chapter 3) held by an individual about themselves and their world are not explicitly definable, especially during the formative years of childhood and adolescence. However, we might anticipate that each experience that transforms the core beliefs and assumptions made about the self and about others would ultimately have some impact upon social relationships in later life.

Skills Component

- Anxieties experienced by the group as a whole are often displayed through the behaviour of a member taking a central role.
- A member taking a central role risks being scapegoated by the rest of the group if acknowledgement of their own anxiety is difficult.
- Group leaders can facilitate the group process by acknowledging the experience of the whole group, freeing members to experiment with, rather than resist, a different experience.
- Communication skills are required alongside an understanding of group processes for practitioners to assist members through transitional group experiences.
- Endings are often difficult and evoke emotional responses linked to previous unresolved losses, including the loss experienced as a result of unresponsive and/or rejecting care by parent(s) or carers.
- A practitioner's primary function is to emotionally contain anxieties within the group in the same manner as a parent/carer would contain anxieties for a child.
- Consistency, reliability and firm responsiveness to the group process enables high anxieties to be emotionally contained.

Stages of Change

Members of groups generally come together because they wish to bring about some form of change in their lives. It might be that statutory agencies demand a change to lifestyle and behaviour and it is this that brings a member to a group. The degree of success of bringing about change for people will be linked to their level of motivation and engagement with the group process. Many factors alongside and intertwined with the group process make change possible. Unless various external matters are tended to, such as providing a safe and reliable environment, anxieties of members can continue to trigger defensive coping mechanisms and, as a result, change can be blocked.

Timing for individual members is also crucial to the change process. If the group is ill-timed for a member, then change that can be maintained becomes less likely. The engagement process for inviting individuals to join a group becomes especially important in this respect. It is during this engagement phase that individuals can be given the opportunity to consider the potential of the group and thus the seeds are sown for active participation and fruitful change. Forcing this stage is unlikely to produce positive results. As individuals are pushed further than they are ready, their defences and automatic patterns of thinking and behaving are evoked and the change cycle closes down.

Transtheoretical Model

Prochaska and DiClemente (1984) developed a model of change based on a period of research. The transtheoretical model considers motivation to be the most important factor when measuring the likelihood of sustained changes over time. This model outlines five 'distinct' stages of change before alternative behaviours become more typical patterns than previous, socially undesirable behaviours.

1. *Precontemplation*: Not seeing a problem
2. *Contemplation*: Seeing a problem and considering whether to act
3. *Preparation*: Making concrete plans to act soon
4. *Action*: Doing something to change
5. *Maintenance*: Working to maintain the change

Depending on the nature of the group, the group members might be at a stage of contemplation or even preparation in bringing about change in their lives. If so, they are likely to respond well to the group processes discussed above, although anxiety about change and about the group process is still likely to be high. If group members attend a group because of statutory requirements *and* as individuals they do not believe they have a problem, it is likely that they would be in a precontemplation stage of change and, without focus on exploring this, engagement with the group process could be difficult. Change that is maintained over time is even less likely to occur at this point.

Velasquez and colleagues (2001) emphasise the need for practitioners to be 'doing the right thing at the right time'. As we raise our awareness of the change process, we can work with individuals prior to participation in a group to attempt to make sense of which stage of change they are in. If the group is an action-oriented group, then including people who are at the precontemplation stage of change is unlikely to assist them to make sustained changes. However, a group that is designed to allow members to consider specific behaviours and/or circumstances relevant to them and the meaning of these for themselves, for other individuals and/or for society, might enable a person to move into the contemplation stage of change and, in time, beyond.

The women's group began to discuss the meaning of breast cancer and of mastectomy to them. All of them had experienced change through surgery that had left them needing to make emotional adjustments to life as a woman with the loss of a breast. The women had been selected for the group on the basis that they recognised the emotional impact of their recent experience and wished to explore this with others in a similar position. This recognition of the need for an emotional adjustment included elements of grief for their loss. Women who had had a mastectomy but did not believe that there was an emotional adjustment to make were not pushed to attend the group. The group facilitators believed that they were probably in the precontemplation stage of change and not ready to explore the emotional impact of a mastectomy.

Those who did attend the group were in different stages of change. Some were still contemplating whether to explore factors such as femininity, body image and the results of pharmacological treatments for cancer. Others were in the action stage of change and would push the discussion towards subjects that others found difficult. Depending on who attended the group at any given time, the focus of the discussion changed. As women found themselves adjusting to their situation and accepting their body post-surgery, some would continue to attend the group on an ad hoc basis and others disengaged from the group. Two group members continued to attend and offered emotional support to other group members. It appeared that continuing links with the group allowed them to maintain the emotional changes they had made. What had seemed to work for the group was the timing of invitation to attend. Those who did attend were ready to begin to think about the impact of breast cancer and were not further traumatised by well-meaning but untimely coercion to address fears before they were ready.

Social Work Application

Often we can find ourselves caught in the dilemma of providing services at the request of other agencies or statutory bodies when the individuals concerned are not emotionally ready to make the change in question. The 'customer' for the service is often not the service user (Carr, 2000). When facilitating groups in social work practice, this is an important element not to be overlooked. The old saying, 'You can take a horse to water but you cannot make it drink' has particular relevance here. For groups to be positive and transforming experiences for people, the timing is crucial. Depending on the purpose of the group, it could be useful for groups of people to come together in the contemplation stage of change to explore the possibilities if action is later

(Continued)

(Continued)

taken, and the consequences if it is not. Health-promotion services often target people where there is no belief that a problem exists or when people are in a precontemplation stage of change. However, in social work practice, unless statutory measures are used to ensure attendance at a group, engagement becomes extremely difficult with people who do not believe that a problem exists or that there is anything that they wish to change.

For those forced by statutory measures to attend a group, leaders need to adapt their expectations of outcome accordingly. The best that might be attained for someone bound to attend a group, with no motivation of their own, is contemplation of change or raised awareness of the impact of their behaviour on themselves or on others. For groups to achieve a degree of success, the anticipated outcomes need to be matched against the stage of change of the potential group members. As motivation towards change increases, the degree of success in meeting tangible outcomes increases accordingly. Including a mix of people at different stages of change can also increase the likelihood of change being contemplated and acted upon through peer relationships. 'Drop-in' groups and open groups are especially well matched to this model.

Skills Component

- Consider the stage of change of each individual identified to attend a group.
- Match the desired outcomes of the group with the level of motivation of individuals prior to the commencement of a group programme.
- Include individuals contemplating change with individuals planning to act towards change, to assist with motivation.
- Exploring potential individual motivational factors at the planning stage of a group increases the likelihood of achieving desired outcomes.

Summary of Key Concepts for using Counselling Skills within Groups

- Groups offer a **Multidimensional** learning experience
- Facilitators of groups **Emotionally Hold** the anxieties of members in groups in a manner similar to an infant with a caregiver
- The **Group Process** takes members through transitions that can be difficult and subsequently resisted until anxieties are addressed

(Continued)

(Continued)

- **Group Cohesion** occurs as initial anxieties are **Contained** and **Managed** within the group
- The group goes through stages of **Forming**, **Storming**, **Norming** and **Performing**
- These stages are not fixed and **Setbacks** occur that move the group to repeat these stages, often several times
- **Endings** can be difficult for group members and can trigger experiences of previous unresolved losses
- Group members are often **Ambivalent** about endings, bringing a mixture of achievement and sadness
- Group facilitators need to **Contain** their own and group members' feelings by remaining responsive, consistent and reliably available
- **Motivation** to change needs consideration at the planning stages of a group to maximise the potential of achieving **Desirable Outcomes** by the end of the group

Conclusion

Groups in social work practice require effective use of counselling and general communication skills comparable to working with individuals or with families. Using counselling skills within a group setting calls for additional skills and knowledge, however. Group facilitators balance the needs of individuals with the needs of the group as a whole entity when managing conflict. Considerations regarding the safety and comfort of the group environment assist members to feel safe enough to explore relationships and activities as part of groups, without which even the most effective use of counselling skills is likely to be ineffective. The group process, regardless of the function of the group, typically results in regressive behaviour that needs to be understood by the social work practitioner as functional to the eventual cohesion of the group. The role of the group facilitator is to 'hold' the group together while conflicts are resolved and anxieties are played out. As the group facilitator offers emotional containment to the group and provides a safe enough environment to protect the group from external hazards, the group is enabled to 'perform'. This requires the group leader to be insightful about group dynamics, consistent and responsive in the leadership style adopted and aware of his/her emotional responses within the group.

Using group work as a medium for change, individuals' perception of 'problems' and motivation to change needs exploration prior to 'forming' the group. As anticipated outcomes are matched with individuals' readiness to make changes, the focus of a group can begin to be formulated. Clearly, the planning of group work is crucial to its success or failure.

Further Reading

- **Velasquez et al. (2001)** offer a detailed outline of techniques and methods that enable practitioners to work with the change process within a group setting. The book is targeted at substance abuse but has a general theoretical base and can be applied to other settings when thinking about change of high-risk behaviours.

- **Barnes et al. (1999)** provide readers with a discussion of group processes and conflicts within groups, from a psychoanalytic perspective and applied to groups. This book is especially useful for making sense of difficult behaviours within groups and problems with group functioning.

- **Benson (2001)** also uses a psychoanalytic basis for group work but broadens this to include a wide range of practical steps that can be taken to enhance the effectiveness of the group process.

- **Brown (1994)** incorporates a social work perspective into his classic text. This book offers a solid foundation to understanding functioning within groups.

Conclusion

There are many different therapeutic schools which offer a foundation for using counselling skills. These various schools often share common themes, although descriptive language for the concepts and techniques are different. Readers will notice the many parallels that exist between the different approaches. The working relationship or therapeutic alliance is fundamental to all models, as is the need to provide service users with a degree of security and reliability. Each school of counselling or therapy that is included within this book draws upon a theory base: and as social work practitioners we also can draw upon a theory base to increase the range of counselling skills that we use in communicating with service users. Knowledge-based practice does require a certain level of scientific rigour and this cannot be completely ignored within social work. We depend upon the research and theoretical developments of other disciplines to shape the direction of our work in many areas. This is certainly the case with developing our counselling and communication skills.

However, crucial to social work is the fundamental priority of considering value positions first and foremost. We recognise that values underpin our practice. As we develop our understanding of the inequalities that lead to oppression in our society, we also recognise that communication, whether using counselling skills or not, will always be biased as a result of our individual history and social position. With this in mind, the first chapter on multicultural counselling skills is important in putting communication into a social context.

Social work practice not only demands an understanding of theories about communication, but also theories in respect of child development, sociological and political concepts, matters relating to physical and mental health, the legal system and the complexities contained therein, as some among many. Thus scientific rigour is not enough for one to become an effective and a responsive practitioner. The use of the self in working relationships is perhaps the most fundamental aspect of practice as it is intertwined with our values. This is difficult to quantify in terms of science. Many of the personal qualities that we bring to our work and the dynamic interpersonal factors that exist within working relationships cannot be directed by the use of a manual of techniques. Spontaneity is required to selectively draw upon techniques used in communication in a timely fashion that fits with the needs of the individual, group or family at a given time. This requires, to some extent, absorbing and then 'abandoning' any manual of techniques (Minuchin & Fishman, 1981). As we read about and experiment with new techniques for counselling skills, we increase our understanding and our ability to be skilfully responsive. However, unless we move away from linear application of techniques, we risk becoming 'wooden' practitioners and overly rigid in our working relationships.

Taking science or knowledge-based practice as a starting point, we can develop the art of social work practice by incorporating spontaneity into our day-to-day interactions. That is not to argue that there should be no boundaries to what we do and say; on the contrary, we are usually tightly bound to act within the confines of the law and agency policy. Equally, our social work values direct us in the decisions that we make and in our conduct. However, to be spontaneous within these boundaries is to embrace creativity to use theoretical frameworks in a flexible and adaptive way in order to best meet need.

Increasing creativity within practice does require a level of confidence and understanding of the various counselling models. To be creative without this theoretical foundation invites us to draw on other knowledge that we might hold, which most often is unlegislated 'common sense' and 'cliché'. Thus we can use the techniques identified within the various models and approaches explored in this book, which have long been established in counselling and therapeutic arenas, to provide a knowledge-based foundation for practice. Using techniques alongside the self brings congruence to our work and facilitates the becoming of social work art through the application of creativity.

Nevertheless, this book does emphasise skill development and describes techniques at times in a 'manualised' format. In doing this, the hope is that this book will bring concepts from other therapeutic disciplines closer to social work practice so that the art of social work practice as a whole might be enhanced. This does require practitioners to avoid being 'wed' to one approach at the exclusion of others; to be selective about the application of counselling and therapeutic techniques according to the needs of the individual; and to use the techniques in a responsive and spontaneous manner.

Bibliography

Adams, R., Dominelli, L. and Payne, M. (eds) (2002) *Social Work: Themes, Issues and Critical Debates*, 2nd edn. Basingstoke: Palgrave.

Ahmed, S. (1986) 'Cultural racism in work with Asian women and girls', in S. Ahmed, J. Cheetham and J. Small (eds), *Social Work with Black Children and their Families*. London: Batsford.

Ainsworth, M., Blehar, M., Waters, E. and Wall, S. (1978) *Patterns of Attachment: A Psychological Study of the Strange Situation*. Hillsdale, NJ: Lawrence Erlbaum.

Alladin, N.J. (2002) 'Ethnic matching in counselling: How important is it to ethnically match clients and counsellors', in S. Palmer (ed.), *Multicultural Counselling*. London: Sage.

Atkinson, D.R. and Hackett, G. (1995) *Counselling Diverse Populations*. Madison, WI: Brown & Benchmark.

BACP (British Association for Counselling and Psychotherapy) *Ethical Framework* [Online]: www.bac.co.uk/ethical_framework

Banks, S. (2001) *Ethics and Values in Social Work*. Basingstoke: Palgrave.

Bannister, A. (1991) 'Learning to live again', in P. Holmes and M. Karp (eds), *Psychodrama*. London: Routledge.

Barclay Committee (1982) *Social Workers: Their Role and Tasks*. Bedford: Square Press.

Barnes, B., Ernst, S. and Hyde, K. (1999) *An Introduction to Groupwork: A Group Analytic Perspective*. Basingstoke: Palgrave.

BASW (2001) *Definition of Social Work* [Online]: www.BASW.co.uk

Bateman, A., Brown, D. and Pedder, J. (2000) *Introduction to Psychotherapy*. London: Routledge.

Bateson, G. (1972) *Steps to an Ecology of Mind*. New York: Ballantine.

Beck, A.T. (1970) 'Cognitive therapy: nature and relation to behaviour therapy', *Behaviour Therapy*, 1: 184–200.

Beck, A.T. (1976) *Cognitive Therapy and the Emotional Disorders*. New York: International Universities Press.

Beck, A.T. and Emery, G. (1985) *Anxiety Disorders and Phobias: A Cognitive Perspective*. New York: Basic Books.

Bee, H. and Boyd, D. (2002) *Lifespan Development*. London: Allyn & Bacon.

Benson, J.F. (2001) *Working More Creatively with Groups*. London: Routledge.

Bion, W. (1962) *Learning from Experience*. London: Heinemann.

Blackburn, I. and Davidson, K. (1995) *Cognitive Therapy for Depression and Anxiety*. Oxford: Blackwell Science.

Boscolo, L., Cecchin, G., Hoffman, L. and Penn, P. (1987) *Milan Systemic Family Therapy*. New York: Basic Books.

Bowlby, J. (1969) *Attachment and Loss I: Attachment*. London: Hogarth Press.

Bowlby, J. (1973) *Attachment and Loss II: Separation: Anxiety and Anger*. London: Hogarth Press.

Bowlby, J. (1988) *A Secure Base*. Hove: Brunner-Routledge.

Brearley, J. (1995) *Counselling and Social Work*. Buckingham: Open University Press.

Brown, A. (1994) *Groupwork*, 3rd edn. Aldershot: Ashgate.

Brown, H.C. (1998) *Social Work and Sexuality: Working with Lesbians and Gay Men*. London: Palgrave.

Brown, H.C. (2002) 'Counselling', in R. Adams, L. Dominelli and M. Payne (eds), *Social Work: Themes, Issues and Critical Debates*, 2nd edn. Basingstoke: Palgrave.

Burck, C. and Speed, B. (eds) (1995) *Gender, Power and Relationships*. London: Routledge.

Byng-Hall, J. (1995) *Rewriting Family Scripts*. New York: Guilford Press.

Carlson, J. and Lewis, J. (1993) *Counselling the Adolescent*, 3rd edn. London: Love.

Carr, A. (2000) *Family Therapy*. Chichester: John Wiley.

Cecchin, G. (1987) 'Hypothesising, circularity and neutrality revisited: an invitation to curiosity', *Family Process*, 26: 405–13.

Clarkson, P. (1995) *The Therapeutic Relationship*. London: Whurr.

Clulow, C. (ed.) (2001) *Adult Attachment and Couple Psychotherapy*. Hove: Brunner-Routledge.

Compton, B.R. and Galaway, B. (1999) *Social Work Processes*, 6th edn. London: International Thomson.

Corby, B. (2000) *Child Abuse*. Buckingham: Open University Press.

Coren, A. (2001) *Short-term Psychotherapy*. Basingstoke: Palgrave.

Coulshed, V. (1991) *Social Work Practice*, 2nd edn. Basingstoke: Palgrave.

Dallos, R. and Draper, R. (2000) *An Introduction to Family Therapy*. Maidenhead: Open University Press.

Dalrymple, J. and Burke, B. (2003) *Anti-oppressive Practice*. Maidenhead: Open University Press.

Daniel, B., Wassell, S. and Gilligan, R. (2004) *Child Development for Child Protection Workers*. London: Jessica Kingsley.

Daniels, D. and Jenkins, P. (2000) *Therapy with Children*. London: SAGE Publications.

De Maria, R., Weeks, G. and Hof, L. (1999) *Focused Genograms*. New York: Taylor & Francis.

De Shazer, S. (1985) *Keys to Solutions in Brief Therapy*. New York: W.W. Norton.

De Shazer, S. (1988) *Clues to Investigating Solutions in Brief Therapy*. New York: W.W. Norton.

De Shazer, S. (1994) *Words were Originally Magic*. New York: W.W. Norton.

De Shazer, S. and Berg, I. (1992) 'Doing therapy: a post-structural re-vision', *Journal of Marital and Family Therapy*, 18: 71–81.

De Shazer, S. and Berg, I. (1997) 'What works? Remarks on research aspects of solution-focused therapy', *Journal of Family Therapy*, 19: 121–4.

Dixon, L. (2000) 'Punishment and the question of ownership', *Groupwork*, 12.

Dominelli, L. (1997) *Anti-racist Social Work*. Basingstoke: Palgrave.

Dryden, W. (ed.) (1996) *Research in Counselling and Psychotherapy*. London: SAGE Publications.

Dwividi, K.N. (ed.) (1997) *The Therapeutic Use of Stories*. London: Routledge.

Elliott, A. (2002) *Psychoanalytic Theory: An Introduction*. Basingstoke: Palgrave.

Ellis, A. (1962) *Reason and Emotion in Psychotherapy*. New York: Lyle Stewart.

Ellis, A. (1999) *How to Make Yourself Happy and Remarkably Less Disturbable*. Atascadero, CA: Impact.

Erickson, M. (1980) *Collected Papers*, Vols 1 to 4, ed. E. Rossi. New York: Irvington.

Fairbairn, W. (1952) *Psychoanalytic Studies of the Personality*. London: Tavistock.

Fairbairn, W. (1954) *An Object Relations Theory of the Personality*. New York: Basic Books.

Fairbairn, W. (1958) 'On the nature and aims of psychoanalytic treatment', *International Journal of Psychoanalysis*, 39: 374–86.

Falicov, C.J. (1999) 'Training to think culturally', *Family Process*, 34: 373–88.

Feltham, C. and Dryden, W. (1993) *Dictionary of Counselling*. London: Whurr.

Field, N. (1995) *Over the Rainbow: Money, Class and Homophobia*. London: Pluto.

Flaskas, C. and Perlesz, A. (eds) (1996) *The Therapeutic Relationship in Systemic Therapy*. London: Karnac Books.

Fonagy, P. (2001) *Attachment Theory and Psychoanalysis*. New York: Guilford Press.

Fonagy, P., Target, M., Gergely, G. and Jurist, E. (2002) *Affect Regulation, Mentalization and the Development of the Self*. New York: The Other Press.

Freud, A. (1936) *The Ego and the Mechanisms of Defence*. London: Hogarth Press.

Freud, A. (1968) *Indications for Child Analysis and Other Papers 1945 to 1956: The Writings of Anna Freud*, Vol. 4. New York: International Universities Press.

Freud, S. (1912) *The Dynamics of Transference*, Standard Edition, 12: 97–108. London: Hogarth Press (1958).

Freud, S. (1935) *A General Introduction to Psychoanalysis*, Vol. 1. New York: Liveright.

Freud, S. (1937) *Analysis Terminable and Interminable*, Standard Edition, 23: 209–54. London: Hogarth Press (1957).

Friedberg, R. and McClure, J. (2002) *Clinical Practice of Cognitive Therapy with Children and Adolescents*. New York: Guilford Press.

Gardner, D. and Harper, P. (1997) 'Using metaphor and imagery', in K.N. Dwivedi (ed.), *The Therapeutic Use of Stories*. London: Routledge.

Garvin, C. (1974) 'Group processes: uses and usage in social work practice', in A. Brown (ed.), *Groupwork*, 3rd edn, 1994. Aldershot: Ashgate.

Geldard, K. and Geldard, D. (2002) *Counselling Children*. London: SAGE Publications.

Gellner, E. (2003) *The Psychoanalytic Movement*. Oxford: Blackwell.

Gilbert, M. and Shmukler, D. (2001) *Brief Therapy with Couples*. Chichester: John Wiley.

Goffman, E. (1961) *Asylums: Essays in the Social Situation of Mental Patients and Other Inmates*. New York: Doubleday.

Gorell Barnes, G. (1998) *Family Therapy in Changing Times*. Basingstoke: Palgrave.

Haley, J. (1976) *Problem-solving Therapy*. San Francisco: Jossey Bass.

Hardy, K. and Lasloffy, T. (1995) 'The cultural genogram', *Journal of Marital and Family Therapy*, 21: 227–37.

Hawton, K., Salkovskis, P., Kirk, J. and Clark, D. (eds) (1995) *Cognitive Behaviour Therapy for Psychiatric Problems*. Oxford: Oxford University Press.

Hiro, D. (1971) *Black British, White British*. Harmondsworth: Penguin.

HMSO (1994) *Children Act 1989*. London: HMSO.

Hoffman, L. (1990) 'Constructing realities: an art of lenses', *Family Process*, 29: 1–12.

Hoffman, L. (2002) *Family Therapy: An Intimate History*. New York: W.W. Norton.

Hollis, F. (1972) *Casework: A Psychosocial Therapy*, 2nd edn. New York: Random House.

Holmes, J. (2001) *The Search for the Secure Base*. Hove: Brunner-Routledge.

Howe, D. (1992) *An Introduction to Social Work Theory*. Aldershot: Ashgate.

Howe, D. (1995) *Attachment Theory for Social Workers*. Basingstoke: Macmillan.

Howe, D. (2005) *Child Abuse and Neglect*. Basingstoke: Palgrave Macmillan.

Hugman, R. and Smith, D. (2001) *Ethical Issues in Social Work*. London: Routledge.

Jones, A. and McCormack, J. (2004) 'The culture of professional teams and the self of the therapist', *Context*, 76: 24–30.

Jones, E. (1994) *Family Systems Therapy*. Chichester: John Wiley.

Kelly, G. (1955) *The Psychology of Personal Constructs*, Vols 1 and 2. New York: W.W. Norton.

Kenny, L. and Kenny, B. (2000) 'Psychodynamic theory in social work: a view from practice', in P. Stepney and D. Ford (eds), *Social Work Models, Methods and Theories*. Dorset: Russell House.

Klein, M. (1921) 'The development of a child', in *Contributions to Psychoanalysis 1921–45*. London: Hogarth Press (1950).

Klein, M. (1952) 'Some theoretical conclusions regarding the emotional life of the infant', in M. Klein, *Developments in Psychoanalysis*. London: Hogarth Press.

Klein, M. (1959) 'Our adult world and its roots in infancy', in *The Writings of Melanie Klein*, Vol. 3. London: Hogarth Press (1975).

Lago, C. and Thompson, J. (2003) *Race, Culture and Counselling*. Maidenhead: Open University Press.

Laird, J. (1998) 'Theorizing culture', in M. McGoldrick (ed.), *Re-visioning Family Therapy*. London: Guilford Press.

Lang, N. (1972) 'A broad-range model of practice in the social work group', *Social Service Review*, 46: 76–89; in A. Brown (1994) *Groupwork*, 3rd edn. Aldershot: Ashgate.

Lanyado, M. and Horne, A. (1999) 'The therapeutic relationship and process', in M. Lanyado and A. Horne (eds), *The Handbook of Child and Adolescent Psychotherapy*. London: Routledge.

Laplanche, J. and Pontalis, J. (1988) *The Language of Psychoanalysis*, trans. D. Nicholson-Smith. London: Karnac (first published 1973).

Leiper, R. and Maltby, M. (2004) *The Psychodynamic Approach to Therapeutic Change*. London: SAGE Publications.

Levy, T.M. (2000) *Attachment Interventions*. London: Academic Press.

Lishman, J. (1994) *Communication in Social Work*. Basingstoke: Palgrave.

Luxmoore, N. (2001) *Listening to Young People*. London: Jessica Kingsley.

Madanes, C. (1984) *Behind the One Way Mirror*. London: Jossey Bass.

Malley, M. and Tasker, F. (1999) 'Lesbians, gay men and family therapy: a contradiction in terms', *Journal of Family Therapy*, 21: 3–29.

Marx, K. and Engels, F. (1965) *The German Ideology*. London: Lawrence & Wishart.

Maslow, A. (1962) *Towards a Psychology of Being*. Princeton, NJ: Van Nostrand.

Maslow, A. (1970) *Motivation and Personality*, 2nd edn. New York: Harper & Row.

McGoldrick, M. (1998) *Re-visioning Family Therapy: Race, Culture and Gender in Clinical Practice*. New York: Guilford Press.

McK.Norrie, K. (1997) *Children's Hearings in Scotland*. Edinburgh: W. Green/Sweet & Maxwell.

McK.Norrie, K. (1998) *Children (Scotland) Act 1995*. Edinburgh: W. Green/Sweet & Maxwell.

McMillan, M. (2004) *The Person-Centred Approach*. London: SAGE Publications.

Miller, L., Rustin, M., Rustin, M. and Shuttleworth, J. (1989) *Closely Observed Infants*. Wiltshire: Redwood Books.

Milner, J. and O'Byrne, P. (2002a) *Assessment in Social Work*, 2nd edn. Basingstoke: Palgrave.

Milner, J. and O'Byrne, P. (2002b) *Brief Counselling: Narratives and Solutions*. Basingstoke: Palgrave.

Minuchin, S. (1974) *Families and Family Therapy*. Cambridge, MA: Harvard University Press.

Minuchin, S. and Fishman, H.C. (1981) *Family Therapy Techniques*. Cambridge, MA: Harvard University Press.

Nelson-Jones, R. (2000) *Six Key Approaches to Counselling and Therapy*. London: Continuum.

O'Connell, B. (1998) *Solution-focused Therapy*. London: SAGE Publications.

O'Connell, B. and Palmer, S. (2003) *Handbook of Solution-focused Therapy*. London: SAGE Publications.

O'Leary, K. and Wilson, G. (1975) *Behavior Therapy: Application and Outcome*. Englewood Cliffs, NJ: Prentice Hall.

Palmer, S. (2002) 'Counselling idiographically', in S. Palmer (ed.), *Multicultural Counselling*. London: SAGE Publications.

Palmer, S. and McMahon, G. (eds) (1997) *Handbook of Counselling*, 2nd edn. London: Routledge.

Parker, J. and Bradley, G. (2003) *Social Work Practice: Assessment, Planning, Intervention and Review*. Exeter: Learning Matters.

Parton, N. and O'Byrne, P. (2000) *Constructive Social Work*. Basingstoke: Macmillan.

Pereira, F. and Scharff, D. (2002) *Fairbairn and Relational Theory*. London: Karnac.

Pote, H., Stratton, P., Cottrell, D., Boston, P., Shapiro, D. and Hanks, H. (2000) *Leeds Systemic Family Therapy Manual* [Online]: www.psych.leeds.ac.uk/research/lftrc/manuals/sft/sft.pdf.

Prochaska, J. and DiClemente, C. (1984) *The Transtheoretical Approach: Crossing Traditional Boundaries of Treatment*. Illinois: Dow Jones-Irwin.

Raskin, N.J. and Rogers, C.R. (1995) 'Person-centred therapy', in R.J. Corsini and D. Wedding (eds), *Current Psychotherapies*, 5th edn. Ithaca, NY: Peacock.

Ridley, C.R. (1984) 'Clinical treatment of the non-disclosing black client: a therapeutic paradox', *American Psychologist*, 39: 1234–44.

Ridley, C.R. (1995) *Overcoming Unintentional Racism in Counselling and Therapy: A Practitioner's Guide to International Intervention*. Thousand Oaks, CA: SAGE Publications.

Rogers, C. (1942) *Counselling and Psychotherapy*. Boston, MA: Houghton Mifflin.

Rogers, C. (1951) *Client-centered Therapy*. Boston, MA: Houghton Mifflin.

Rogers, C. (1957) 'The necessary and sufficient conditions of therapeutic change', *Journal of Consulting Psychology*, 21: 95–103.

Rogers, C. (1959) 'A theory of therapy, personality, and interpersonal relationships, as developed in the client-centered framework', in S. Koch (ed.), *Psychology: A Study of Science*. New York: McGraw-Hill.

Rogers, C. (1961) *On Becoming a Person*. Boston, MA: Houghton Mifflin.

Rogers, C. (1962) 'The interpersonal relationship: the core of guidance', *Harvard Educational Review*, 32: 416–29.

Rogers, C. (1969) *Freedom to Learn*. Columbus, OH: Charles E. Merrill.

Rogers, C. (1975) 'Empathic: an unappreciated way of being', *The Counselling Psychologist*, 5: 2–10.

Rogers, C. (1977) *Carl Rogers on Personal Power*. London: Constable.

Rogers, C. (1980) *A Way of Being*. Boston, MA: Houghton Mifflin.

Rogers, C. (1986) 'A client-centered/person-centered approach to therapy', in I. Kutash and A. Wolf (eds), *Psychotherapist's Casebook: Theory and Technique in the Practice of Modern Therapies*. San Francisco: Jossey Bass.

Roth, A. and Fonagy, P. (1996) *What Works for Whom*. New York: Guilford Press.

Rowbotham, S. (1973) *Women's Consciousness, Man's World*. Harmondsworth: Penguin.

Russell, S. and Carey, M. (2003) 'Feminism therapy and narrative ideas', *International Journal of Narrative Therapy and Community Work*, 2.

Rutter, J. and Friedberg, R.D. (1999) 'Guidelines for the effective use of Socratic dialogue in cognitive therapy', in L. VandeCreek, S. Knapp and T. Jackson (eds), *Innovations in Clinical Practice: A Sourcebook*. Sarasota, FL: Professional Resource Press.

Sandler, J. (1987) 'The background of safety', in J. Sandler, *From Safety to Super-Ego: Selected Papers of Joseph Sandler*. London: Karnac.

Satinover, J. (2002) *Homosexuality and the Politics of Truth*. Grand Rapids, MI: Baker Book House Co.

Schön, D. (1991) *The Reflective Practitioner*. Aldershot: Ashgate.

Scott, J., Williams, J. and Beck, A. (eds) (1991) *Cognitive Therapy in Clinical Practice*. London: Routledge.

Seden, J. (2005) *Counselling Skills in Social Work Practice*. Buckingham: Open University Press.

Solly, A. (2005) 'Mindfulness and cognitive therapy', *Clinical Psychology*, 45.

Speed, B. and Burck, C. (eds) (1995) *Gender, Power and Relationships*. London: Routledge.

Stern, D. (1985) *The Interpersonal World of the Infant: A View from Psychoanalysis and Developmental Psychology*. New York: Basic Books.

Strachey, J. (1934) 'The nature of the therapeutic action of psychoanalysis', *International Journal of Psychoanalysis*, 15: 127–59.

Street, E. and Downey, J. (1996) *Brief Therapeutic Consultations*. Chichester: John Wiley.

Tarrier, N. (1987) *Living with Breast Cancer and Mastectomy*. Manchester: Manchester University Press.

Thompson, N. (2001) *Anti-Discriminatory Practice*, 3rd edn. Basingstoke: Palgrave.

Thompson, N. (2003) *Communication and Language*. Basingstoke: Palgrave.

Tolan, J. (2003) *Skills in Person-centred Counselling and Psychotherapy*. London: SAGE Publications.

Trevithick, P. (2000) *Social Work Skills*. Buckingham: Open University Press.

Tuckman, B. (1965) 'Developmental sequences in small groups', *Psychological Bulletin*, 63: 384–99.

Velasquez, M.M., Maurer, G.G., Crouch, C. and DiClemente, C.C. (2001) *Group Treatment for Substance Abuse*. London: Guilford Press.

Vetere, A. and Cooper, J. (2003) 'Setting up a domestic violence service', *Child and Adolescent Mental Health*, 8: 61–7.

von Glasersfeld, E. (1987) *The Construction of Knowledge*. Seaside, CA: Intersystems.

Walsh, J. (1995) 'The external space in group work', *Group Analysis*, 28: 413–27.

Weeks, J. (1986) *Sexuality*. London: Tavistock.

Whitaker, D.S. (1995) *Using Groups to Help People*. London: Routledge.

White, M. (2002) *Externalising Conversations Exercise* [Online]: www.dulwichcentre. com.au/workshopnotes.htm

White, M. and Epston, D. (1990) *Narrative Means to Therapeutic Ends*. London: W.W. Norton.

Wills, F. and Sanders, D. (2002) *Cognitive Therapy*. London: SAGE Publications.

Winnicott, D. (1945) 'Primitive emotional development', in *Collected Papers*. London: Tavistock (1958).

Winnicott, D. (1951) 'Transitional objects and transitional phenomena', *Collected Papers*. London: Tavistock (1958).

Winnicott, D. (1960) 'Ego distortion in terms of true and false self', reprinted in D. Winnicott (1965), *The Maturational Process and the Facilitating Environment*. London: Hogarth Press.

Winnicott, D. (1975) 'Hate in the countertransference', *Through Paediatrics to Psychoanalysis*. London: Hogarth Press/Institute of Psychoanalysis.

Yelloly, M. (1980) *Social Work Theory and Psychoanalysis*. Wokingham: Van Nostrand Reinhold.

Zuckweiller, R. (1998) *Living in the Post-mastectomy Body: Learning to Live and Love your Body Again*. Washington, DC: Hartley & Marks.

Index

Compiled by INDEXING SPECIALISTS (UK) Ltd., Regent House, Hove Street, Hove, East Sussex
BN3 2DW. Tel: 01273 738299.
E-mail: richardr@indexing.co.uk Website: www.indexing.co.uk